Scandalous

Things Good Christian Girls Don't Talk About But Probably Should

Emily Dixon

Edited by
Joanna Rempel-Knighten
and
Lacey DeAnne Riggan

Cover Art
by
David and Patricia Stiles
of
D&P Photography

Shoes thoughtfully and lovingly provided by
Ty Dixon,
in response to his wife's obsession with great
foot apparel for Christmas 2011.

ISBN: 1477645780
ISBN-13: 978-1477645789

For my girls.

CONTENTS

Miscellaneous
or Scandalous Tidbits

Emily Dixon

Why I Don't Mind Being Scandalous

I am hoping that when you picked up this book you knew we were going to spend a good deal of time talking about sex. Over the years, I have become the "go-to-gal" for most of my friends when it comes to this subject, and my reputation has become such that even complete strangers approach me saying "so-and-so" recommended that they talk to me. I never set out to become a "sexpert" nor do I consider myself to be one. I think that the word just got around that nothing embarrasses me and I have a compulsive habit of honestly answering any straightforward question with an equally straightforward answer.

In the course of my life, I have had to actively seek out the answers to the questions that so many women have about their own sexuality, but most importantly, I have tried to discover how the teachings of the Bible play out in the real world. I have discovered the simplistic answer so often provided in Christian circles have failed to provide all the information needed to live out our faith boldly and with confidence in a world that would try to use our sexuality against us. This was a truth I lived in my first marriage, and confronted again as a divorced woman trying navigate a vast region of uncharted territory.

Later, as an instructor at a local college, my students began to voice the same questions that I had faced, and I found that even this more sexually enlightened generation struggled with many of the same issues I did. Learning to share not only the answers I had discovered, but also my story, was a point of healing for me and a source of empowerment for them. I also learned that our girls didn't need our pretty answers, or even our polite ones. They needed the plain unvarnished truth spoken in a language they understood and left no room for misinterpretation. Even more importantly, they needed someone to ask them the hard questions that compelled them to be honest about their faith and their struggles so that they would have the chance to face the fight for their purity free of half truths and self-delusion. And since I have never known when or how to keep my mouth shut, I seemed to have been tailor made for this task.

Over the past eleven years, I have spent countless hours reading, researching, and trying to understand this great mystery. I have talked with a handful of women who were brave enough to willingly share their insights and many more who have struggled to overcome their fear and embarrassment in talking about this sacred subject. Now, I do not have a degree in sexuality, nor am I doctor, so much of my information is anecdotal and gleaned from the medical research of others. And that is okay, because I am not trying to write a how-to book or even to address the topic of biology from a technical standpoint. I merely desire to facilitate those conversations we as women should be having with each other and share a few of the things I learned along the way.

If I am blunt, it is because I believe the gravity of the topic deserves the honor of our honesty. If I am shocking, it is because I believe some truths shouldn't be candy coated, and if I make you uncomfortable, I do not mean to offend you. Throughout the Bible a reader can find writings on sex that range from the raucous and scandalous to beautiful and inspiring, and even more shocking is some of these moments are one and the same. If our Lord deemed that such language is appropriate for this topic, who are we to do less?

I will try to be as genteel with this as I can possibly be, but those of you who know me best know not to expect too much in this area. Gentility cost me years of heartache and torment, and I would be perpetuating the same system for another if I allowed gentility to have a greater sway than it deserves. Our God is a good God, but a quick perusal of the prophets' writings shows that even a good God will not serve our social or cultural restraints when it does not teach His people truth.

So I promise to shoot straight and pull no punches if it will save one more woman from the nightmare I endured.

Emily

My Apologies to the Moms. . .

I am truly sorry for what you are getting ready to go through, but I wanted you to know there is a reason for the madness. When I originally sat down to write this book, you weren't the ones I had in mind. (After all, I figured that since you already had kids you probably knew a thing or two about sex.) When I pictured my audience, I pictured the many high school and college students who asked me the questions that sparked this whole endeavor. In our discussions about sex, I found that many of our young people feel as if the Church just doesn't speak their language and so they simply did not know how to communicate with their elders about many of these issues. And being the glutton for punishment that I am, I decided that I would do my best speak frankly in the most contemporary terminology I knew. (Even at that, I am pretty sure I still manage to date myself just a little). I also determined that no matter how controversial the topic, if anyone had ever asked me the question, I would answer it again in these pages. All I can say is brace yourself.

So, Mom, here's what I am asking of you – use this as a tool, a chance to learn a few things about how our kids communicate, and push through the form to find the function. I'm not saying that you need to integrate these terms into your vocabulary, but at least you will know what your daughter means when she uses some of these terms.

I am also asking that you at least consider the possibility that your child is dealing with or will deal with these topics. As a mom, I know there are just some things we never want to think about in the same context as our children, but after teaching in a Christian ministries program at a local college, I can truly say almost all of these issues universal to our kids. The media has forced them to grapple with sexual topics that you and I did not even know existed until recently (or for some of you, maybe not until you read this book). My hope is that you will put down this work a little better informed and better prepared to guide your daughter through this minefield.

Learning to Have the Conversations
or
She Said What?

I am learning how not to be surprised anymore, but there is still some part of me that remains mystified at how little we know about our own anatomy. Many women with whom I have spoken recount their "sex talk" from their mothers as follows:

Mom: You will start bleeding soon, and no, you aren't dying. There are pads in the bathroom cabinet. Use them when you need them. Let me know when I need to buy more.

So goes the introduction most girls get to their periods. If it weren't for sex education in schools, they would never know the mechanics or the reason for such a troubling phenomenon. Others learn a multitude of myths from other girls their age who are just as ignorant, and few of the more ambitious ones will seek out information carefully hidden in books and through covert internet searches, a dangerous way to learn about something so important.

When it comes to the actual sex act, many have reported a conversation that sounded like this:

Mom: Do you know about sex?

Embarrassed teenage girl who would do anything to avoid this conversation: Yes.

Mom: Well, you need to wait until you get married. You don't want to get pregnant or catch an STD.

Girl: Absolutely! (She almost yells over her shoulder as she runs out the nearest door or window)

I hope that you see the holes in this conversation and the multitude of problems that can arise from the failure to communicate some basic facts on a deeper level. I personally believe that our inability to talk about sex stems from one basic and universal source – shame.

From the time we were young, we were taught that you keep your body covered up, don't talk about bodily functions, and never allude to this intensely private experience. We learned that what was said by our parents, teachers, and the respected adults in our lives was sometimes less important than what they didn't say. Added to that is the constant critique of those women who do bare it all, the bikini clad girls on the beer commercial, the avoidance of swimming pools and beaches, the strict dress codes of Church camp, and even the lack of sexuality in the dress of a typical Church woman. All of these things coalesce in our psyches as a single message: Our bodies are bad.

Men's bodies are okay. Dad runs around without a shirt. He passes gas, belches, scratches where he itches, and makes jokes about his bathroom habits. He even steps around the corner of a building to relieve himself. His behavior is not questioned or even referred to. Such things are accepted because his body is accepted, and the boys of our families follow in his footsteps bragging about who smells worse or who can pee the highest on a wall. If you haven't experienced this, then I will ask you to examine who set the tone for your family's interactions, your mom or your dad? Because when I talk to families where the male dominates, this behavior is normal and not the strange and exotic ritual of uncouth males. It is simply part and parcel with being male, but we will get back to them later. If it was mom, however, the boys frequently receive the same message as the girls, and this can lead to some interesting problems for them. (But that is a topic for another book.)

Women within the Christian culture have received a schizophrenic message about our sexuality. We should be honored and treated as the weaker vessel, in all the various interpretations that phrase has received, but we should hide anything that betrays our femininity. We should be pretty and pleasant, but we should not be sexy or alluring. We should be sweet and hospitable, but never be too inviting. Friendly, but reserved. Well dressed, but not allowed to take pride in our appearance. We should focus on our inward beauty, but ignore the inner parts of our anatomy. We should marry, but not discuss the act of marriage. We should have children, but never reveal how they got here.

Combine this with unceasing pressure of the world to celebrate our sexuality by flaunting it in our dress, having multiple sexual conquests, and indulging in uninhibited experimentation, is there any wonder that so many otherwise good Christian girls end up confused about their own bodies?

Many Church programs focus on purity and chastity, preaching a message of abstinence, but never answer our true questions about who we are or how we were created. In this way, we learn avoidance but never acquire the tools needed for dealing with our bodies responsibly. We discover ways to deny that we are women with needs, desires, emotions, and dare I say it – a sex drive! I wish I were exaggerating when I say that some Christian women see their sexual impulses as a fatal flaw within their design, but more than one woman I have encountered believes that experiencing these natural desires is evidence of how wicked she truly is. How liberating to know the truth, that God created us this way for a reason and with a purpose, and believe it or not, it wasn't simply so we could procreate.

God designed women to be wonderfully complex in body, mind, and spirit. It was no accident that we are round and curvy, or that our bodies have the ability to transform the smartest of men into blithering idiots. God knew what He was doing, and guess what? He likes us this way. He is not embarrassed by our nakedness. He sculpted our forms just as surely as He sculpted Adam's. He was the one who placed breasts upon our chests, rounded out our bums, and gave us rich thighs. He took delight in making a well-turned ankle and in creating that bloody uterus that gives so many of us fits. He crafted the ovaries that hold so much potential for life and entrusted them to us. He made our skin soft, our bodies touchable, and our hair for fingers to run through. And He did all of this all for His glory, so that we can marvel at a God who could create a being so magnificent she could enshrine future generations within her flesh.

Unfortunately, the wonder of our bodies is often lost in a battle for our purity. We cover up, hide the beauty of how we were designed, sometimes to the horrifying extreme of becoming asexual.

We try to be the good girl, blushing at the off comment, acting appropriately shocked when someone uses those awful words like vagina, nipple, clitoris, or (horrors of horrors) orgasm. We don't even teach our children the proper terms for their bodies, resorting to euphemisms and nick names that protect our sensibilities. Imagine for a moment if we did the same thing with other parts of our anatomy calling our nose, eyes, arms, or legs by names like "ninnies" or "pouties." Do we realize that in this seemingly harmless act, we are implying to our children that even the proper names of our body parts are offensive?

But outside the world of the Church, there is another world one where the most basic parts of me are celebrated, displayed, and desired. It is a world where my breasts are seen as a badge of honor, my backside is applauded, and men will do anything to catch a glimpse of what I keep hidden beneath my skirts. Here I can be sexual, and I can stop worrying about what people think if I inadvertently show the lacy edge of a bra. And when I cross into that place, I no longer have to work so hard to suppress this part me. Freedom of this style is like being able to breathe after a life time of holding my breath.

This type of high makes it easy to forget the dangers of ignoring of all those things I was taught in Sunday School. The affirmation feels so good, is it any wonder that so many good Christian girls live a dual life? One in which everything is properly concealed, and another where they bask in the adoration of people unembarrassed by their sexuality?

Yet the Church seems shocked when time and time again the good girl, the leader of the youth group, and the winner in all the Bible trivia games ends up pregnant or in a bad marriage. We shake our heads and click our tongues wondering how "such a sweet girl" could end up in such a "bad situation". The answer is simple, but not one that we want to hear. Learning that answer means that we have to set aside some of our scruples and those icky feelings of embarrassment. We are going to have to have some real conversations, and we are going to have accept that fact that our girls are being targeted at younger and younger ages. We can't wait until puberty to start talking about sex, and we may have to be more specific than we've ever been before.

We have to guard our conversations, not against honesty, but from any undercurrent that devalues our sexuality. For each time we fail to approach women as a beautiful and amazing part of God's creation, we are confirming the secret fear that almost every woman harbors somewhere deep in her soul – there is something deeply and fundamentally wrong with her. She is somehow deficient, and what she is . . . is terribly shameful.

Girls, now is the time to start telling the truth to ourselves and to our daughters. It's time to have the conversations that will free us from shame and teach us about the awesome gift and responsibility of being a woman.

Our Bodies

or

Oh, What a Bloody Mess!

I can't sugar coat the fact that we in the Christian community have really messed with women's perceptions of their bodies, but simply pointing out the flaws in the system is insufficient. We have to start actively seeking solutions.

A good place to start is to stop telling the story of Eve like it begins and ends with her temptation. We can also stop telling it like it is the only story about women in the Bible. Too often we forget that she walked in the garden with God, naked and unashamed, not only before her husband but also before her Lord. She talked with Him, learned from Him, and shared in one the most unique relationships with God known to history. Yes, she made a mistake. She was tempted and she gave in, but her sin did not revoke her calling to be the mother of humanity. God was not punishing her for her sexuality. He was allowing her to receive the consequences of her sin, and it is time we started making the distinction.

Yes, I know the consequences included pain in childbirth, but the gift of being a mother was not taken from her. God did not take the beauty of our sexuality away. He merely pointed out how our sin makes following our destiny more difficult. Eve went on to have three sons, two of which were a blessing and pleasure to God. What a great legacy for any woman to have! She should be remembered not only as the woman who sinned, but also as a wife and mother and a revelation of how our sexuality is a gift that serves the world.

Some of us need to go back and actually read her story. Too often we Christians fall into the trap of simply "knowing" a Bible story without ever taking the time to read it for ourselves. Even more often, we read the Bible as if we are already aware of the great truth it has to reveal to us, and Eve's story is just one example. I want to encourage you to take a moment right now and read the story of her creation. Go on, I'll wait . . .

Now let me ask you a question, where did you start your reading? Did you begin in Genesis chapter one? Or did you skip on over to chapter two? You see the story is told twice, once in chapter one giving the creation of mankind in unity with the rest of the universe, demonstrating our place and significance in this wonderful thing God had called into being. Then the writer does something unusual – he goes back and gives another version of the same story. There has been a lot of debate about why he did this, but one of the most widely accepted explanations is the first account is poetic. The story has a rhythm and a flow, and if he had paused to share the details at this juncture, he would have broken the format that he had so carefully constructed. And there is simply so much that is revealed in how he told the story that we would have lost some of its significance if he had shifted gears too soon. However, we did need to know more and like any good narrator, he takes the appropriate detour at the appropriate time.

So what important truth is he revealing to us in chapter one? For our topic, the answer is in verse 27,

> So God created man in His own image, in the image of God He created him, male and female He created them.
> Genesis 1:27 (ESV)

Some of you are thinking, "Wait a minute. I was taught that God was just creating Adam here." But the Bible clearly says that He created "male and female", so it had to be more than just Adam. Eve has to be in there somewhere, too. The answer I was taught to that little mystery was the verse is only referring to the Adam's rib, the soon to be Eve, but we can do a bit of debunking for that theory by simply continuing to read. Go on to verse 28.

> And God blessed THEM. And God said to THEM, "Be fruitful and multiply and fill the earth and subdue it and have dominion over the fish of the sea and over the birds of the heavens and over every living thing that moves on the earth."
> Genesis 1:28 (Emphasis added).

Note that the commands are to both of them, not just Adam. How many of you were taught that God never spoke to Eve, that she had received her instructions secondhand? I did. And yet, this has to have been said to them both, not just because that is what the Book says, but because it includes the command to be fruitful and multiply. Not a feat that Adam was capable of doing on his own. Dominion was given to them both, not one or the other, but to each of them with no discrimination.

Within Jewish circles, it has been taught that it is only in the first account of creation that Adam retained his image of God, because if we look at the second account, there is no mention that man has been created in his Creator's image. So what are the distinguishing aspects of these two stories? In the first account, woman is still considered to be a part of man. In the second, she is separated from him. Think about this, girls, what are the implications of this teaching? Man, in and of himself, is not the image of God. Only when we are united with him do we bear the likeness. To lend further credence to this teaching, we simply need to examine the name of God as it was given at the burning bush. (Exodus 3).

The name of God is a brilliant revelation of God's nature and character. The lessons from this one word are staggering, but we simply need to look at one. The name of God is called the Tetragramaton, and is often translated as "I am that I am," but a better translation is "I will be what I will be." The name is made up of four Hebrew characters, the first two being a ׳ (pronounced yode) and an ה (pronounced hey). According to Jewish custom, these two letters are masculine in nature, and demonstrate the masculine characteristics of our Lord. The second two letters are a ו (vaw) and an ה (hey), and if you haven't already guessed, they are feminine. Male and female revealed and presented as the most Holy name of our Lord, a name that is so perfect and so awe inspiring, it was only allowed to be spoken once a year by a priest specifically chosen by God Himself.

Can you see how these two ideas weave together, creating a more perfect picture of our Lord and what we as women must mean to Him? We, just as much as Adam, were created in His image. We were not some silly afterthought created simply to keep men company. God placed us here, creating us and crafting us as a revelation of Himself, a God who is big enough to encompass both the feminine and masculine aspects of humanity.

The second thing that we should take away from these verses is the fact that God called His creation not only good, but "very good" (Genesis 1:31). I have sat in classes where the leader has specifically stated that God never called woman good. Even more disturbing were the number of women who eagerly nodded their heads in agreement, as if they could take the sting out of the statement by quickly agreeing to it. And if you bypass the account of our creation in Genesis one, He doesn't, but what we need to bear in mind is that in the second creation account – which tells of the creation of man and woman, nothing is called good.

Perhaps the most well known "fact" of woman's creation is that we came from a rib. A trifling bit of the body that is redundant and, when only one is required, expendable. However, this is another fact of the story that we have gotten wrong. The Hebrew never specifies that we were a rib, and when we truly study this passage in the original language, we find a phrasing that is difficult at best. Simply trying to decipher the words is nearly impossible due to a lack of context and rarity of the phrasing, but if we go back and hear the words of the rabbis, the men who lived in this culture, spoke this language, ate, drank, and breathed the Torah, we learn that this phrase means so much more. The idea being presented, according to these great teachers, is that woman was an equal half of Adam. Think about how that changes our understanding of the story. No longer are we simply a rib. Now we are the other half, the completing piece of this magnificent puzzle.

Please, hear me. I am not a feminist. I have no use for the idea that women are superior to men, or even identical to men. Far from it. I celebrate our differences, and I love the fact that we have them. I can find no place in the Bible where women are superior to men. What I do find is that we are supposed to respect women for who God created us to be. I also find that we should be equally valued, not held up as superior or ignored and discounted for our differences. Our respective sexual roles, as taught in Scripture, are beautifully complimentary and completing the other. Everything about us from our emotions to our anatomy, demonstrates that we are supposed to operate together, meeting each other's needs and blessing one another through our unique natures.

The story of women in Scripture does not end with Eve. Instead the Bible is full of women who used their unique position and abilities to protect and promote God's purposes in this world. Jael who lulled a great warrior to sleep and drove a tent peg through his head, because he made the mistake of underestimating a woman. (Judges 4). Deborah who led a nation in war, and whose wisdom compelled others to seek her out for counsel, including the great leaders of her day. (Judges 4). Esther who knew how to use her feminine wiles to bend a king's will to her desire and in doing so save a nation. (She was important enough to get her own book, the Book of Esther). Ruth the seductress and Naomi the wise widow who knew the appeal of a young woman's beauty. (She has her own book too.). Hannah who prays with an honesty that shamed a priest, and whose joyful heart is the first to announce that God is sending His Messiah. (I Samuel 1 and 2). The cast of women in the New Testament provide even more reason to celebrate our role within the Christian faith. We have been the first to anticipate our Lord's coming. We served Him and with Him. We were the last to leave the scene of His death and the first to discover the empty tomb. It was a woman who housed our Lord in her flesh, and through her body delivered Him as a baby into a waiting world. Women supported the early Church and opened their homes to those who brought the good news to their lands. We have done so much right, and it is time we shared that good news to our daughters.

So often it seems as if women are only told about Eve's failure or are "encouraged" to be more like the woman of Proverbs 31. And God knows how many women have gone insane trying to emulate (read that copy, imitate, and otherwise be like) this particular little gal that I think we should take a moment to clarify something about her. She was fictional. She was the figment of a man's imagination, and quite frankly, a man who hoped for the impossible. Neither should we forget the fact that many of her accomplishments were facilitated by a husband who provided her with resources, the likes of which none of us will ever see. Do you know how much more I could accomplish if I had servants? That one thing alone would probably allow me to take over a third world country.

Does that mean that we shouldn't strive to emulate this amazing woman? Of course not, she is the epitome of all that a strong and vital woman can be. She is the potential that lies within us all, but we shouldn't beat ourselves up when we fall short. If such a woman did in fact exist, she should be an inspiration, but we should recognize that she accomplished none of this on her own. She was surrounded with a network of people all aspiring toward the same goal – the success of her family. And even a woman like this had to have experienced few bad days. She just had a man who was willing to see all the goodness she brought to his life while graciously overlooking that one week out of the month.

The women of the Bible were vital and alive, fully aware of their bodies. They lived in a culture that recognized and accommodated their needs as women, and did so in far more dramatic ways than even our liberated culture does for us. Provisions were made for the needs of her body, and it was more than a broken, coin-operated tampon dispenser in the ladies room. Nor were the women ashamed to speak up when they needed such accommodations. Rachel once used her period as an excuse not to rise before her father. Boldly, she told him in no uncertain terms that Aunt Flo was in town, (Genesis 31:35). Surprisingly, there is no mention of either being embarrassed by her speech. Why? Because God had insured that under His law the physical needs of woman could not simply be ignored or swept under the proverbial rug.

Under the laws of the Hebrew nation, women were considered to be unclean during their periods. This is not a point of shame, but rather, a natural state of being that came with some pretty great benefits. Women were allowed to take a break from their routine duties of being a wife and mother. Since she was unclean, she could not cook for her family. Having her clean the house would have been pointless, since anything she touched would then be unclean too. Girls, can you imagine a full week off, each and every month? I want to cry just thinking about it, and makes me wonder just how liberated we truly are in this society where even this most elemental evidence of our sex must be discreetly hidden away.

To make things even more fun, at the end of her period a woman was required to offer a sacrifice so that she can be declared clean once again before her God and His people. You can imagine how obvious it would have been to anyone present what had happened when a woman approached the priest with her prescribed offering, (Leviticus 15). The priest knew, her husband knew, and so did anyone else with eyes in their head. Consider for a moment what it would be like for a modern woman to tell her pastor each time she finished her period. Would you be embarrassed by such an action? Or would you quickly become accustom to sharing what we have been taught to hide?

Marriages were arranged when girls were young, way before they had reached puberty, and then the groom would anxiously await the day when he could claim his bride. How did he know when that day had come? When her father declared that she had "come of age", or, to be a little more blunt, started her period. The customs of their day did not allow for prudish behavior about this normal biological function. Nor did the technology of their time – no easily flushable tampons or pads discreetly wrapped in toilet paper for these gals. The women would gather together at the river to wash out their bloody rags, gossiping, comparing notes, and sharing tips on how to deal with this evidence of their womanhood. Joining the gaggle at the river and taking part in these conversations would have been a rite of passage, and I can only imagine the laughter and good-natured teasing that greeted the young girls who approached the banks for the first time with her own bundle of rags. How quickly she must have felt accepted and celebrated as she became part of this special society. No hiding, no shame, but rather a community event where women learned to be women together.

I love this image. I love the idea that there was a place where women could talk through the questions they had about their bodies. I love that there was no room for shame in this community and that the girls had a chance to learn, not from other giggling teenagers, but from women who had already been there and done that. It wasn't a formal education full of charts and line drawings. Instead, it was a time of being drawn into a conversation that had been going on since the day that Eve first told her daughter of what was happening in her body. Each young girl would now share in what was a natural and organic event that allowed her to move with grace into the realm of womanhood.

Okay, okay, so I really have no desire to beat bloody rags on river rocks, but I do believe one of the best things we can do is provide a place where girls can join in the conversation. We need to let our daughters listen as we talk with our friends, comparing notes about which tampon is the best and why one brand of pad works better for us than the other. We need to include them as we bemoan our chocolate cravings and laugh about the midnight runs for salty potato chips. We should share our tips on dealing with cramps and heavy flows. In short, we need to let them know that this isn't anything to be ashamed of, nor is it to be treated as a disgusting event. And we do this by talking about it as simply and as graciously as we do so many other biological events in our lives, by inviting them to join in the conversation, not talking at them.

If all this weren't enough, we haven't even looked at the living situations of those times. Houses were small, and the personal bedroom had not yet been invented. Families slept in common areas where the beds of children surrounded the parents', and while I am pretty certain that most of their intimacies were not displayed, kids aren't stupid, and we are never as discreet as we think we are. I also have a suspicion that this probably led to some pretty steamy mid-day trysts between husbands and wives looking for a little privacy, out there somewhere in the daylight where the women weren't able to hide their bodies in darkness.

Nor should we overlook the fact that for most of the Bible we are dealing with an agrarian (read that farm living with the "Green Acres" theme playing the background) culture. This meant that sheep, cattle, and horses were busy doing their thing. Having grown up on a farm, and currently living with a bull in my backyard, it is amazing to see what kids pick up when they are not kept in the dark about the simple truths of nature. They see it and accept is as part of a system that just is no – thing alarming or disturbing, just one more part of this crazy world.

Why do we need to know this about the women in our Bible? Because we need to know that they were real women. We need to understand that in some ways they were far more conscious of their sex than we are of ours. They didn't have the option of regulating their periods with birth control pills, reducing or enlarging the size of their breasts, dulling the pain of childbirth, or opting for baby bottles. So often we tell their stories as if they happened in a sexual void, as if these women were blissfully unaware of their bodies and its demands, but in many ways their understanding of sexuality was far more clear and poignant than ours ever will be. And yet, these are the women who are offered as our example, the ones God deemed worthy to be remembered. They are our teachers, showing us how to live our lives fully as people of faith and as daughters of a God who was pleased in His creation.

My hope is that by reexamining some of our ideas about what the Bible teaches us about being women, we can confront some of the ideas that we may have simply accepted without considering their implications. And while, I did not offer a complete or in-depth study of women throughout the Bible, I hope that you are beginning to see that we are a celebrated part of God's creation. The importance of this cannot be overstated.

By simply discovering who God says we are, who He declared us to be, we can discover the answers to the questions we all face and find the courage to live these answers boldly and gracefully before the world. If we appeal to the Bible for guidance, we will discover that the Word of God is fully alive, fully responsive, and fully able to direct us to the appropriate expression of sexuality and faith.

Every Christian Woman's Dilemma
or
Cover That Up or Dress to Impress?

Of all issues that women face, none is as basic or elemental as that of our dress. What to wear is an issue we ponder and grapple with from the time we are old enough to realize that our bodies need to be covered. We wrestle with issues of modesty, function, and style, while balancing our innate need to be beautiful with the hazard of being considered (gasp!) too sexy.

For centuries, women have been cautioned against dressing provocatively, but the problem we face here is that there is no set rule on what determines if an article of clothing, or even a body part, can be deemed as arousing. I have read that at one point in history the mere sight of a woman's ankle could send a man into lustful fantasies that would make you blush. Now obviously, ankles have failed to retain their status as a mainstream turn on, but that begs the question, when are we showing too much? When have we crossed that invisible line in our dress that makes our bodies a temptation?

Allow me pause for a moment to make a confession, I have an obsession. I love shoes – the higher the heel, the pointier the toe, and the more outlandish the better. I love being four inches taller and balancing my body on a pencil thin stiletto. I feel beautiful when I don them with a great pair of jeans, or add them as the finishing touch to a knock out dress. I like shoes because I never felt as if I had to question if I was displaying my assets (read that boobs or butt) a little too obviously, but I found out that not everyone agrees. Over the years, I have been accused of wearing "hooker" or "slut" shoes, and even have been told that I am actively trying to seduce men, all because I dared to stand just a little too tall.

The point is there is always someone who is ready to throw a stone at anyone who dares be a little different, and often the first rock we throw is "immodesty." Now I cannot honestly believe that my shoes are a major source of temptation for any level-headed man. Could there be some men out there who see my shoes as deliberately seductive when I am merely celebrating the fact that as a woman I can enjoy this small indulgence? Absolutely, but I am not responsible for them. There are men, who can be turned on by a stiff breeze, but I cannot stop the wind, and it is wrong for a woman to be held responsible for a man's problems.

The idea that we as women are solely responsible for the thoughts of men has been carried to the extreme far too often, and in many parts of the world it is a mindset that still reigns. Women are refused the right to show their faces and have even had their hands cutoff for wearing that oh-so-tempting fingernail polish. Victims of rape and abuse have been severely punished and even killed for seducing men through wanton behavior, some of these "women" being mere children who were too friendly with family members two or three times their age. Thankfully, I can say that our faith is not guilty of these atrocities, but neither are we guiltless in perpetuating the idea that women who are victims of sexual abuse somehow asked to be victimized. I wish I could say that the American Church had left this mentality back in the Dark Ages where it belongs, but the truth is many women have heard an implied warning in our discussions of dress. Wear the wrong thing, and you will be raped, and it will be your fault.

As a result of this warning, many a Christian woman has adopted a dress that denies her sexuality. We hide every curve and disguise every bit of womanhood that doesn't smack of the maternal. Necklines are strangling, hemlines touching the tops of our crew socks or even the tops of our tennis shoes. We avoid make up and scrape our hair against our scalps. Jewelry is eschewed and being soft or womanly is confused with being trampy. Okay, so not all of us go to these extremes, but many do. And those who don't get snagged by that particular trap often fall prey to those styles (I use that term loosely) that make us look old before our time.

Ladies, there is absolutely nothing wrong with being beautiful or womanly in our appearance. We are even warned that we are not to dress as the opposite sex (Deuteronomy 22:5), and most of us are sure not to fall into that sin, but isn't dressing as an asexual creature just as wrong? Aren't we denying our God-given identity when we fail to celebrate our femininity in our dress?

Can you imagine Sarah, the wife of Abraham, dressed in the attire of today's Christian woman? Sarah, who was considered to be one the seven most beautiful women of the ancient world? She was so appealing that kings desired to have her as their wife, and Abraham had no illusions about the power of her beauty. He went so far as to pass her off as his sister in hopes that he wouldn't be killed just so another man could claim her. To make matters worse, he did it not once, but twice, (Genesis 12:10-20; 20:1-18). These events make me think that she wasn't shy about dressing as the knockout she had to have been. And how about Ruth? Do you honestly think she went to the field clothed in such a way that her beauty was lost? Read her story. Boaz noticed her. Why? Why do you think? You can't see a woman's character or brain from across the field. And when she showed up at the threshing floor – bathed, perfumed, wearing her best dress – do you think she was hoping to win him over with just her charming personality? If you do, we seriously need to have a talk.

And we haven't even touched on Esther, Shulamite of Song of Songs, or even the Proverbs 31 gal. All of them are remembered, at least in part for what they wore and how they presented their bodies.

I know, I know. Paul chastises the New Testament women who are busy braiding their hair, piling on the makeup, and jingling their jewelry, (I Timothy 2:8-14), but gals, we have made this our pet excuse to be lazy about our looks. He was addressing a time and culture where these girls were using their sex to distract men away from God. Many of our New Testament Churches were located in cities where idol worship, along with temple prostitution, was simply part of the culture. And some of these gals, formally employed by those temples, converted. When they started attending local Churches, they found out that some of their old habits weren't so easy to kick, and Paul is delivering a corrective word to these girls in particular.

Now, I know that none of you have ever delivered a corrective word, especially not you moms out there. You know those times when you say to your kids, "I don't want to hear another peep out of you." "Don't move a muscle." "If you bat an eye. . ." "Don't you even think about it." "If you so much as look in that direction. . ." Are you starting to get the idea? Corrective words are harsh and sometimes a little extreme to get our attention. And well, if anyone was going to go overboard when talking to the gals and leave it sounding like blanket statement, it would have to have been Paul. Is he saying don't be beautiful? I don't think so. I think more than anything he is trying to tell us it doesn't matter how beautiful the outside is if the inside doesn't match up, and this is an idea that we can all get behind.

I have already brushed past the topic of arousal when I was waxing eloquent about my shoes, but it deserves a little more attention. The truth is our bodies were intentionally designed to arouse men. Unfortunately, our society has become so muddled in its thinking about sex and sexuality, this term has lost much of its original meaning. To arouse someone is to awaken them, to make them aware of a situation or circumstance that needs a response. Girls, we need men to respond to us, and they need to respond to us. Arousal is all part of a system that God put in place for a reason, but this response doesn't necessarily mean that they want to have sex with us. Allow me to explain it this way:

As a woman I should evoke, or arouse, a certain response from a man – any man. If I approach a door, he should reflexively open it on my behalf. If I fall from atop my pretty shoes, he should rush to my aid. And if I am starving, he should feed me. The role of a man is one of protector and provider, and one, as a woman who was divorced for eleven years, I appreciate.

When I am fully a woman, I present a challenge to every man before me – can you fully be the man you were created to be? When I inhabit my sexuality with all that it entails, I am provoking the men in my life to fully inhabit theirs. I am telling them, "I am female enough for this situation. Go find your own job, one that doesn't infringe on my right as a woman to be the woman in this situation."

Look, we have two choices when it comes to living out our sexual roles, male or female, and no matter how much some people may desire that we have the third option of gender neutral, it just does not exist. Every time I try to be asexual, I am really taking on masculine traits and infringing on the rights of the men in my life to be men. When I deny them the right to respond to my femaleness, I am robbing them of the right to fulfill their God ordained roles. When I appreciate my womanhood and live my life as a celebration of who my God has created me to be, I am not tempting them to fill the void and take on feminine traits. I am not giving them permission to be less than the men they are supposed to be.

Think about this for a moment. Think of those young men, sometimes as young as eight and nine, who gallantly hold the door open for you at Church. Why are they doing it? Because either their mother told them that this is what good men do for women or a great dad modeled this for his sons by responding to his wife's role as woman. Even at this age, our willingness to let them wrestle with that door is affirming that we value the fact that they are men – or will be. We are giving them permission and praise for responding to our sexuality, and there is nothing dirty or wrong with this.

And it goes way beyond doors. If we as women would give men permission to be men in every area of our lives, we would be amazed at the lengths they would go to celebrate the women who valued them this much. Having recently remarried, I have been blessed with an amazing man, and he is all man. He gets up every morning and goes to work no matter how bleary his eyes are from sleep. He works hard all day long, and when he comes home he comes home to me, for me, and because of me. He knows that his wife is waiting with a hot meal, a hot kiss, and the hope that the temperature in the bedroom will climb before the night is over.

Some of you are cringing over that last paragraph. "Are you his doormat?" you are thinking. Not by a long shot. I am celebrating his affirmation of my sexuality and all that it means for us as family. By being the man who fulfills that role as protector and provider, I am able to fulfill mine as his wife and as one who has a call to share a message. He is responding to the fact that I am a woman in a completely appropriate fashion, and as such he has never had the opportunity to think of me as a doormat. He knows I can take care of myself. I can change the brakes on the car, pull a transmission in my truck, lay a hardwood floor, and haul hay with the boys, but now, I don't have to unless I want to because he is responding to my needs and desires. In case you were wondering, I know what it means to be a man's doormat, and believe me, this isn't it. What we share is a simple expression of how we have aroused each other to be more than we would have been alone.

This power of arousal extends to all women. Little girls make the men in their lives feel protective and awaken the desire to please them with pretty things and kind acts. Old women arouse a respect and kindness within men who have the ability to appreciate this woman's wisdom and sacrifice she made for the men in her life. An anonymous woman standing by a broken down car alongside the highway causes a real man to at least wonder how he can help. Arousal is our right and privilege as women and that is why there have been so many stories about damsels in distress. Somewhere deep inside we want a man, who is inspired by our beauty and virtue, to fight on our behalf, and they want the same thing, but when we fail to be women, they forget that we are the ones they should be fighting for.

Now, lest you misunderstand me, we should not be, nor were we created to be, helpless and tragic little things. There is a strength in women that is astonishing, and we should exercise it to its fullest extent. Part of celebrating our womanhood is being strong, and the right demonstrations of that strength demands respect from those around us. In our strength we are enabled to join in the fight, and participate in the battles that protect our homes, families, and our hearts but we do it as women, not as sexless warriors. Being a strong woman does not mean the denial of our sexuality, but rather, it is having the strength to embrace it.

When we discover the power we have in our gift of beauty, and we stop running from our responsibilities as stewards of God's creation, we treat ourselves better, and in doing so, we will be able to teach our daughters to love themselves and make wise decisions that honor our King. Not to mention, many of the traps that we as women fall into could be avoided, because the bait wouldn't look nearly as tempting as the love we already possess in our God.

I know that a few of you are waiting for my comprehensive list on how to dress as good Christian woman. Some of you are thinking that now is the proper time to give you a complete system of measurements for your skirts, and detailed explanation of how to tell if a blouse is cut too low. Well, brace yourselves, because I am unapologetically going to disappoint you. There is no list. None. And I really don't think that there ever can be such a list.

Dressing as a good Christian woman is based on our ability to appropriately determine what clothing both honors our Lord both by concealing those parts of us that should be reserved for spouse and celebrating our God's creation of someone beautiful. I believe that the Lord desires us to choose the clothing that is appropriate for the situation and circumstance of our lives. As women who engage in full and hopefully active lives, our clothing choices should be made with wisdom.

For most of us, the question isn't whether we are being modest or not, the question is whether we are dressing suitably for demands of our lives. As I explained to my girls once upon a time, you do not wear your bathing suit to Church, but you also don't wear your Church dress to the lake. In other words, what is completely acceptable in one circumstance is questionable or even objectionable in others. As the wife of a biker, my leather chaps are essential for long rides and cold weather. Wearing them at bike rallies or benefit rides is not only okay but expected. They keep me warm and if we would have a wreck they would help preserve some of my skin. However, that cute little cut out that nicely displays my butt would draw the wrong type of attention in other situations. The fact is that cute little cut out is not a fashion statement. It is part of a functional design that allows my body to bend and move as leather pants never could.

Allow me one more example, and in doing so, I will totally rip one of my good friend's stories. Thanks, Joanna.

Joanna recently began working out in order to take better care of herself. During the planning stages, she had commented on the skin-tight clothing so many women wear at the gym, and she did not believe that she would be comfortable wearing something so revealing. However, once in a work out class she bent over and discovered that her more modest, loose fitting shirt left everything about her on display for anyone who might be looking. Soon she was wearing more fitted clothing that did not flash her other class members.

Learning how to be appropriate isn't always easy, and we need some help. As someone who speaks in public, frequently from a stage, I have to be very aware of my skirt length. I often opt for pants just so I do not have to worry about accidently exposing myself. And as I tend to be somewhat animated when I talk, I wear tight tank tops under my blouses, so I don't accidently expose myself when I lean into the audience. I only learned to do this when my husband made me aware of how much moving I do when I speak. His observations provided me with the help I needed to make more appropriate choices.

While we are on the subject of skirts versus pants for women, I want to throw this out there for you. The argument that women should only wear skirts is often set forward in Christian circles. The reasoning being that pants are for men and women should not dress like men. Okay, but does that mean that men should not wear skirts? Should women wear kilts? They are definitely men's wear. After all pants are a fairly recent fashion phenomenon, and Paul and Jesus wore something very skirt like. What determines what is men's wear and what is women's wear? I, and I emphasize "I" with no other authority than my own observations, would say whatever society dictates as such, and pants no longer belong to men alone. When the Bible commands us to dress appropriately for our sex, God was not talking about wearing a specific article of clothing that belongs to the opposite sex. He was talking about trying to *appear* as the opposite sex, and I don't think that the way I fill out a pair of jeans allows anyone to mistake me for a man.

I know one family where the women do not cut their hair, wear pants, or use makeup. This is their choice, and I think we need to respect their convictions. However, one day when I happened to drop in unannounced, the wife was working in the yard wearing her husband's old work boots. Self-consciously, she explained how his boots fit, and they were warmer than any of the women's boots she had found. The men's boots just seemed to be better made, and she had even bought her daughters the same type of boots to work in.

Now, here is the question – if wearing pants is wrong because they are men's wear, how is wearing his work boots any different? I agree with my friend's conclusion, and I think it is a logical solution. I have no fear for her morality simply because she dared to wear men's boots, nor do I think she is leading her daughters down a path of destruction. What I don't understand is how did she determine this line was okay to cross but not the line on pants?

I have heard it argued that pants reveal too much, and allow me to say what I think about that – hogwash. If you have ever walked around in a skirt on a windy day, especially a modest full skirt, you know that you are in grave danger of pulling a Marilyn Monroe. And if you have ever played in the floor with a toddler, I don't have to warn you of how exposed you could easily become. Tight pants can be revealing but so can a tight skirt, even an ankle length skirt, and this is why simply following the "rules" cannot help us in our attempts at modesty.

I could easily make the argument that tight pants are safer for girls to wear. I recently saw on a sticker – If I can barely squeeze into these jeans, what makes you think he can get into them? There is something to be said about all that buttoning, buckling, and zipping. It takes a lot more work and thought than a hand ran up a thigh under the cover of a skirt, and if he manages to get a hand in your jeans – you almost always have to let him. For me, jeans were the clothing of choice on a date, and in fact, my husband asked me not to wear skirts while we were engaged. As he put it, skirts were way too convenient, and he didn't have to elaborate.

While I have very few definite rules about how we should dress as Christian women, I do want to address one issue that is often over looked – the proper care and grooming of our girls (read that as breasts). I do not understand why we fail to teach our daughters how to buy a proper bra, but we do. I don't know if it is because we were never taught, (because most us of weren't) or if we think, once again, that if we ignore it, it is not a problem. Too many Christian gals are walking around with sagging breasts or the double boob, and ladies this is not good. Not only does it draw the wrong sort of attention to our breasts, it is also uncomfortable and unflattering. So here's a quick piece of advice – measure. Measure first below the breast directly against the rib cage. The number you get is the number you should look for on your bra. Now, measure directly across the fullest part of your breast, subtract the first number from this one, and for every inch of the difference substitute a letter – 1 inch = a, 2 inches = b, 3 inches = c, etc. This gives you the proper cup size, and now you know what to buy, and can stop guessing. So if you first measurement is 36 and the next one is 39, you should wear a 36C.

If you are still having difficulties or have large breasts, because this method doesn't always work for those of you who are "blessed among women", simply go to a good department store or a specialty bra shop and ask to be measured. They have clerks there that have been trained to take the right measurements and help you find the right bra. And go on, spend the money for a good one. You will feel better and look better, too. I firmly believe that this is not vanity. We would never think of wearing shoes that were two sizes too small or clunking around in ones that were too large. We know that it makes no sense and would make us miserable – the same goes for the girls.

Look, here's what it all boils down to – if you feel like you are displaying your assets a little too boldly, you are. If you feel over exposed, you are. If you are dressing with the intent of seducing men, you are, and you need to rethink your choices. However, if you are dressing as a celebration of your sexuality, adorning your body as befitting the artistic creation of a wonderful Lord, then you are properly celebrating His work.

As an artist, this is exactly how I like to think of my body – God's own piece of art, and that has helped determine how I dress or, in keeping with the metaphor, frame what He has given me. If you visit my house you will find numerous pieces of art. The ones I love get displayed properly, befitting the value I put on them. Those I don't like so much are kept hidden. I ask my friends who visit my home not to leave their dirty fingerprints on my paintings and drawings, but I will give them all the coloring books they could desire. (If they do a really good job, I will even put it on my fridge.) It is a matter of respect for the things I hold dear, and they are willing to abide by the rules because they care for me. If I was a little more neurotic, like some people I know, I would insure the safety of my art work by keeping it safely out of sight, but I think we all know that defeats the purpose of having beautiful things. Nor do I set them out in the sun, or even hang them where the sun can hit them directly, because while their beauty would be stunning in such light, the overexposure would quickly destroy them. So I display them but set boundaries and take the appropriate steps to insure they are preserved. It is what we do with works of art and beauty. They were created for our enjoyment and pleasure, and our bodies are the first piece of art we are given. We should care for them as such. So if I were to write a list of rules for our dress it would go something like this:

- Use an appropriate frame
- Make sure it is properly supported
- Display it gracefully – don't hide it away
- Prevent unauthorized handling – remember no fingerprints
- Use the proper lighting – enough to appreciate it, but always avoid overexposure.

The Truth About Love and Romance
or
Why You Can't Believe the Movies

As girls, we are raised on the hopes and promises of romance. We are told that we are little princesses, and we easily insert ourselves into the stories that sent us off to sleep each night. Every chore confirmed that we must be Cinderella, each time someone spoke the words that threaten to cut our hearts out we knew we must be Snow White, and that horrible guy that no one else appreciated had to be our Beast or Frog Prince.

Some moms buy their daughters tiaras and plastic "glass" slippers. We watch the Disney movies and remind our girls that someday their prince will come. Of course, we never tell them that this never quite happened for us. We hope that their lives are going to be different. We pray that they will never face the fact that happily ever after may not include a castle or even some sewing mice. Maybe we think if we keep the fantasy alive for them, they can escape the realities of difficult relationships and broken hearts.

The problem for too many girls is their hopes become reliant on finding that perfect man, the modern day Prince Charming. We Christianize the image by including such attributes as being a good boy who goes to Church, comes from a two parent heterosexual home, a boy with a good job, and a fine singing voice. He is the boy we want our daughters to fall for, the one we hope to have at Thanksgiving dinners, and as the father of our grandchildren – oh wait, that means our girls will have to have (say it in a whisper with me) sex.

Which begs the question, why do we teach our daughters about romance but forget to tell them about the facts of sex in the real world? After all, I don't know about you, but all my teenage fantasies about Prince Charming were pretty steamy. I wanted a man who got my motor running, and let's face it, the good boys aren't always so good at that.

So who does our daughter bring home? A long haired, tattooed, and pierced freak claiming she's in love with him. And who can blame her? With those sultry dark eyes, brooding brow, and fierce air of untamed passion (or could it be hormones?), he is stunning. I know I fell for him once upon a time. He was fierce, and he was dangerous. He sent tingles down my spine and into the pit of my stomach (not to mention a few other places). Just his presence was overwhelming and delicious. Cotton candy clouds and fairy godmothers melted out of sight when he let his ripped-denim-clad thigh rest next to mine on that Church camp bench. Mama's hopes and dreams were way too tame for me now. I wanted the promise of adventure I could see in his eyes.

And when all three of his whiskers brushed my ear . . . yowzhers! It was all I could do to remember that I had made a commitment to save even my first kiss for the man I would marry. Thank God, God is gracious to the stupid and the naïve.

I was a teenager when the "True Love Waits" campaign took the Southern Baptist Churches by storm, and as the grandchild of a preacher, I was one of the first ones handed a pledge card in hopes I would set an example for everyone else. I managed to escape my teenage years unscathed, holding hands for the first time at eighteen, receiving my first kiss at nineteen, and holding out for the wedding night for almost everything else, but let's face it – when you give kids rules, you are also handing them a truck load of loopholes, loopholes to be exploited and used as brazenly as they dare.

And if you need some help, there is always some smooth talking guy who has had his tongue freshly lubricated with a surge of hormones demanding release. He has an amazing ability to think of ways to bend rules that most of us good little Church girls had only entertained on the darkest of nights but never actually thought that we would do. He whispers things like, "We aren't really doing anything wrong," "You promised to stay a virgin, and you will," "I love you, and it will be years before we can get married. God will understand." And those defense-shattering words – no, not I love you – "You are beautiful."

So hands go meandering, kisses, even kisses that aren't allowed to land on the lips, become impassioned, and your body starts curling around his before you know what you are doing. Suddenly the voices in your mind start telling you, "Well, if you did this much, a little more won't hurt, and it feels so good." All logic centers shut off and morals fly out the window, as you struggle to remember why you aren't suppose to be doing this – and when his tongue snakes into your ear, you swear that there isn't a bit of oxygen left in the universe. For the first time, you know the power and glory of being woman, and it is intoxicating.

We had been taught that love was supposed to be magical, earth changing, and what can be more magical or earth changing than that pulsing between your legs? Surely this is what mama was talking about when she said love was beautiful and grand. Or that is how it seems. Only my Prince Charming can melt me into this pool of quivering goo, so he must be it! And so begins the tale of the modern day Romeo and Juliet. Death will not be literal, but hopes and dreams will be sacrificed for the illusion of true love.

Our fairy tales and romance novels taught us that there will only be one great love of our lives, one man who can make us feel this way. So we fight to hold on to it, giving in and putting out when we know that it is wrong. Yet, we were taught, conditioned, and groomed to believe that all great love stories face difficulties and require sacrifice, even of ourselves. This is it, we believe. It has to be. We tell ourselves, because we know that we will never have another chance to feel this way.

In some ways this thought is absolutely correct. You won't. It happens this way only once, the first time, when all systems are go and that wash of hormones is one hundred percent brand new, and the discovery is more exciting than the event. This is a moment that can never be reclaimed or relived, but we will try. Going to new heights of excitement and new lows of scandalous behavior all in search of something that we lost, usually to a boy too young to realize our dreams of manhood.

For so many of us, remembering that time in our lives is difficult. Most of the Church programs about sex that I have attended were led by women who had been married for years. Many of them had married their high school sweethearts and forgotten how mind numbingly intoxicating first kisses can be for a girl who is just discovering that her body is capable of feelings that had previously been nonexistent. Some of us don't want to remember.

We want to think that the girls we have raised are unaware of their bodies, that they aren't wired like we were, and they don't know the sensations I just described. So we give the proper sex talks – Wait until you are married. It will be so much better with your husband. Sex outside of marriage is dangerous. You don't want to be a teenage mom. In short, just say no.

But say no to what exactly? Kissing? Holding hands? Petting? How do they know what they are doing until it's too late? When he is so worked up that he forgets what the word no means? When you suddenly realize you are topless in the front seat of his car? Or is it after some fully-clothed bumping and grinding led to a crazy explosion in yours and his pants?

Look, all the good Christian advice is right. There is no way to deny it. Studies, even secular ones, indicate that the most stable and rewarding marriages are often the ones in which the couples chose to abstain until the wedding night. The problem is most of our girls don't know where to draw the line, or even how to pick up a piece of chalk.

As a teenager, I used to joke that you shouldn't do anything in a car you couldn't do with your seat belt on. Later, I discovered there are a lot of things you can do with your seat belt on, there are a lot of things you can do with your clothes on, but I don't think that they are all activities we can endorse from a Biblical stand point.

To be honest, knowing where to draw the line was much easier as a divorced woman with some experience under my belt. Oh, the line was harder to draw, but I had more of an idea of where it should have been drawn. I found that some of the things I would have never dreamed of doing as a virginal teenager were completely all right, but some of the things that I had once considered an innocent past time were the sexual equivalent of strolling through a minefield. As you might imagine, eleven years of being divorced gave me lots of time to think about how to handle these potentially explosive (pun intended) situations.

And allow me to add, that as a divorced woman many of the myths that I had been taught about love and romance came right back to me. All the stuff that I been led to believe about that one and only true love colored my thinking yet again, and the first man that I allowed to be physically close to me had the same draw and power over me that any teenage romance ever did. Only this time, I didn't have the added incentive of protecting my virginity. Not to mention, I knew what I was missing out on, and I wanted it. The forbidden nature of it all only added to the excitement, and the temptation to forget everything I believed was almost too great to endure.

Making matters even worse, I was told that the Bible did not teach us that celibacy was required of divorced women or any woman who was already sexually experienced. A man in Church leadership told me God knew that we had opened those doors, and we were allowed to enjoy sex as freely as any hedonist. While I never bought into the lie enough to completely act upon it, I did toy with it long enough to cause some major confusion in my life. The repercussions were not pretty, and I have had to deal with the consequences. The major consequence being that for eight years I stayed in a relationship that left me and my children in an emotional limbo, unable to leave behind a man who at least partially fulfilled my physical needs without ever being willing to fulfill my emotional ones. Looking back, I can see how foolish this was, and I know now that the person who told me this was simply trying to take advantage of a woman in a vulnerable circumstance and was exploiting his position of authority to do so.

So what do we teach our daughters? And for those of us who are single with experience, how do we protect ourselves from these dangers? I don't claim to have all the answers, but here is what I have learned.

The first thing we have to do is somehow disentangle our hopes for romance from our bodily reactions. We need to be honest about how we were designed to respond to the male body. We get all tingly, light headed, our breathing changes, and our heart races. Faces become flush, nipples become rock hard, and our pelvis feels like it is molten lava. These are all good and appropriate responses to the smell and feel of a man's body. We want to have them, and we should be glad that we do. In the proper time and context, these responses are mind blowing for both parties and should be enjoyed. What we need to know is these are just biological functions that have no special significance when it comes to true love. Under the proper circumstance just about any man who is the least bit masculine can illicit these responses from us, and we need to be aware of them. We also need to control them.

you right tho!

The problem is we don't want to be this specific with our girls. We have a hard time telling them what to watch for so that they can know when they are becoming aroused. I think that we have this idiotic hope that they will never experience these feelings until they can engage in a proper sexual relationship, but this is naïve and dangerous for them. The truth is once we reach this state of excitement we are sending off an ocean of pheromones the man is picking up on and causing him to have some pretty intense reactions of his own. In turn, he has become a biohazard of male hormones, and his pheromones are working together with ours to send us into a mating frenzy. Everything in us is wired to send the very clear message that now is the time to mate, and the naive ones are taken by surprise.

Being truthful means that we stop thinking that denial is the answer. If we are single, we need to be conscious of our physical responses, and if we are teaching young girls, we need to help make them aware of what is going on inside their bodies. And we need to stop acting like these things only happen when a girl is out prowling for sex. Our bodies are fascinating, and as we age, it sometimes does test runs and warm ups for the big event. Reading through some of my journals as a girl, I found where I once became completely fascinated by a man's neck and reading the words about that day, it all came back to me. I wasn't thinking anything sexual. I had just notice the nice clean line where his hair was cut and how it revealed where his neck had not been tanned beneath the hair. My response was dynamic. I couldn't breathe and my lips began to tingle, both sets, and I all I wanted to do was run my finger along that line.

To this day, I still love that place at the base of a man's skull, and it began as a very innocent and uncontrived observation. I wasn't pursuing or plotting anything. The natural systems spontaneously took over. For years I was embarrassed that I was so moved by something so small, but now I know that it was an adolescent surge of hormones telling my body that this was the correct and proper response to a man. I hope I don't disappoint you when I say nothing happened that day. I was in my parents' living room and he was a friend of my father's who had never seemed all that appealing before. Having run into him again not too long ago, I realized that that place on his neck may have been the only attractive thing about him, ever. Why do I tell this story? Because I am not the only one who has had this reaction, and by calling it what it is, I believe that girls who have never had a sexual experience can begin to take note of the signals their bodies are sending them before they get into a compromising situation.

Love and sex are two distinct entities, but so often in Christian circles we have made them synonymous. We have done this in hopes that our young people will understand that sex should be reserved for the person who loves you enough to marry you. And while that is a totally correct idea, too many of our young people have heard our message backwards. To them a great sexual response – especially when they weren't looking for one means they must be in love. Should sex be a part of a healthy expression of love? In a marriage covenant absolutely, but having sexual response should never be confused with being in love.

The burning in your loins is not romance. It isn't even affection. What you are feeling is hormones plain and simple, but as women who were told that only bad girls have hormones. We think that the source must be something higher than our dancing clitoris – even if that is where we are feeling it most. So we justify our actions because we don't recognize that we are getting sucked into the lie that the world has presented and the Church has unwittingly confirmed.

We need to find a clear vision of what love and romance really are. However, finding that vision is difficult. The world has equated romance with sexual desire, and the Church has painted it in shades of pastels. As smart women, we know that romance is scarlet and crimson, never anything so weak as pink. Christian marriages seem passionless to our eyes, more of a friends with benefits arrangement, wherein she does his laundry and he mows the yard, than a torrid love affair. How many times have we heard the women in Church speak of sex with disdain or outright declare that it was their duty without the slightest indication that they may actually find this "duty" to be the least bit enjoyable?

Do you see why so many girls and women are so confused? Even our message as Christian women is muddled. Love should be romantic like a fairy tale, but tame like the marriage their good Christian mom has. A young girl's Prince Charming should sweep her off her feet, and yet when she looks to mom and dad, she's pretty sure the only sweeping that happened between the two of them was the nightly sweeping of the kitchen floor because mom acts as if she never knew what romantic adventure was. Or she acts outright afraid of them. Always warning her daughter against anything remotely resembling one. And dad? Well, he might be sweet and all, but when did she ever witness him doing anything romantic for her mother? Surely, mom and dad just missed out on that great adventure, but you can bet, she isn't going to.

Television, movies, romance novels, and songs tell us that the love of our lives should make us quiver with desire. Kisses should inflame us with passion, and sex should be as sultry as a July afternoon in Savannah. All of these things make it seem as if the Church's way of doing love and romance is seriously lacking, and so we go off looking for it in greener, if thornier, pastures. Ladies, it is time we started telling the next generation the truth about love, romance, and sex and stop hiding behind what is good and proper. God never did that to us, ever. He told us the truth, and if we listened we were better for it. It is time we do the same favor for our daughters.

We can start by learning to share our stories of romance. We need to let our daughters know that what may seem like a quietly proper marriage in the living room is a sexual adventure in the bedroom. They need to know that romance abounds in quiet unobtrusive ways between us and our husbands. We need to share the joy of a love that is unapologetically expressed through a healthy and God-ordained love affair called marriage. No, they don't need the details, but they need to know that true romance does not belong to the world. It belongs to those of us who have a loving and passionate God living inside of us, blessing our marriages, celebrating our unity with the men who love and desire us as women.

We need to be vocal in our praise of our husbands. We should compliment him freely in front of children, demonstrating our appreciation for the way he works to provide and protect your family. Our words should reflect the value we place on his masculinity and care. Our eyes should betray our desire for him, and we should guard our bedrooms as a sacred place, conveying that what occurs behind that closed door is special and precious to us. Flirting with him openly, touching him appropriately in public, and unashamedly stealing a quick kiss, all of these actions tell the girls that there can be passion in Godly marriage without being crass. And this type of passion is supposed to be modeled for our daughters. They need to know that our sex life is hot.

Don't believe me? Pick up you Bible and turn to the book of the Song of Songs. A lot of the meaning is lost to the English audience, but let your mind play with the euphemisms and metaphors. It is hot, not just warm or tepid, outright hot. We should all be so lucky to have a man who adores our bodies and personalities as much as he did hers. I should add that studying the Hebrew and learning a bit more of the "slang" for that time was one of the most difficult things I ever did as a single woman. I never knew that the Bible could be such a turn on, but it was and is.

When we model passionate and loving marriages for the girls, we are helping them set realistic expectations for what romance should and can be. Not to mention, this type of open adoration can send a man into a tailspin of appreciation and desire for his wife, making it a win/win situation for everyone involved, but we will explore this further in a later chapter.

The second thing we need to do is to debunk the theory that our first love will be our only true love. I have met far too many Christian girls who feel compelled to stay in a relationship that is horribly wrong for them because they did not want to admit that they made a mistake. We need to kill the idea that dating is always the first step to marriage. Now, I know that I just lost a lot of you with that statement, but let's look at it rationally, shall we?

The pure and simple truth is, we don't have very many places where we can get to know someone. This is especially true if you are out of high school and college. I know someone is yelling at me right now, "What about the Church?" To that I have to ask you, have you attended a Church single's function lately? Most of them are seriously flawed, and with no signs of recovery. If you have found one that is really great, congratulations and enjoy. If only I could have been that fortunate.

To begin with, around 80% of all the people there are giant horny toads just hoping for the chance to have Church-sanctioned sex. Their end game is marriage, pure and simple, and they are ready to dive in within minutes of meeting a potential victim . . . uh, I mean, spouse. Which leads us to the next problem, any person involved in a Church singles group who is even remotely normal will get married in a matter of a few months, leaving an "interesting" blend of people behind.

Before you get mad, let me just state, I was one of the ones left behind, and no, I am not normal nor do I ever hope to be.

In addition, the pressure in Church single groups is suffocating,. The very fact that it is related to the Church means that people are on their best behavior. They have all the Church answers down pat, and getting to know the real person is often next to impossible.

We don't have enough community activities anymore. Places where married and single people can gather together to play and work, free of the pressure to pair off with someone, are almost nonexistent. So where are we suppose to meet that great guy? Beats me. Honestly. I met my husband at a bar, and later found him again on the internet, not the ideal ways to meet a good Christian man, but God has a sense of humor. So let's turn our attention to the dating world, and examine why we may need to rethink our approach, and why it is so important to destroy that idea that our first love will be our only love.

How to be an escape Artist
or
I'm Only Here for the Food

Dating serves the vital function of allowing us the time and place to converse with someone and get to know them in a neutral location. If we use our heads and some common sense when we date, it can be a really fun and safe activity, but we have to take the pressure off the singles to date like it is a job interview for marriage. I tell young women it is all practice, a learning experience where you learn to spot those things in men that you love and hate. Perhaps most importantly, I remind them there is no need to jump into a boyfriend/girlfriend relationship just because he buys you dinner.

I also advise saying yes to almost everyone who asks. I did not like my husband when I met him, but after a few dates where we honestly spent hours talking to each other, I realized that he really was the man of my dreams. Fortunately for him, I had just made up my mind to date as much as I could a few weeks before he did ask me out the first time, or he would have missed out on a lot. Sure there are some guys you really don't need to spend time with to know that they aren't for you, but when in doubt, say yes. You never know who is going to wow you when you take the time to really get to know them.

Also, the more men we know, the more likely we are to know what we are looking for in future mate, because sometimes you find that what you thought you wanted really isn't what you need. Even some of the most prince-like qualities can turn out to be less than endearing once you actually get to spend some time with a man who is everything you thought you wanted.

I once dated an amazingly gorgeous man. His manners were superb. He was charming and witty. When he looked into my eyes, I felt as if I was the only living creature on the face of the earth. I had never felt so beautiful. I loved to go out with him, but after a couple of times out, I realized that he treated every woman this way – and I do mean every woman. Young, old, short, tall, ugly, and beautiful, he would rest those big brown eyes upon their face, and they felt the same magic I did. And I began to realize that I did not want a man who acted this way. Sure it was fun, but I knew that he would forever need the affirmation of a woman's mesmerized eyes staring into his. We remained friends, and I wasn't surprised when he called a few months later to tell me that he and his new girlfriend were having problems. He felt that she was ignoring him, and he had cheated on her.

I could share at least twenty different scenarios that I have personally experienced while dating, but it all boiled down to this – by meeting and talking with many men, I learned to identify those traits that I loved and hated. This meant as I got to know my husband, I learned that he possessed the traits that I wanted in a mate, and perhaps even more importantly, I knew that he did not have many of the ones that I did not want. Knowing these things made saying yes to the right man so much easier.

Many people will argue that dating in such a willy-nilly fashion is dangerous, and if we went by the rules of the 1950's, it is. Times have changed and our approach to dating has to change with it. We can begin by recognizing there are no set rules for dating in the Bible, and the reason for this is that dating did not exist back then. Women did not decide who they were going to marry. Their fathers chose a groom based on finances and social standing. Marriages were business contracts, and things like love and desire played no part in the selection of a mate. The best the girl could hope for was that her dad picked out someone who would treat her well, but even that was a gamble she had to take.

Since prearranged marriages simply do not happen in our culture, we have to make a way for people to meet, learn about each other, fall in love, and marry. For so long the Church has upheld the idea that by limiting the number of men we dated, we limited the chances that we are going to get caught up in a dangerous situation. However, from what I have seen and experienced, it is usually just the opposite.

I feel that there are three important reasons why we need to stop claiming that dating must end in marriage, and they are:

1. We need to feel like it is safe to get out whenever we need to get out. No strings, no pressure, and no thoughts of failure. We gave him a shot. It didn't work, and now it is time to move on with no shred of guilt for making a wise decision now.

2. We tend to romanticize the relationship if we think that we are obligated to stay. Once we think we are in it for the long haul, we start trying to overlook and accept attitudes and behaviors that should be tip-offs he is not the one for us.

3. It also means that many girls feel like it is okay to be freer with their bodies since they believe they are going to marry this guy. Recognizing that it could end at any second helps us be a little more guarded with our hearts and our breasts.

Dating may lead to marriage, and ultimately, I think that is what we all want, but we need to stop thinking that it *must* lead to marriage.

I believe that if you desire a marriage, there is an amazing man out there somewhere for you, and now you just have to find each other. No one can tell you how that will happen, but I am pretty sure we can rule out royal invitations and fairy godmothers. Usually it is trial and error, and this is a good thing because dating is all a chance to learn.

Earlier I stated that we needed to use our heads and some common sense when we are dating, and I cannot overstate this. Christian dating is stuck in some crazy 1950's time warp. Dating according to those rules is flat out dangerous in this day and time. Over the years, I developed my basic protocol for dating, and it served me well, so I will share it with you.

1. Do not give out your number.

Despite the fact that there was a day when good girls never called a guy, this is not that day. If a man wants to talk to you further, get his number and call him. When you do, be sure to block your number. With all the technology around today, giving out a phone number is the same as giving him a road map to your house – and trust me, there are some men that you don't ever want to know where you live. If you have your address listed on a social networking site, take it off before you move into the dating arena.

And for all you single gals living alone who are included in a Church directory, consider having your number withheld. Ask to be listed with an email address instead, and then you can determine who should and should not have your number. I once had a man that I had spoken with only briefly at my church use the directory to get my number and then find my house. I was not pleased when he appeared on my doorstep unannounced and uninvited.

2. Google! Or other internet searches like Pipl and Linkedin.

Yes, that's right. Google him before you call. There is so much you can find out, and you can pretty much bet that if he is really interested in you he is doing the same. Is he a registered sex offender? You don't have to guess about it, look it up. An arrest record? It's on the internet if it exists. Bankruptcy? Divorce? Owes back child support for a child, or twelve, he forgot to mention? Any news worthy items about him? His professional history will give you clues as to who he really is too. It's all at your fingertips, so take advantage of the technology. After all, if it is on the internet, it's a matter of public record and fair game, but be aware just because you don't find any dirt doesn't mean that he's clean. Proceed, but proceed with caution.

3. For first dates, pick a very small window of time.

A lunch or a coffee date is a great way to start. If all is going well, then proceed to the next time to get together. In the meantime, you aren't feeling pressure to actually endure a whole evening with someone you may not even like.

4. Drive your own car on dates.

Not only does this keep your home a mystery for a while longer, it also means you can leave anytime you wish, with the added bonus of getting to say good night in a public parking lot – not under the front porch light with him expecting the almost obligatory good night kiss.

Girls, remember you have the ability and right to determine who you are going to invest your time in. This means if you find yourself on a date with a jerk, you have the freedom to leave. Dating is not the time and place for politeness to dictate your actions – our goal in dating is to be appropriate, not polite. If he gets out of line, makes suggestive remarks or any remark that makes you uncomfortable, gets a little free with his hands, or forgets the importance of personal boundaries, leave. You can do it, and you should. Which brings us to. . .

5.   File a flight plan and stick to it.

For this you need the help of a friend, and make sure it is someone you can rely on. Tell them your plans, where you are going and when you plan to be home. Give the friend your date's number and full name.

Check in with them on your way home, or once you get there, so they know you arrived safely. Plus, no date is complete without the after-date-debriefing, but we will talk about that more later.

6.   Have an exit plan.

Go on each date planning to leave early. I have a really good friend who would call me an hour into a date and tell me her kitchen was on fire. If I was having a good time, I laughed at her, and she told me to have fun and hung up. If I was dreading spending one more minute there, I gasped and told my date I had to go.

This call actually serves a number of purposes. First of all, it allows you a way to get out of date where you may feel threatened in some form, without escalating the situation. Second, if you tell him what the call was really about (I usually did if I stayed), you can see how he reacts to the fact you were being smart. Some guys hate the fact you would dare even consider walking out on an evening with them, but others take it in stride.

Hint: if he doesn't react well, you should probably leave anyway. A guy who thinks he can control you that early in a relationship, especially a casual one, will only get worse.

7. If you decide to stay after the phone call, keep in mind you can still leave at any point and time.

Have a departing line ready. Practice it at home until it flows smoothly and gracefully off your tongue. Here's a sample of ones I used:

"Thank you for this chance to get to know you and a lovely evening, but I really don't think this is where I need to be right now."

"I know that you are somebody's prince, but you just aren't mine. I hope you find what you are looking for."

"This has been a lot of fun, and I do enjoy your company, but I think we both know that this isn't going anywhere."

Once you have made your closing remarks, get up and leave. Don't hang around or invite further conversation. Be polite, but firm. If he is not gracious about your leaving, so be it. That is not a quality that you need in a future mate, and you need to leave as quickly as possible to avoid sending mixed signals.

Sometimes, you just know that a date isn't going anywhere. Sure he was nice, but for whatever reason it just isn't happening. In those cases, I usually waited until the check had arrived and offered to pay half before letting him down as gently as I possibly could.

8. Stick to public places.

A quiet table at the back of a restaurant is a fine place to have a good get-to-know-you conversation, and while he may have Netflix at home, any place where you cannot call for help is a bad idea.

If you are the more active type, go bowling or play pool. Movies are an awful choice for first dates, because even if you do talk, no one else will appreciate your conversation. Hiking and rafting are also bad choices, but outdoor fairs and festivals can make for a great time. And if you share a common interest in the outdoors, go to a camping store and design your dream set up together. My husband loves to antique, so we have spent hours just browsing antique stores and talking about what we would buy if we had the money.

Get creative, but above all stay public and do things that allow you talk to each other. After all, the whole point of this exercise is to get know this person.

9. Have an accountability phone call about two hours in to the date.

My wonderful friend would call and ask me (in a faintly insinuating voice), "Whatcha doin'?"

If the date is going well enough for you to still be there, then there is probably a nice amount of chemistry happening and that's great. After all, we want chemistry in a relationship, but we need to keep in mind getting physical is still not a wise idea. Knowing that I had this phone call coming helped me stay focused, and knowing that my friend knows me well enough to know when I am being evasive kept me honest.

When I began dating my husband, she called almost every time we went out, even after we were engaged because she knew my raging hormones were testing my restraint.

10. Know when you are leaving.

Of all my rules, this one was the most difficult for me to stick to. I am the type of person who can get caught up in a conversation, and if it is good, time has no meaning. So set an alarm, and when it goes off, use the snooze to let you wrap things up and then leave.

11. Know your limits and state them up front.

Have in mind how far you are willing to go up front. If a good night kiss is on the menu, then make sure that's all it is. I would announce my limits early into, even before, the first date by saying, "I have two rules about sex. One is, it is to be enjoyed within marriage only. And the second is, then you should make up for lost time." It let the fellow know that while I wasn't a total prude, he shouldn't hold out hope of getting any. Now there are two things to be aware of about stating your limits up front.

Some men will run, and good riddance. At least you know why they wanted to go out with you in the first place, and it wasn't to admire your mind.

Some men will take this as a challenge to see if they can get you to compromise for them. They just think they are that great, and no girl needs a man who is that arrogant in her life.

A very small percent will think it's fabulous that you are willing to live by your convictions. These are the keepers.

12. Every date requires a debriefing.

The debriefing is vital for a healthy dating life, and for this you need a really great friend. She needs to be someone who loves you and wants the best for you. She needs to be someone that will ask you the hard questions, and someone you can answer honestly, but most of all, you need someone who isn't awash with raging hormones.

Recount the evening, every little detail, and get her perspective. Does she see things you didn't? Does his behavior bother her? Why? Did something bother you, but she is not worried by it? She may extend some grace for the nerves that you would have been too rough on, or she may call him on something that you missed because you are just too nice. Listen to her. Her perspective is unclouded by all the new guy mania you may be experiencing. Or she may see some qualities that you overlooked in your attempt to extend grace.

13. If you had even an okay first date, go on a second one.

Remember the first date can be misleading. There are way too many emotions and jitters flowing about for things to be normal. So cut the guy a break and give him one more chance to make a good impression. You might be surprised at how much fun he really is once he's had a chance to calm down from the excitement of getting to go out with you.

Obviously, these are only guide lines and are open to interpretation. Take what works for you, and tweak it to make it better for your situation. The only one I consider indispensible is accountability. We all need back up, and we girls need to look out for each other.

While we are on the topic of dating, allow me to throw this out there. I am not completely opposed to online dating services, but I do have some reservations which might just be a product of my age and generation. In previous times, men and women met each other through the aid of a matchmaker, usually an older woman in the community who was able to spot those traits that would make for a happy pairing. Her task was to sort out all the blatantly wrong and mismatched people and make arrangements for those who had potential to meet. While her decision was respected, it was not the final word on the matter. Her couple now had to make the final decision on their own, or under the guidance of their parents.

I think this is a pretty safe way to approach online dating. The computer makes suggestions for possible matches, and we check them out. It may or may not work out for us, and that's okay. Given the dearth of ways and places to meet new people, this one is far safer than even meeting someone at your local Church or bar. If you find yourself in one of those limbo places, that place where there really is no one who interests you in your established social circles and you desire to have someone, give it a shot. There isn't a lot to lose and who knows, you might just find someone. Just remember, as in all dating, you can call it quits whenever *you* want to, and you are in no way obligated to do more than check out the suggestions – no matter how scientifically selected.

So now that we have opened the door for dating, this leads to so many more questions. If I haven't already made you mad or shocked you enough to put this book down, thanks for hanging in there, but you might want to brace yourself, because here is where it gets real.

The Three Questions of Dating
or
How Pure Is Pure?

Invariably there are three questions that I am asked when young women talk to me about dating and relationships.

- How far is too far?
- Is oral/anal sex really sex?
- What about masturbation?

Some of you moms want to put this book down right now, but I encourage you to keep reading. Young women come to me for the answers to these questions because they know I will answer them, but what would shock you is how young many of these girls are. Thirteen and fourteen doesn't even faze me now. Twelve makes me cringe a bit, but it is the eleven year olds that still leave me questioning what the world is coming to. In my college classes, these issues were often brought up by students who were unafraid to discuss these issues in mixed company, and they shared that they had wrestled with these issues from a very young age. And these weren't just the girls who came to class questionably clad. They were the good Church girls who could not speak to their mothers, so they listened to the advice of their friends with questionable results. Not talking about it does not make their sexual desires go away, it just makes them look for other sources, and the world is ready and willing to pick up where we lay down our rights as mothers.

Last night, I watched a few of the television programs marketed to our kids, and these three issues were freely referenced by the teenagers on the screen. I know that you may not let your kids watch these programs, but many of their friends do. We need to accept that not all parents are conscientious about what their kids are consuming as you may be, and guess who your daughter is talking to at school? You may even think that you have taken all the right steps in guarding your children from bad influences by taking what some would consider extreme measures like homeschooling. As a former homeschooling mom myself, allow me to say that I am frequently amazed at what my kids hear from other homeschooled children and their friends at Church. Fortunately, my girls speak with me openly and candidly about these issues, but even I had to collect my wits when my eleven-year-old uttered the words "anal sex". I had no clue that such a thing existed when I was her age, but the girls today do, and my daughter isn't the only one.

Now, lest you think that this is only for the moms, I want to encourage you single gals to keep reading too. If you have not asked these questions yet, let me assure you, you will.

In the context of dating, questions one and two can pretty much be answered together. First of all, there is no Biblical handbook for this one, but I think we have some pretty good principles to follow. The number one being, to flee from temptation. So the answer really becomes a question – what behaviors are tempting for you?

Let me put it another way, what types of physical interactions turn you on? The answers will vary from person to person based on their temperament and past experience.

I have always had a very short fuse, and I can go from comatose to raring to go in a heartbeat. So I learned to set my boundaries pretty tight. With few, but disastrous, exceptions I would not even kiss a man until we were seriously talking about marriage. Kissing for me is foreplay and not something I take lightly. On our second date, my husband asked if it was too early to ask for a kiss, and I told him it was. Like the gentleman that he is, he accepted my verdict and asked for another date instead.

For some people kissing can be just kissing, and for those I would say that kissing doesn't have to be a taboo. For others holding hands or snuggling on the couch watching a movie is a turn on and should be avoided. Wherever you need to draw the line is fine, and you need to accept it as such. A real man will be okay with being told he will have to wait for what many may consider an innocent display of affection.

So my first answer for those two questions is rather simple, do you consider this a part of foreplay? Or to be more blunt, would this be something that would lead you to desire an orgasm? If the answer is yes, stop. Take a cold shower, and don't cross that line again until the proper time.

The second answer I have for those two questions is this – when it is time to get married, what do you want to have to confess to your husband? Honestly sharing your sexual history is essential for a good marriage. It doesn't mean that the only marriages that can survive are the ones where two virgins get married, even though that is ideal, but it does mean that when we marry, we should marry someone who can cope with our stories, even our mistakes. Girls, not every man can get over the idea of his future wife being intimate with another guy, no matter how much she may regret it or how many times she apologizes.

Take some time and really think about having that conversation, about telling that man who adores you enough to devote the rest of his life to you what you have done. Picture having to confess doing the most intimate acts with someone other than him, all because you got impatient – because you didn't love him enough to wait. How does that feel?

I can tell you from experience, it doesn't feel good. Nothing will ever erase my then soon-to-be husband's troubled eyes from my memory. And while I could honestly say that I had never had intercourse with any man other than my first husband, I hated having to admit how close I had come to crossing that line with a man I believed would one day marry me. Of course, he forgave me, and I forgave him of things in his past, but there are still some consequences that we have had to deal with in our marriage that stem from our lack of self-control.

Make a list, decide what you can stand, and then stick to it. Be specific. Would you be ashamed to admit that you had kissed another man? That you allowed him to play with your breast? Slide a hand up your skirt? Oral sex? How about some dry humping in a parked car? Now say it out loud and listen to the sound of your voice while imagining the man of your dreams listening to you recount the times when you allowed another man to handle what should have been reserved for him alone.

And don't think that you can do any of this stuff and keep it hidden from him. Every sexual encounter leaves a mark, marks you may not even remember until some random event brings them to mind. We can't erase our memories. They are always there waiting to pounce on us when we least expect it, and when it does, we have no choice but to deal with it.

An even more fun thought is – what are you going to tell your kids when they ask about your sex life before you were married? As a single mom, I had built in chaperons, and I know that they were watching. I know that one day they might try to use some of my past mistakes to justify doing some of the same things I did. My only hope is they have seen that chaos it caused in our lives and that they are better prepared to deal with their sexuality than I was.

We have to take the long term view of our lives when it comes to sex. Living in the moment can lead to a life time of consequences. There are the obvious things like pregnancy and venereal diseases, and there are the more subtle effects upon our minds and hearts. Even if you escape physically unscathed, the subtle effects will linger for years and perhaps never entirely fade. So begin protecting your marriage now, begin loving your husband today. Knowing that he is out there and you have a reason to wait makes it easier. Decide what you want to experience with him alone and guard those parts of you for him. Your whole life will be better for it.

For those of you hoping for fuller answer to question two, don't worry, we will get there, but I want to look at it separately in the context of marriage. For now, let's stay focused on the single life.

On to our final question, masturbation.

I wonder how many of you cringed when you read that word. If you are going to read this section, I request that you read the entire section or skip it entirely. For a number of reasons, I have looked into this issue extensively, and I will share more of those reasons in the section over pornography. I do not take this lightly, nor do I think it is an issue that we should avoid, but before we jump in, we need to do a little homework.

First, the Bible is very specific about sex. Leviticus 21 is nothing but a list of people and things that we are not allowed to have sex with. Some of them are so obvious you almost have to wonder what type of people has to be told these things. The prophets used graphic sexual metaphors that even in their toned down, proper English still shock modern readers. Song of Songs is downright erotic and is accepted as the Bible's final word on romance and sex. So I don't think the topic was avoided because God was too embarrassed to bring it up.

God seems to take sex very seriously, and I am told that He knows everything about everything. That makes me pretty confident He did not miss the fact that people can give themselves an orgasm. So let's think about this for a moment – God who is serious about sex, very detailed in His instructions about other sexual activities, and knows we can give ourselves orgasms. Either He left a glaring oversight in the pages of Scripture, or He did not see a reason to address it. Nor can we say, as with dating, that it was not addressed because it did not exist back in those days.

We also can't claim that God wasn't aware that someday in the future people would scratch their heads and wonder what He thought about this issue. You know one sentence in this big ole Book would have settled everything, but for some reason He chose not to include it. And I don't think it was because He could not find space for "Thou shalt not masturbate".

I can almost hear someone out there asking, but what about Onan (Genesis 38)? He masturbated and God struck him dead. Hey, I know that is the way we were taught the story, but this is one more time when we need to go back and read the Bible for ourselves and stop listening to all those pious know-it-alls who never bothered to read it for themselves. Onan did not get in trouble for masturbating, or spilling his seed on the ground, if you want to say it in good King James English. He got in trouble because he was being a selfish rat and not getting his dead brother's wife pregnant – like he was supposed to do. In an effort to keep her childless, he was practicing coitus interruptus, known today as pulling out. So she has to go and sleep with her father-in-law while disguised as a hooker. It's a great story, really. Beats any day time soap you will ever see on TV.

But that story doesn't help us with the question of masturbation, because masturbation is never addressed.

Oh! But wait! Someone is screaming, Jesus said if you lust after a woman in your heart it is the same as committing adultery. Yes, you are absolutely correct, but what does that have to do with masturbation?

Do people sometimes lust when they are masturbating? Yes, usually. Do you have to lust to masturbate? Nope.

For women in particular, masturbation frequently has nothing to do with lust or any other fantasies. It is simply a stress reliever and a way to deal with certain physical discomforts. We were made to have sex. Our bodies were designed for it, and they run better when we get it on a fairly regular schedule. For some of us, having sex on a regular basis is out of the question for a number of reasons, for me it was eleven years of being divorced. Masturbation is not a substitute for a real relationship and does not have nearly the same health benefits as a healthy sexual relationship, but it can be of some benefit.

As a sufferer of severe menstrual cramps, I have found that this gives me some relief when medication can't even touch them. I have friends who promise this is the ultimate cure for migraines. For women who don't have a sexual partner, this sometimes used as an exercise to strengthen the vaginal muscles and help ward off a prolapsed uterus or bladder (read that as having your innards falling out).

There is no doubt lust is wrong. Reading romance novels or watching porn is not healthy for us in so many ways. We should be doing everything in our power to stay away from anything that stirs up sexual desire for anyone but our spouse, and if lust even threatens to enter the equation, we have stepped over into sin, just as we sin when we allow hunger to morph into gluttony. Masturbation is also a sin when we use it to avoid seeking out a healthy relationship that would include sexual intimacy. We were never designed to meet all our own needs. We were created to be relational creatures, but I think there is a reason why masturbation was never specifically forbidden by God.

Look, there is a reason that we can't hug, kiss, or tickle ourselves, and this leads me to believe there must be a reason we can do this for ourselves. We need to be checked in and aware of how we are using this tool. Are we dependent on it for a sense of well being or to enable us to avoid real relationships? If we aren't doing either of those things and if we aren't lusting, then I personally do not believe it is a sinful activity. After all, God filled us in on all the other stuff, why wouldn't He do the same with this?

Allow me to offer one last caveat. We should never do anything that violates our conscience. God gave us one for a reason. If you feel that this act is wrong, then it is for you. There may be a reason why He would have you refrain, and you should listen to that prompting. On the flip side, carrying around false guilt is never right either, and we need to be aware of what the Bible really teaches on these issues and not be a slave to cultural mores that have no basis in Scripture. Work it out with God. Ask Him to show what He would have you do about this issue, and then listen. Don't just take my word for it.

Protecting our Purity without a Chastity Belt
or
Harnessing Those Thoughts

As Christians we are really good at telling girls that no is the proper response to sexual activity outside of a marriage covenant, but if that is all we are telling our girls we are setting them up for failure. Saying no starts way before we move into a tempting situation. Saying no begins with the preparation of our hearts and minds. I have already addressed where to draw the line when you are with that smoking hot boyfriend or potential mate, but in reality we have to begin drawing the lines in our day to day life, even before the fella enters the picture. Knowing where to draw those lines means we need to know how we are wired.

The first thing we must recognize about women is that sex is never just a physical act. Science has confirmed that the largest sex organ known to humanity is our brain, and that is the first thing we have to deal with. Our thoughts set the tone for all of our actions, determining what we will or will not do, why we will or will not do it, by placing a specific value on that action. Like most creatures the value of sex is somewhat predetermined by our genetic code, with our past experiences and familial values all influencing the final tally.

When sex becomes just another physical experience, it is usually the result of trauma or desensitization. Neither of those things are in keeping with God's intended purpose for sex, both should be addressed with the help and understanding of people trained in these areas. I know the idea of therapy or counseling can be disturbing to some, but let me just say there are some types of crazy that need expert management. This is one of those times, trust me, I've been there, and I am better for it.

When most women think of sex, their thoughts rarely race straight towards the image of a rock hard penis. (Honey, you need to pick up your book). Instead our minds are flooded with images of spine tingling kisses, breath taking caresses, or even that awe inspiring power of the cave man approach. Eventually our thoughts do turn to that bizarre piece of equipment God gave the male, but those thoughts are merely a reaction to the preceding thoughts that turned on all our instinctive responses.

So what are those preceding thought? The chase, the pursuit, the wooing, the affection, the seduction – all those things that men do that tell women they are desirable. Intercourse is great, but if you don't have the rest of it, all the emotional build up and romance, the event falls flat. Sex breaks down into an emotionally empty biological process, and as much as that is okay for most men, women weren't designed to work that way.

The irony is that so many of our Christian circles encourage, especially young, women to think along these lines. Okay, sure, we stop right before things get explicit, but we eagerly share in a girl's fantasy of pursuing a life that is full of sex.

I can feel some of you pulling away from the page in horror with the thought, "I never do that." Let's explore this for a moment, shall we?

Ever talk to a girl about her dream wedding? Ever talk to a young woman about how many kids she would like to have? Ever discuss how to be a good homemaker? The attributes she should look for in a husband? What did you think you were talking about? Sex! Sex! Sex!

Is there anything wrong with this? Absolutely not! Having these conversations is what we are supposed to be doing with the young women in our lives. The problem occurs when we fail to take the conversation farther. Our role as older women is to equip young girls and encourage the older single gals out there to embrace their sexuality as a healthy and valuable part of who they are. We are to teach responsibility, not denial, and we need to stop deluding ourselves about what we are doing.

I know that as a girl when I planned my dream wedding, even as a thirty-four year old bride-to-be, I envisioned the dress, the flowers, the guests, but most of all I envisioned the loving way my groom would look at me when I walked down that garden path towards him. I dreamt of how his voice would sound as he repeated the vows and how he would kiss me before my friends and family. And then I would think about being whisked away, on his Harley, so we could retreat to a private place and fulfill, in part, the vows we made to each other.

I pictured arriving at our honeymoon destination. I wondered whether he would carry me over the threshold or not (he didn't). I picked out the proper negligee and hoped he would like it (he did). And from there the script was steamier than any romance novel. Notice how none of it began with thoughts of having sex?

My day dreams were in keeping with a natural progression of how things should work. As a bride, I was focused not on sex itself, but as I considered the plans we had together, hoped and dreamed of the life we would share, it was only natural and right that my thoughts would stray into the arena of sex. My man should, and does, turn me on. It was proper that I desire him this way, that I should love him so much that I want to express my feelings in this manner. However, notice that expressions of love gave rise to the desire. A sexual entanglement did not give birth to otherwise nonexistent feeling. My task as a bride was to keep it all in check until the proper time.

So what does this have to do with protecting our purity? We have to be aware of how these hopes and dreams for our future are affecting us. As a divorced woman, I found out that focusing too much on the hope of finding a mate stirred up my desire to love and be loved. Stirring that hunger could leave me feeling lonely and sometimes even desperate for one sign that I could have love in my life. With sex and love appearing to be so synonymous, a man's sexual interest could easily be misinterpreted by my lonely mind as proof of his love and affection for me.

And I am not alone. Too many girls have fallen into the same trap, because let's face it, waiting on the right man to come along is a lonely thing. We begin to think that we must be doing something wrong, are too ugly, or maybe just a bit too guarded. So we let our guards down, lower our standards, let the next fellow come a little closer, find something that feels so right and good in their touch, and because we want it to be true, we believe they must truly love us. We accept the sexual excitement as a testament to his love, and we become attached to man whose only appeal is his ability to evoke that magical biological response in us. Frankly, this is how so many women wind up in relationships they hate, situations where they compromise or violate what they believe, and discover, in the most painful way possible, why we must distinguish between sex and love if we are ever going to find a man who values all of us and not just what we can do for his body.

When we disentangle love and sex, we empower our daughters to recognize the difference. But when we talk about marriage and the dream wedding without making a clear distinction between love and lust, we are not telling our girls the whole story. To make matters worse, once some girls get caught up in this confusion, they feel that having any type of sexual response makes them nothing but sluts with no value apart from their sex appeal, and give up any right to hope for a healthy sexual relationship with a Godly spouse. The next generation needs us to speak up and share what we have learned, through the good and bad experiences of our lives. We need to stop fearing the mistakes of our past, those moments when we fell for the lie, and begin using what we had seen as shameful as the weapons they are. Remind our daughters that God is big enough to redeem all things, including our sexual mistakes, but also reminding them His ultimate desire is to protect us from making them in the first place.

Ladies, this takes guts on our parts, and for some of you, the idea of sharing any of your misadventures in sex is terrifying. We want our daughters to think that we automatically got it right, that we never struggled with our sexual desires, and that we expect the same from them. We call it setting a good example. Our girls call it what it is, being a hypocrite. Look, our daughters are smart. By now they have probably figured out that we have had sex, at least once for every child in the family, and if you do have a history, there's a good chance they at least suspect that too. So let's stop living the lie, quit doing the big cover up, and shoot straight with them about why we are concerned for them. You aren't doing them any favors by acting as if sex never held any attraction for you. Even worse, you are giving up any right to speak to their sexual issues when you act as if you have never dealt with any of your own. Girls don't want to talk to virgins or asexual women about sex. They want to talk to the women who are brave enough to embrace their sexuality. Like I said, they are smart, and they know that in order to get the real scoop, they have to talk with someone who knows the power and the pitfalls of being a woman.

I am not saying that you had to have made mistakes to be credible. All they are asking for is a woman who has at least wrestled desire. Those of us who got it right serve as a testament that waiting is not only expected, it is possible. At the same time, we can acknowledge that it is a struggle, and that it is not an easy choice, but it is a good one that protects them and their marriages. When it comes to the future of the young women who surround us, there is no place for false pride or modesty. We need to fight on their behalf, and if fighting means that we have to expose some aspects of ourselves that vanity or pride would rather we keep hidden, so be it. Our girls are worth it.

So moms, dream with your daughters, but never let the fantasy obscure the truth. Let them know that love is out there, but don't sell them a dream based on the unrealistic hopes that so many mothers have for their daughters. Give them a dream tough enough to endure the trials and pressures of real life, one big enough for their sexuality, and filled with a beauty that makes it worth defending.

Some of us gals have been in the game for awhile and quite frankly lugging around any dream for too long gets tiresome, and maybe we just need to put the dream down for a bit. We need to stop thinking about a romantic future. We need to stop thinking about what things will be like with our future spouse. Some of us need to turn off the romantic movie, put down the Christian romance novel, and step away from the wildebeest. I know because I had to do it. I stopped watching anything that smacked of a love story. I didn't even go to Church during Valentines season and avoided even the grocery stores that were filled with hearts shaped balloons and chocolate boxes. The reminders of what I was missing were just too much too bear.

Now, I never stopped hoping to get married. I wanted to be married for many, many years before it finally happened. And I never stopped complaining about being alone – ask any of my long suffering friends. In fact, I was even quite vocal about the lack of sex in my life, and my friends proved their worth by enduring it all. I just had to stop doing those things that fed into the fantasy, even the innocent fantasies, because it stirred up emotions that were too big to tame.

Protecting our purity isn't just about saying no. It is about finding a reason to say no and avoiding those things that weaken our resolve or blur our vision. Going on the defense requires that we know who we are and why we are worth the wait and actively pursuing who God created us to be in full knowledge of our sexuality.

The number one thing we can do for our girls is to help them see a vision for their life – where do they want to be in five years? What do they want to accomplish? And we need to stop talking like marriage is a foregone conclusion or as if it is the only way to be a good Christian girl. Young women are getting married later and later in life, meaning decades of celibacy, and many Christian women who have survived a divorce are having to deal with purity issues on an entirely different level than the lucky virgins.

If you are struggling with your sexual desires, allow me to share a few things I learned. Maybe you can save yourself a few years of suffering and make my travails valuable for something other than my own character formation.

Stop focusing on sex, or any relationship or dream that could lead to you focusing on sex. But let me caution you, your mind, just like anything else in nature, abhors a vacuum. You are going to have to fill that space with something, and frankly, knitting and scrapbooking just aren't going to cut it.

You have to find a vision for your life. A vision that makes every fiber of your being come to life with longing and desire, something that consumes you, something bigger than you. It doesn't matter what it is really, if you are passionate about it. I sometimes think that we are all born with a certain level of passion that sits inside of us demanding release, and if we don't release it in healthy ways it will take us over like lunatics in an asylum. Soon we will be doing things we never knew we were capable of doing – all because we failed to respond to this dubious gift God has given us.

Too often girls have no clue as to who they can be or what they can accomplish apart from being a wife and mother. Girls, let's step out of that box, shall we? And while I don't like all the repercussions of the feminist movement, there have been some good things that have come out of it. One of the best is that we are only as limited as our belief in ourselves. So, where do they keep those types of visions? Because, as I am sure you may have noticed, they simply do not stock life-changing visions in most major department stores. The truth is they are buried somewhere inside of us, and if we look, we can find them. And that type of soul searching requires energy, like the type we often squander looking for Mr. Right.

Don't overcomplicate this. Keep it simple. What do you like to do? Eat? Then how about cooking school, starting a catering business, or volunteering at a local shelter and an aerobics class on the side? Decorating? They have schools for that, too. Helping people feel better? Medicine, massage, and counseling are all options. Gardening? If you have some dirt, you can start, but what about horticulture class? Cars? Yes, some girls like cars. Check out your local Vo-Tec. Woodworking and welding? Same thing. Jewelry? They have classes for that, too, or maybe it's time to start making a business plan.

Look, it doesn't really matter if you love whatever it is you are doing, and if you don't know where to start, ask a friend to help. Have them list the things they know that you enjoy and are good at, and check out the possibilities. Sometimes they see the things in us we miss.

For years I had no idea what I wanted to do with my life, and I eventually stumbled into a bad marriage, all because marriage was next logical choice for a good Christian girl who had no idea what to do with her life. After the divorce, I went back to school, not even sure if I liked the degree I was getting, but along the way one of the teachers rocked my world. He asked me what I had written. I thought there was a problem with one of my assignments, but no, he wanted to know what I had written with the intent of publishing. He said I was that good! And since he was a former editor, I believed him – kinda. I have been writing since I was twelve, but only for school and in my journals. The idea that I could write something and get paid was like being told I could get paid for breathing. It seemed almost too ludicrous for words, and yet would you look at what you hold in your hands? I think that's my name on the cover.

The second step is determining how your gift is going to serve your faith. Honestly, I could just as easily, or more easily, write romance novels that would spontaneously combust, but I don't. And I don't because I believe that God desires to use my gift in His kingdom. Knowing that keeps me from writing smut, or even an insulting status on my social network. My desire to honor my God is why I was able to say no in those sexually charged situations even when I was choking on a yes. I just couldn't deny myself that type of pleasure if it was only for me, but it's not. I knew that by being involved in a sexual relationship, I would be destroying my chances to fulfill the vision that God had given me in my life. And frankly, I wasn't willing to give that up, because I believed this book, and the others that will follow, are far more important than any momentary pleasure I may have experienced.

Whatever your vision is, chase it. And it doesn't have to be some highfaluting Church sanctioned endeavor for women. Your vision doesn't even have to be overtly Christian at all. It just needs to be something that you love, and through it, your integrity and excellence will make it an expression of worship.

Now here's the beautiful part: that love of your life that you have always wanted, will fall in love with the real you, (not the clingy, needy you who just wants to get laid and experience a little relief in the moment), will get to see the woman who passionately pursues her dreams, who made the sacrifices required to be true to who God called her to be, and everything grand and great within him will respond. Any true man, who wants a real woman, will know that all those qualities so beautifully exhibited in this area of your life will bode well for your future together.

We should also develop a network of support. I cannot stress this enough, and I will say it a few more times before we get done here. Isolating yourself, even if it is easier, is the quickest route to disaster. We need other women in our lives to help us navigate the waters. For a long time I did not believe this was true. I had always been one of the guys, and I had little use for female companionship. Not until my mid-twenties did I discover that the women in my life were amazing blessings.

In this network you need an array of women: single, married, divorced, widowed, mothers, professionals, old, young, and in between. Each one of them has something to teach you and share with you, but you should not think that this is a one-way street where you simply receive. You should be actively participating in their lives because you also have something to share. (And you should never feed the poor-pitiful-me-whining-and-crying-because-

I-am-alone-victim mentality, and one of the ways we starve it to death is by deciding that you can and will make a difference in the life of another.) These should be women who desire to see you succeed and live a victorious life, single or with a mate. They should be women that you can speak freely with about your struggles and your victories in your sexuality.

I have one single friend who has determined that she will remain single, and she is fine with that. She has an outsider's perspective that is sometimes clearer than those who are in the middle of a crazy love relationship. Since she has no husband to answer to, she has no problem with the late night phone call or even the late night drive to discuss what is going on our lives. Not to mention, she never let me forget that being single didn't mean my life was over, and she never let me use it as an excuse to give up on the vision for my life. Over the years she has proven time and time again that she is capable and willing to help me regain my balance when I have teetered off course. (Whether I want her to or not).

Among my friends are a few married women who adopted me and my girls as a part of their families. They share their insights on relationships from hard-won experience and helped me cope with the demands of being a single mom. Their husbands have been trusted big brothers who were ready to offer a man's perspective on the men and dilemmas in my life, and their children have accepted me like a trusted, eccentric aunt. Together they helped keep my life full and meaningful when I might have been tempted to wallow in despair.

One of my all time favorite friends is the mother to one of my married friends. She is called Mammie by those who love her. Not bound to convention, she speaks with bluntness and brutality that is a right reserved for only those whose heart and character have withstood the challenges of life. She has threatened dire punishment both to me and the men in my life when things were not as they should be. And I had no doubt of her sincerity or capability to do what she promised. Unwavering in her loyalty and unapologetic in the truth she speaks, she is who I want to be when I grow up.

I do not have a formula for how to create such a network, but I believe that it is essential both for your sanity and to help you grow in all areas of life. I found most of my friends at Church, and later they introduced me to the women whose friendship they valued.

Together we have laughed over our insanity, cried over our losses, studied, practiced, and reclaimed our faith. We have called each other on our stupidity and our arrogance. We have threatened fist fights and never to speak to each other again, but in the end we are the ones who fight most fiercely for each other. Together we have learned how to resolve conflicts and express our emotions, first one to another and then taking what we have learned into other relationships. I truly believe that my marriage now owes much to the lessons they taught me about God, love, and myself.

A final note on my network, when I did get married, they helped me pull off the wedding I wanted. They arranged a bridal shower that would have made most good Christian gals blush or run from the house in terror. They helped me be the beautiful bride I hoped I could be. Even though funds were tight, together they insured that I was tanned, polished, and styled beautifully in a pretty little garden next to a stone cottage. They wanted this day, and even this night, to be fabulous. As my good friend Joanna says, "When it comes to sex, Christian women should be the best." And they gave me all the trimmings to help with that goal. My wily friends even invaded the honeymoon cabin and stocked it full of food and blush worthy goodies so my husband and I could leave in style on his Harley, unencumbered by luggage.

If I was only allowed one prayer for the women of the world, it would be that they could have such friendships, because I truly believe that if everyone had friends like mine, books like this would never need to be written.

Men

or

How to Drive a Woman Insane in Three Easy Steps

Look, but Don't Touch

Of all the fundamental facts of this life that we need to be reminded of, one of the most significant is – men are different from women. I know it seems self evident, but girls, too often we forget this simple truth. They look different, smell different, act different, speak different, and think different. And like the fast food commercial says, different is good. We want them to be different, and we need them to be different. However, simply knowing that they are different isn't enough. We really need to understand how these differences affect us, in both good and bad ways.

Please note, I'm just hitting the high points here. There is no way we could talk about all the differences between the sexes, mainly because we keep discovering new ones each time science discovers a new way to scan the brain. I just wanted you to be aware some rather basic and fundamental things that help us understand these bizarre beings just a little more.

One of the most fascinating and infuriating things about men when it comes to sex is that they are so gosh-darn visual. They love to look at beautiful things. The sight of a beautiful woman does things to them that we can't even imagine. We can shake them to the core, causing their brains to become a useless puddle of mush, all because they liked the shape of our booties in that pair of jeans. Girls, we can't fault them for this. It was how they were made. God designed them this way, and it's why He designed us to fill out those jeans so well.

Now, I know that there are a lot of people out there who would try to convince us that this is a horrible wicked part of the male that

61

should be snuffed out completely. I disagree. When we look at the Song of Songs, we find page after page of the man reveling in the sight of his beloved's body. He is enjoying all the wondrous sights she offers up to him, and frankly, she is enjoying the attention. His admiration of her body, and her delight in receiving it, is one of the ways that we were designed to complement each other. He likes to look and we like to be looked at, again all part of God's design in how we can bring pleasure to the ones we love.

Girls, we need to be aware that for men the desire to look came hardwired in his being, just like his receding hair line and back hair. There just isn't much he can do about his hair (both the wanted and the unwanted) or the fact looking at us is such a source of pleasure. Plain and simple, looking at women is just part of being a man. In and of itself, the desire to gaze upon our beauty is neither wicked nor evil. Looking only becomes a problem when it crosses the line between the appreciative gaze and the lustful leer. And, I think that we should appreciate the difference.

Once we accept that this is how men are built, we find new motivation to be careful in our dress. Not because we are responsible for how they deal with their impulses, but rather as an act of grace and our desire not to lead them into temptation. No man, unless he is gay, super disciplined, or dead, can resist gazing upon our bodies without some tingle of excitement. If we prop our boobs up and leave them half exposed, he is going to talk to your tits and not to your face. If we walk around with our G-string pointing the way down into our jeans, he is going to ogle butt. And they assume, usually rightly so, that we were wearing these things as an invitation for them to follow their natural instincts.

Look, we are never going to stop men from looking at our bodies. To try and achieve this we would have to gouge out their eyes and this really isn't a good solution. As Christian women we have a certain obligation to help them guard their hearts. We are beautiful, and we should never be ashamed of that beauty. However, we should be trying to dress in ways that are flattering but avoid deliberately tempting men to think of us in inappropriate ways. Men read how we dress as a statement of how we expect to be treated, and the truth is, if we dress like a slut, we are telling them to treat us like a slut. But we need to keep in mind that the converse is also true. If we dress like we are ashamed of our bodies, like we don't value what we have, they won't value it either. Women who dress attractively are more likely to catch the eye of the man she wants, and a woman willing to work towards achieving that balance between modest and slutty will be more likely to find the quality of man she desires.

I have heard people trying to discourage women from dressing attractively. I have heard that any thought given to being beautiful is considered vanity and should be routed out, but gals, let be honest. Men don't chase the frumpy girls unless they feel that is all they can get. And honestly, that's not the man you want. No man ever crossed the room to speak with a strange girl because she had a beautiful mind, but they will cross a room to talk to a woman who presents herself as the beauty she is – then he might just fall for your beautiful mind.

While we are on the topic of beauty, we also need to be aware that men don't see beauty as we do. We get all worked up about cellulite, the size of our breasts and hips, that gnarly scar, or our hairstyle. And all the while, they really don't care. If you ask a man what type of breast he likes, and I have asked several, the most natural reply is a naked one. Believe it or not, they care less about size than we do. (As one of my guy friends put it, more than a mouthful is a waste and he never minded reading Braille.) Men love women in all shapes and sizes. There are some who adore huge bottoms and rich thighs (to which I say thank you, Jesus!). There are men who love nothing more than a freckled face and cute crooked teeth. There are men who love bony girls, and men who think that skinny girls are gross. Scars, even stretch marks, are often seen as something interesting and uniquely you, and isn't that the idea, that they love you as uniquely you?

When you talk to men who are truly in love with their wives, they will tell you that while they love the sight of her body the thing they love the most about her is her eyes, her laugh, the way she speaks, or something that didn't make our list of typically tempting body parts. I have one male friend who said he realized his wife was the sexiest woman alive when she slipped her beautiful feet into the cold mountain stream. In that moment, he decided he had to marry her. My husband says he knew I was the most dazzling woman on earth when he watched me planting tomatoes in my family's garden while my hands were covered in dirt.

My point is – men love the female form. They love the feel of our skin and scent of our bodies. They don't care that it isn't perfect. They love that it has been designed for their pleasure and enjoyment. So we can put aside some of our insecurities and trust that when God brings that right man along he will see you as the beauty that you are. Who cares what others might think? And if you don't believe me, look around you sometime. See how many good looking guys are with women that you or I would not consider to be beautiful. They are everywhere.

We need to accept this so we can be free to work on the things that really matter. We can't do a single thing about some of the "gifts" that genetics gave us, but we can learn to work on our sense of value and purpose. We can become well versed in our identity and discover the dream that leads us to our destiny. As hard as it is to believe, these are the things that turn a man on even more than DD breasts.

And girls, we really need to stop thinking that men who admire our form are just dirty perverts. Of course, we shouldn't accept a coarse or crude comment about our bodies as complimentary. These types of remarks reveal that our bodies are all they are looking at, but we shouldn't fault them for appreciating the fact that we are women, a fact largely defined by flesh. Men should show us more respect than reducing us to an inventory of body parts, and a good man will recognize that his physical desire for us as simply a part of his enjoyment of who we are as a complete person.

However, we have a responsibility in this, too. As women we need to acknowledge the power we have over men, and there is no doubt that we do have it. We should be aware how our actions are affecting him, recognize that a hand innocently laid on his thigh is doing crazy things to him. Things that are happening in the vicinity of his zipper. We need to know that a whisper in the ear is not communication in his mind. It is your lips brushing his ear. A fun wrestling match over a spoon full of peanut butter is really full body contact, and water polo is really your legs wrapped around his neck. All of these actions set off a chain reaction and gets them thinking of other places your lips, hands, and legs would feel good against, or around. Their response is a natural and good thing in the right context. And while these gestures may not have the same effect on us, we need to recognize most men's reactions are much more immediate and much more visceral than ours.

Our fuse for arousal is so much longer than theirs. On average women have to think about sex for fifteen minutes before they are ready for sex, but men only need three. Teenage boys, who are always thinking about sex, need a mere second. Women think of sex as the result of seduction and affection. We tend to view sex as the culmination of the right words, actions, and circumstance. We envision the candlelit dinner, the exciting situation, or the heated kisses and the well-placed caresses. All most men need is something vaguely reminiscent of something sexual. They don't need all the build up and hype to make sex an appealing option. A blouse pulled tightly over a breast, the warmth of a hand on the inside of their arm, the smell of peaches, or the sight of '68 Mustang convertible, all of these things can be enough to send them reeling into the realm of desire. If we know this, we can help them avoid the pains of getting too worked up, and we can help prevent compromising situations.

Of all things that I have discussed with young women, this is probably the most difficult thing for them to grasp. Men get turned on a million times more easily than most women. (Yes, that is a scientifically accurate measurement).When I advise that women minimize physical contact, I know it seems like overkill, and with some guys it might be, but if it is you might want to check his pulse. Ever since the dawn of time we have held temptation in our hands. Like Eve, we make the choice to extend the forbidden to them or to discreetly withhold it until the proper moment. In this we have been given a great honor and a great responsibility, and we need to respect ourselves and them enough to use it wisely. We don't tempt the ones we love, and we don't lead them into situations that would cause them to sin. So we must be on guard, monitoring our actions and words. We need to be sensitive to their needs and the design placed within them, not belittling them for being weak or the sexual creatures that God created them to be.

As a side note, a really good guy, the type that makes a great husband, will guard you from his urges. He knows that he sought you out, pursued you because he was attracted to you. He is already well aware of the way you affect him, and is probably more in tune with the messages his body is sending then you are to yours. If he ever decides that he needs to go home, or leave the situation for awhile, let him. He is probably getting away so he can cool down a bit, and in doing so honor you as the woman he loves. Stepping away from something they want so badly is not easy for them, and we should not make it any harder than it already is.

So, no coy remarks about staying just a bit longer, we can just cuddle, or another kiss or two won't hurt. It can, and probably will, if you push the boundaries too far or too often. Remember by the time you are getting that warm and tingly feeling in your nether regions, he's already experienced it a few times over. Let him go, encourage him to leave, and rest in the satisfaction that you both had the wisdom to stop playing with fire before somebody got burned.

I share all this with a bit of trepidation (read that worry, fear, and outright gut-wrenching terror). I worry that someone might use this information for evil. Taunting and flirting with a guy just to watch him squirm. I won't deny there is some type of perverse thrill comes from seeing a man completely overcome with desire for you. Experiencing the intensity of such a feeling is a wonderful and deeply fulfilling sensation. I adore those moments when I see that mist fall over my husband's eyes, but outside of a marriage where you can find satisfaction together, it is cruel punishment. For his sake, you should not indulge in this game, and for your sake, it should be completely avoided.

Too many times girls have pushed a man to the edge of all reasonable control. They have played with his head, heart, and body so that they can bask in the affirmation that they are beautiful and desirable. They have said no with their lips, but yes with their bodies. Pushing him away with one hand while pulling him closer with the other. Eventually the men realize that their no doesn't really mean a thing, it is just a pretense at being a "good girl" while getting to enjoy the danger of being bad. Taken too far this is a "game" that can end in disaster.

Hear me. When you tell a man no, mean it! Do not send mixed signals. Get up, get out, and move away. If you are okay with what he is doing then own that, too, but don't say no just so that you can feel better about what you are doing and later be able to blame him. Understand what you are doing, the chances you are taking with your body, your life, and your future.

I am not trying to justify men who fail to hear or heed a girl's no. Date rape happens far too frequently and is a heinous crime. I believe that at whatever point a woman decides to stop, her no should be respected, but a woman who truly loves a man will not place him in a situation where there is any doubt as the sincerity of her words. Be wise in your actions, protect the both of you by avoiding those sexual taut situations to begin with, and all will go so much smoother.

Romance in a Foreign Language

Another major difference between men and women is we see romance differently. Women tend to think of things like the candlelit dinner, the bottle of wine, the roses, and the soft music. For many of us these ideas about romance are encoded in the very fiber of our being. They just don't change whether you are single girl of fifteen or married for fifty years. We may add items to our romance list over time, but these original ideas never go out of style. However, if you talk to men who are married and men who are single, their ideas of romance vary widely.

When men are single, romance is often more accurately described as a description of their lust. They are looking for the girl who turns them on. They are looking for sex, and romance is more the tool of seduction than the results of love. Now, obviously this isn't true for every man, and there are some good guys out there who want to give us that dream night, but we need to be on the lookout for the men who use our favorite fantasies as the key to our panties. Honestly, I never had one of these story book dates with a man who wasn't trying to get laid. The guys who really wanted a real relationship usually kept dates rather low key. Men are fully aware that these types of romantic gestures come with certain expectations, the primary one being sex. And in the right context, there is nothing wrong with that, I love it when my husband takes me on one of these dates, and I am more than willing to fulfill our shared expectations of the evening.

With the good guys, romance is often far more organic and far less contrived. Romance springs out of the simple things that you share in your time together. Maybe it's a push on a swing simply because it was there. An impulsive gift of seashell found on beach, or being handed a drink before you knew you wanted one. A shared look, enjoying a sunset, or just recognizing that perfect moment and how much better it is because you are together.

Married men tend to see romance as something you live out. Romance could be washing his clothes, or preparing him a meal. Remembering he doesn't like spinach or black olives. Romance could mean keeping the car cleaned out or the dishes done. Little things like meeting him at the door with a kiss when he comes home from work, and making sure he never leaves home without the feel of your lips on his. It can be as simple as getting up to share a cup of coffee with him before he leaves for his job, or listening to what happened in his day. A really great husband will see these as the romantic gestures they are and appreciate them as such. And gals, just a tip, when we do these things, we free up his time and energy while providing him with the incentive to set up those romantic evenings we tend to want. Also, we need to remember that every day our men go out and work to provide for the family, keep the car running, and mow the yard – they are telling us that they love us. Sure, it isn't as pretty as bouquet of roses, but would you rather be homeless and starving to death and have the lovely flowers?

The Silent Game

An additional difference is men are far less verbal than women tend to be. They don't need to talk about their feelings as much as we do. They just don't, and what's more some of them find it to be a physically grueling event. We need to be watching what they do and stop worrying so much about what they didn't say. Men tend to speak up when there is something wrong, but remain silent if everything is going alright. We can drive them crazy with our persistent questions about what they are thinking, what they like or want, and our attempts to get them to verbalize their feelings. Now this is not carte blanche permission for them to say nothing, we need them to talk and they need to be responsive to that need, but gals, we need to loosen up a bit when they fall silent and stop imagining the worst.

In my life experience, I have encountered three types of silence from men. The first is the angry silence. Gals, this needs little or no explanation. He's mad, and he wants you to know it by withholding the communication you need. This type of silence is a form of control and self-serving manipulation, trying to get you to do what he wants. And it resembles a sulky three year old having a tantrum. Trust me on this one, if you encounter this guy in your dating relationships, get out. Being controlled or manipulated strictly for another's pleasure is not part of a good relationship, and if you experience it while dating, you can rest assured it will only worsen after you get married.

The second type of silence is the noncommittal or avoidance silence. This type of silence is one where the man lets you fill in the blanks however you wish, and unfortunately, we girls have vivid imaginations. We can fill in the blanks with the worst, leading us to crazed acts of desperation trying to get some sort of response, or we can believe the best and build a future on nonexistent foundations. These men are typically the ones who like having you around, care enough not to intentionally or actively hurt you, but are unwilling to make promises they have no intentions of keeping. So they keep their mouths shut, fully aware that you will read their silence incorrectly, and yet do nothing to correct your perceptions. And when they decide it is time to get out, well it wasn't their fault you drew the wrong conclusions. Once again, we are talking about control and manipulation, but this time we were willing partners in it.

The third type of silence is the "everything's great" silence. This type of silence is the silence of contentment. Nothing is wrong, so nothing needs to be addressed or fixed. It is a little unnerving if all you have ever experienced are the first two forms of silence. The men who offer this type of silence are sublimely happy in your relationship, and indulge in the luxury of not having to speak. When they do speak, it is to affirm that they love you, love what you are doing, and want to be with you. These words may be seldom and far between, but the sincerity is so rich that you really couldn't stand more of them any way. Indulgence in those wonderful words would border on some type of emotional gluttony. The only other time these guys may speak is when there is a problem. They tend to be brief and to the point, telling you their concerns honestly, perhaps even painfully, but with the intent of including you in the resolution of the problem. I shouldn't have to tell you that these men should be held onto.

Since men tend to be less verbal, and we are so very verbal, we need to make allowances for these differences and set some provision in place for them. Once again, this is where your network of friends comes in. They are not a substitute for the vital conversations you need to have in a healthy relationship, but they often serve as the winnowing ground of words. Our friends help us pinpoint the real topic we need to address, clarify our emotions, and just blow off steam. Allowing us to be a little more clear minded when we do approach our man with an issue we believe needs to be addressed, and allowing him not to be overwhelmed with the multitude of words that we have been mulling about in our minds.

Obviously, not all men are the strong silent type. Some men are great talkers (most of them are related to me). These guys can talk about any and everything ad nauseum. However, when you listen to their conversations, rarely do we hear their hearts. Sure they may talk about their emotions, but when you get to close to the real feelings, they draw back and hide behind a multitude of words, keeping us as distant as the silent ones. We have to be careful not confuse pointless or emotionally bulimic conversations as revelations of love. Men who compulsively tell about their heartaches, wounds, disappointments, and pain are really just looking for a band aid. They want a girl who will fix them, pet them, and make them feel better about themselves. And if you think you are the only one to hear these deep revelations, think again.

I never seriously dated this type of man. I just never really found them all that appealing, probably because my ideas of the masculine were bound up in images of John Wayne and Sam Elliot. (Sorry, younger gals, but I didn't have a modern equivalent and I would be whipped before I used a Twilight analogy. So rent the *Searchers* and check out *Connager*, it will do you good.) However, while I was bartending, I saw this guy a lot. He was the one who told every girl that he had "never told anyone this before, and I can't believe I am telling you now. I just feel so comfortable with you." The sad thing is he really believed that he was telling them the truth.

I know that for many of these guys this little routine was a gold mine for female compassion and sympathy that was eventually expressed in sexual terms. So girls, don't be taken in. Men feel better when they have the attention of a woman, especially when it is sexual attention, but you don't ever want to be as gross as that used band aid you avoided stepping on in the parking lot.

Sure it seems like you are doing a good deed, helping someone in pain and in need, but all you are really doing is reinforcing his martyr complex and enabling him to keep on using women as pain medication. If you really care about the guy, you will not offer yourself up as yet another sacrifice to his emotional instability. Yes, he will probably walk away when you don't give him what he thinks he needs, but it only proves how little he cared for you and how much he loves himself. And you shouldn't think that he will stay with you if you do show your concern for him in a sexual manner. Eventually he will blame you for his pain and seek out consolation from someone more sympathetic to his needs. And he will find her, just like he found you.

When we are talking about how men express themselves with the spoken word we need to bear in mind that not only do men tend to speak less, but they also perceive even the act of talking in different manner than we do. The spoken word is often far more intimate for men than women. In a lot of ways, saying how they feel or sharing their experiences, especially the painful ones, is very similar to what we experience in physical intimacy. There is the same element of vulnerability and personal revelation that exceeds a casual encounter. For many men this type of exposure can only occur in a safe, stable, and secure relationship. Yes, you can go through the motions with a stranger, but ultimately, it is far more rewarding and terrifying to say the words to someone who has vowed to love you for the rest of their lives.

As women, part of our role in a love relationship is to create an environment where men can be free to speak about their emotions with no condemnation or ridicule. We need to provide a place where they feel their words are valued and heard. Just as we would be reluctant to engage in a sexual encounter with a man, even our husbands, if they criticized or ridiculed our bodies, a man will be hesitant to speak to a woman who attacks or criticizes his words.

Conversely, we need to recognize that since men's words are loaded with intimate import, we need to be guarded in the conversations we have with them. As a woman, I always request permission from the wife before entertaining more than a casual conversation with a married man. Now that I am married, I always make sure my husband knows about any conversations I have with other men. Too many men have had their marriages crumble due to emotional affairs where no physical infidelity ever occurred.

Contrary to what you may have been led to believe, most affairs do not begin with a wanton sexual overture. Instead, men who feel undervalued and stifled at home wake up one day to find that the conversations they are having with a co-worker or other female friend is far more satisfying and stimulating than the ones they are having at home. With the internet and social networking sites, this is becoming more and more of a problem as men are learning they can find a sympathetic ear of a stranger with just a few mouse clicks, and she is easier to open up to than a wife who ridicules him about the issues that affect him the most. The sexual component often comes later, when the woman in question reaches out in an expression of friendship and finds an often unexpected but natural sexual response.

Does this mean that we can never have a meaningful conversation with a member of the opposite sex? Absolutely not. It simply means that we need to be aware of how men feel about these types of conversations, and we need to be careful that we never mislead them into thinking that our gesture of friendship could or should lead to something else. Just as the good guy guards us from making sexual mistakes, we help guard them against emotional ones by carefully placing boundaries around our conversations.

And lest you misunderstand, this does not simply mean that we avoid conversations of a sexual nature. We avoid intimate conversations that involve deep feelings and impassioned revelations, especially ones involving complaints about their wives. If a man ever approaches a woman, especially a single woman, with a grievance against his wife she should put an immediate halt to the conversation and advise that he speak with another man or a counselor. This should be a nonnegotiable point for all women.

Allow me to run the scenario for you – a man, a good man, is in a situation where he is working with or has close contact with a woman. Say they are painting the Church together, long hours of boredom, and to kill the time they begin to talk. The conversation is innocent enough, perhaps even theological in nature. She affirms his beliefs, ideas, and feelings. Maybe it is something that she has strong feelings about, and it is the first time that either of them have had a chance to articulate this idea. Soon they begin to compare life notes, nothing raunchy or crude, just where they grew up, what schools they went to, or what they did last night. The atmosphere is safe. Neither one thinking they need to be on guard, they are just enjoying the moment.

Soon they find that they are running into each other often. They have a good time talking about things that seem new, fresh, and exciting. He remembers what it is like to be appreciated, and she is enjoying not feeling so lonely. Almost invariably there is a fight with the wife, and he lets it slip out. The girl thinks "if I had a man like him I wouldn't treat him that way". She expresses her sympathy, perhaps offers him a hug . . . da dum da dum . . . you can feel it starting to heat up, but they ignore it. Maybe nothing ever happens but that intimate part of who he is has just been shared with someone who had no right to it. The wife begins to look less appealing to him, and she is becoming a lunatic because she knows something is wrong. Things spiral out of control, and soon no one is happy. The wife is miserable. The husband is at war with himself. Unable to reach out to the wife he should be leaning on, because another woman has offered support that is far easier to accept. Meanwhile, the single gal is experiencing jealousy and the pain of disappointment. No good can come of it, but too many Christian couples are in this place all because of unguarded conversations.

And girls, it happens to the best of us. I hate to think of the number of Christian women who have confessed to being in this situation, as either the wronged wife or the unwitting adulteress. For my younger readers, perhaps you think that this has no bearing on you, but it does. Even now, in your teen years, you need to be learning how to spot those conversations that can be a temptation to men. You need to be honing your senses and learning how to respect the marriages of our sisters. One day it maybe your marriage that needs the sensitive response of another woman to help keep it intact.

As a divorced mom in the Church for eleven years, I never fell prey to this scenario, but I have seen the door opened to it many times. Later I learned that many of these men did go on to get embroiled in this very situation. I quickly learned to keep my conversations with men in public settings, with full knowledge of his wife and including her when possible, and I conducted all conversations with the assumption that everything that was said would be repeated to their wives – even if it didn't happen. Above all else, I learned that if I ever got the vibe that the man I was talking to was getting some type of fix or high from our conversation, the conversations ceased. I would rather err on the side of caution than to have a failed marriage on my conscience.

"I'm Sorry, Babe" and other Signs of the Apocalypse

Finally on the matter of the spoken word, we need to realize that even when men do speak the words they use are different from the ones we use. Take apologizing for instance: men hate to say the words "I am sorry" or "I was wrong" and will go to great lengths to avoid them. I applaud the man who can actually articulate the sentiment, but gals, we need to understand that this is a terribly difficult thing for guys. It isn't that they don't want say it, but it costs them so much. So most men find some other way to let us know that they are sorry for anything they may have done to hurt us, a way where they don't actually have to say it.

One of my friends complained that her son never said he was sorry, but moments after an argument he took out the trash when it was not his turn and had not been asked. I pointed out to her that he was "saying" he was sorry, but just could not find the words. Do we hope that one day he will be able to make the statement with some grace and tact? Absolutely, but as women we need to give men some space to be men. If they can't find the words, putting pressure on them will not help matters, and will probably result in bitterness from them. So if your fellow brings you flowers but never actually said that he was sorry, know that he is doing the best he can. Cut him some slack. Don't rub it in that he is doing it wrong. He tried, and he deserves some credit for that.

Conversely, men aren't really all that good at receiving an apology. They don't like to be that emotionally raw, and it makes them uncomfortable to see others, especially someone they love, be that vulnerable. However, their way to avoid this discomfort can often lead to a bigger confrontation. They tend to deflect, move back to safer ground, and stay away from your naked emotions. Often they do this by going back over the events, replay the problem, and with a seeming death wish of inciting all of our wrath when we were simply trying to do the right thing.

Not too long ago, Ty did this with me. It took everything in me not to rip his head off and use it for a basketball. Thank God, I had the presence of mind to look at him and state, "I just apologized for that. I acknowledged that I screwed up, and I am taking full responsibility for my actions. Now, is our first fight really going to be over a stupid skillet, or can you please quit rubbing salt in my wounds." Inspired by my good example, it was his turn to grin sheepishly and say, "I'm sorry, babe."

Men's verbal handicap also means they give lousy compliments. Ty's biggest compliment is "You did good, babe." It lacks the poetry and elegance I had hoped to have in a husband's words of praise, but once I realized that he really meant to say all the sappy and beautiful things lovers are suppose to say, I learned to appreciate these words a lot more. However, I will admit I am still not too happy about his, "That'll work." To him, they mean roughly the same thing as the first one, but to me, it still sounds like whatever he is complimenting is barely sufficient. So girls, if you are looking for effusive and Shakespearean compliments, you are going to have to look long and hard or you might want to reevaluate exactly how important the words are to you.

Another area where men's verbal constipation becomes a problem is in how they address problems. Men see problems as something to be fixed as quickly and as efficiently as possible, so when they do address a problem or concern head on it is exactly that – head on. Often there is no easy lead in and no breaking it to you gently. They just want to get the messy task over with as soon as possible. To our delicate female ears, they can sound harsh and critical when all they were trying to do is address the facts and only the facts of the situation. Actually articulating the emotions behind what is going on seems irrelevant to them, mainly because emotions cannot be weighed and measured like tangible results. Gals, this means that we need to work at being okay when they are straight to the point. If you are worried that there is some serious issue beneath the circumstances they address, ask them, but try to be specific in your questions.

If they say they don't like your mother's casserole, don't ask if they hate your family. Ask if they don't like casseroles period, or if it was something about that particular one. If they say they don't like what you are wearing, don't ask them if they don't like your body. Ask them if it is the color or the style or if there is something they like better. If they say they are having a bad day, don't just ask them what's wrong. Ask them if it is work or home. And if you want to help, don't just ask if there is "something" you can do, specifically offer what you know you can do.

I must admit that there is one trait common to men and their use of language that makes me want rip out their vocal cords and use them as shoe laces. Turns out the men are born with the apparent inability for them to ask a question. Now, I am not just talking about asking for help. No man likes to do that and will usually avoid making that request at all costs unless it falls under the heading of events specifically covered in the male code wherein help is merited. These types of event include certain mechanical tasks, like pulling a transmission, home improvement projects, like tearing out a rock wall, or outdoor work, such as removing a tree stump. And in all of these things, it is recognized that the men do not ask for help because they were unable to do it themselves, or did not know how to do it themselves, but rather it would be more enjoyable with a few of their buddies and some cold beer. We are often not asked to join them because the primary tenant of accepting any real help in these situations is the need for pure brute strength.

However, we may be pressed into service if no other men are available. Of course, we are included in these events without ever actually being asked if we would be willing or able to help. Instead, we are told that we are helping because to be asked would mean they had to ask the question and acknowledge a supposed weakness on their part.

The only question we might be asked is "Honey could you come here for a second?" Girls, when you hear these words, be prepared for a prolonged stay. From there expect statements, not questions. For instance, "Hold that right there." "I need you to come this way with that." "Hand me ____" "Just grab on to it." Etc. I think you get the idea. Gals, there won't be any "pleases" or "thank yous" during the course of this event, so don't expect them. Your man will be in "task mode", and this means that all power supplies for speech have been redirected to the "Git'er done" portion of the brain. So if he seems a little short, remember it isn't personal. It is just a man being a man.

A man's inability to actually form a question can also lead to some interesting methods of communication when faced with a situation where a question is the only way of obtaining information. He may ask questions that seem insulting or condescending as a way to avoid actually having to make a request that might be refused. The world champion at this is my father. If my mother ever fails to serve a beverage along with his meal he will never ask for something to drink. Instead, he asks, "Did we pay the water bill this month?" or "Did all the glasses go missing?" If he wants something to eat, he asks, "Been to the grocery store lately?" or "Did you let all those peaches go bad?" Thirty-seven years of marriage have not made this trait any more endearing to my mother than it was when they were dating.

Such an approach can be rough on us when they are trying to get emotional or sensitive information out of us. Ty has a habit of watching me and then offering advice that I didn't want. For a long time I did not realize that he was really trying to gather some intelligence on how to deal with my artistic moods. Not wanting to get his head bit off for asking the wrong thing, he chooses to make a statement that I can object to or accept. He determines how good his observations are by my reaction. If he is right, I snarl and growl at him a bit before agreeing with his often wise suggestion, but if he is wrong I calmly tell him so (with a bit of an edge to my voice) and then reveal to him what is going on. What seems like a rather roundabout way of gaining information, allows him to feel less vulnerable while still trying to tend to my needs. And truthfully, it allows me the luxury of opening up as I feel ready. Funny how that works.

The main reason men use this approach is they hate anything that might reveal that they are wrong, don't already know an answer, or might be refused or rejected. Not asking a question is a way to keep their feelings from being injured, because despite how it may appear, they are just as emotional as we are. The only difference is their pride runs a lot deeper than ours. So we can do a couple of things to make this easier on everyone. First, we can learn to recognize when some of their statements were meant to be questions. If you are dealing with an emotionally volatile topic or situation, let it go and tell them what they need to know. Second, we can create an atmosphere were questions are valued and safe to ask. It will take time for them to trust this, so don't rush it. Intentionally, ask them "Is there anything you want to ask me?" He will say no, but don't be surprised when he comes back in a few days with a profound question. Remember your promise to make this a safe place for him to do this, and that means you can't get mad at him for not asking the question you wanted him to ask. If there is something you want him to know, tell him, because you cannot wait for him to win the game of twenty questions when he can barely form one. Third, we can teach them how to ask questions both for asking our help and seeking information.

Reserve the teaching process for things that aren't a big deal, and keep it fun. The other day Ty told me he was starving and then continued to sit in his chair. I got up, kissed him, and said, "Honey, I sure could use something to eat. I'm starving! Would you mind making me a sandwich, please?" I replied to myself, "No, Babe, that's not a problem. I am so glad you asked, because I didn't realize you were hungry." I continued the conversation on his behalf, "Thank you, hun. I am so glad I can just ask for what I need and that I have lovely, beautiful, hot, sexy, amazing wife, who takes care of me so well." By this time, Ty was out of the chair and chasing me around the kitchen, laughing. When I did let him catch me, he kissed me and said, "Baby, can you make me a sandwich, please?" Unfortunately, by that time he had forgotten he was hungry, and the sandwich had to be put on hold for more important matters, but the next day, he asked unprompted and with a gleam in his eye.

Do I tell you this so you will know how to seduce your husband with the promise of a sandwich? No, I am telling you this so that you can know that men just don't speak the same language we do, and that's okay, *if* you know how to interpret his lack of words and *if* the two of you are willing to work at it. Remember, speaking can be difficult and even a painful process for them, and we need to be sensitive to their needs, but we can both learn some new things about ourselves and each other if we are willing to use some grace. In the end, you will find that it is completely worth the effort.

Breathe with Me

One of the things we share is men hate to be alone. Ever since the Garden of Eden when God looked down at Adam and saw that it was not good that he was alone, men have had a special type of dread for loneliness. Men will go to just about any lengths to not be alone. This is not to say that they want to spend every second of the day with you. Some are perfectly content to be away for days at a time and then celebrate their return, but they want to know that there is someone to come home to. They like knowing that there is someone they can call even if they don't bother to pick up the phone. So if you have a man, don't let him get lonely, but if you haven't found one yet, there are few things you should keep in mind. While some men don't need constant contact, a man who is truly smitten with you will hate to be away for any serious length of time.

If the man in your life is calling only when it is convenient for him, only wants to go out when he wants to go out, or has to be pressured to keep in contact with you – he's using you. You are nothing more than his security blanket, and you are letting him treat you that way. You are allowing him to keep up a pretext of a relationship and avoid the fact that he truly is alone because he never let you in. Girls, if you are worried that this might be your relationship, decide not to call him for a week. See how many phone calls you get. None? Two? But he has a great excuse when you confront him on it? And he really does love you? You can tell whenever you are together?

Please repeat after me – "I am lying to myself, my friends, and my family. And the only person I am fooling is me."

If that hurt, hold on. This one is worse. So once again, repeat after me. No cheating; say it aloud. "He does not love me like I love him, and I am being used."

This one is a bit better – "I deserve more than this. God created me for better things, and I will wait in faith for a man who will love me for who and what I am." Now do it.

I know that was rough, but if you can face the truth now it will can possibly save you years of hurt and disappointment. And I know from whence I speak. I once spent years hoping that one of these relationships would work out. Guess what? Despite all my hopes, prayers, and pleas to God and the man in question, nothing changed until the day I decided that I would not tolerate being treated like this anymore.

One great quality of men is they like our presence, and not just sexually. They like having us around. We don't need to be talking or doing anything. They just want us to be breathing the same air as they are. For a man, a girl who is willing to sit on the lake shore while he fishes is quite the catch, even if she is just using the time to soak up a few rays or do some reading. They want us to sit with them while they watch the game or the movie we have no desire to see. They like us standing nearby while they fix the car, even if we aren't the slightest bit of help.

So many men have told me how much they wish their wives would go with them to __(fill in the blank)__ or do ___(fill in the blank)__. They don't care that she may not be any good at it or that the dishes don't get done that day. They just want their women with them.

Girls, this is why it is so important to fall for a man who loves at least some of the things you do. I am not saying you have to love everything he does, but there should be a few activities that you share. If you aren't an outdoors person, don't marry someone who loves to camp. If you don't like sports, don't marry someone whose life revolves around the game schedule. If you don't like video games, run if you see an Xbox, Sega, and Wii all stacked on top of each other before his TV.

Yes, opposites do attract, but the things you share are the things will that keep you together. And this doesn't mean there is not room for compromise. Ty loves to fish, but I had no interest in spearing a worm on the hook. So I took my laptop or a book, and when he yelled he had a bite, I cheered for him. (Right up to the day I decided to give it a try and actually caught one! Now we fish together, and we have a great time enjoying some friendly competition – which I typically win.) We both love to ride the Harley, go antiquing, and eating good food. So, we share those things every chance we get. I don't care to go camping every weekend, but I trade him out for the occasional opera and sushi dinner, things he doesn't care for. We work it out, and we work it out so that we can be together most of the time. We recognized that togetherness is something we need for our relationship to retain its intimacy and stability.

And girls, we need to be honest. Too many of us are more than happy to tag along while we are dating, but think that we will be exempt when we get married. Honey, he isn't going to change what he loves once he says I do. He loves you and whatever hobbies filled his time before you came along, and he will see marriage as a way to have both. Not to mention, you fostered the idea by all that tagging along you did. Don't pull a bait and switch. Changing who you are after you catch him is not fair to either one of you. So be picky when you are dating, because I don't care how wonderful he is, if you don't have something you can share it is going to be difficult to find points and times to connect – and no, sex is not enough.

The truth is, if you aren't out there doing the things he loves, there is always some other woman willing to take your place. And if she can do it in that arena don't think she can't do it in the bedroom. So much of a man's identity is tied up in what he does, and when we fail to appreciate the things he appreciates, he feels as if we are not appreciating him, leaving the door wide open for some other "appreciative" woman to console his wounded ego and pride, and this is not a door you want to leave open even an inch.

Does this mean that you are condemned to a life of doing things you hate just to have a man in your life? Could be, but have you made that commitment yet? If you have, honey, you need to work out some way to enjoy it. Even if you have to constantly remind yourself of how beneficial this is to the rest of your marriage while you endure one more car show or trip to the hardware store. If you haven't, choose wisely. Remember marriage isn't a weekend road trip. You will be dealing with his hobbies for the rest of your life. Be sure you can deal with them and hopefully enjoy them together.

I know that some of this may seem to be geared more for women who are married, but honestly, affair-proofing your marriages starts way before you exchange vows. Protecting your love begins when you start dating, when you start becoming the woman who will one day be a man's wife. Making your marriage a success begins when you start selecting the type of man you choose to date and how you approach those dating relationships. A wedding isn't a magic cure all for any type of difficulty or concern you may have about a man. Instead it is a magnifier of all things troubling, and you need to be constantly comparing the men you date to the man you want. And all of us gals have had that man's image emblazoned in our hearts and heads since we were old enough to know that men existed.

The problem arises from the fact that we never bothered to put together a cohesive image of this man. We have seen snippets of his perfection and untarnished glory in our minds, but the totality escapes us so we begin to impose this image on the latest great guy we just met. And too often we fail to see who the man before us really is, warts and all. Once again in the effort of full disclosure, I think I should warn you, all men of every type have warts, some of those warts are just harder to find than others. Having a few flaws doesn't mean they are automatically disqualified from being our Prince Charming, but we need to understand that even Prince Charming has bad days and maybe even some bad habits. So we need to find that balance between being realistic and critical, seeking the good and being delusional. The truth is most men are pretty good fellows and can be quite enjoyable, our job is finding one who is the best complement for who we are.

So girls, drop your impossible standards. Men scratch, belch, and fart with great regularity. They make crude comments about their bathroom habits, and they tend to stink from time to time. They may even cuss a bit when they get mad, but it doesn't mean they don't have a solid faith. They are sexual and may even get a little overly excited to be near you, but if they truly try to maintain some type of respect and honor towards you, you might want to give them a chance. They can be blundering idiots when they are faced with the woman of their dreams, and may even resort to cheesy pick-up lines when they don't know what else to say. Sometimes we just need to give them some space to calm down, regain some sense of themselves, and get over the nerves.

Men are looking for someone to love them as much as we are looking for someone to love us. And they often find it difficult to say the right things or live up to that image of a man society has foisted upon them. Most guys out there are trying to be someone worth having, but most guys out there have no clue as to how to be that person. The best of them are working it out, actively acquiring the tools to become a better person, and this is the man you want. Sure he may not have it all together, and his presentation may need some work, but we have to give them some type of a chance. Because believe it or not, they are fumbling through this just as much as you are. There are still few who really want to know you as a person. They want to find a wife, a lover, and a mother for their children. There are even a few who are diligently trying not to get in your pants, and they are fighting a colossal battle to keep it that way.

These are the men we should love. The ones we shouldn't let get away, and should even fight for. However, most of us aren't smart enough to tell the difference between a great guy who is screwing it all up and the predator who is seeking out some fresh meat. Obviously, I don't have the corner on male psychology, but I have noticed some basic trends among the men I have met. I am offering a few examples of the most prevalent types, and I am focusing on their flaws. Not because I don't like them or they don't have few good traits mixed in, but rather to remind you that if you fall for one of these guys, these are the things you might miss in your excited state of mind. So, let's begin with the worst.

Oh, the Variety!
or
Is That All There Is?

I don't think that I can emphasize it enough that we have unrealistic expectations about men. Our images of men are many and diverse, but we think that we know what a good man looks like and, for some reason, we think that bad men are indelibly marked in such a way that we will immediately know who they are. Good guys wear suits, clean shirts, have great breath, and impeccable manners. Bad men have bad breath, bad skin, and greasy hair. They are slimy in our imaginations, and we think they will helpfully comply in real life. However, a little time in the real world should dash any of these ill-founded fantasies.

Shark!

As much as I hate to say it, the dirty perverts that we need to be on guard for are usually a little more polished than the good guys. They don't come on to us with cheesy pick-up lines. Those are normally reserved for men with less experience. These guys come on to us with smooth compliments and easy conversation. They are pros at what they do, and they know that if they want to get in our panties, they can't run us off in the first five minutes. I call these types of men sharks. They are docile and cool, just floating along with the situation. You can feel at ease with them, find yourself opening up to their casual ways of affirming who you are both as a woman and a person. Sharks can shift gears so serenely and quietly that you have no idea what is going on if you aren't paying attention.

The shark laces his conversation with sympathy and affirmation. If you are a teenager, then he will tell you how he understands what it is like to have overbearing parents and how painful it is to be alone in this world. If you are older, he will sympathize with your financial problems, the pain of past relationships, and other wounds you may have revealed to him. He knows the right time to offer a comforting touch and when to withdraw. He is in tune and aware of the things that lull you into a false sense of security and what might trip you off to his trap. His touch is unobtrusive and easy to accept, innocent even, at first. As you become more and more at ease in his presence, he will begin to open up to you, share some things about himself. If you are a sympathetic and compassionate person, he will tell you of his wounds as if you were the only one special enough to see his most intimate scars. If you are bolder and independent, he will challenge you to take a risk. He has no difficulty in finding the one thing that would cause you to act contrary to your morals.

He is sometimes willing to invest hours, days, weeks, or even months getting to know what makes you tick. He will get inside your mind and slowly dismantle the reasons behind your actions. He has a thesaurus of lines ranging from, "God made sex to be enjoyed. Shouldn't we enjoy what He has given us?" to "How will we know if we really have any chemistry if never try it?" or "I love you, and I just want you to feel my love. How can that be wrong?" And I shouldn't forget, "I just want to see how beautiful you really are."

Girls, I hope I don't need to explain the flaws in all of these lines, but let's go over them, shall we? Yes, God made sex for us to enjoy, with our spouse. God does want us to find pleasure in the bodies of the men that we marry, but He does not want us to suffer the ill effects of having experienced this sacred and amazing act outside of the covenant of marriage. And there are consequences. I am not even going to go into the physical ramifications, but some studies suggest that breaking off a relationship in which sex has been a component is just as devastating as a divorce. If you have never experienced the painful consequences of divorce, let me just say you never want to. How good is a God who desires to save you that pain!

As for the second lie . . . uh, I mean line. Allow me to ask you this, is there any chemistry already going on? Are there sparks when you touch? Is there tension in the air when your eyes meet? Then you have chemistry. Having sex will not change this conclusion, nor will it provide anything that is not already there. And if you don't already have chemistry, why would you want to move on to anything else, anyways?

Sometimes the "chemistry" line is phrased this way, "How will we know if we are sexually compatible if we don't try it first?" Okay, fact – 98% of all human beings are sexually compatible if we are talking about all the parts fitting together in the right way. Do you know how long you would have to look to find someone you were not compatible with? Me neither (I never was good at math), but I know it would take a lot of time and dangerous experimentation. Besides if I truly loved someone, I would be willing to accept any physical limitations they may have if I knew that he truly loved me. Shouldn't a man who really loved you feel the same?

As for the "I love you" line, really? Really? You love me so you want use me so you can get your rocks off without offering me the safety and security of a committed relationship – you want to take without giving, so you can express your "feelings" without honoring mine? What type of man is that?

Look, I get it. Men do express their emotions through their deeds so much more easily than words. Wanting us physically can be a genuine expression of their feelings for us, but this is one time when their actions of respect and honor do far more to demonstrate their love than any sexual act. A real man is willing to do what is right, even when it is not easy or natural for them, and anyone who is willing to make the more difficult choice for our good truly loves us and not merely using us for their own selfish designs.

The last line is a favorite of the sharks. They love beautiful women, and for them almost all women are beautiful. They do want to look at our beauty. They want to admire our bodies, and they want to find their pleasure in easing the greatest fear that we face as women – whether or not we are truly beautiful and desirable. Their words are a heady mixture of adoration and affirmation that can leave us breathless. Deep down inside, we want what he has to offer. We believe that the man God intended for us will love us this passionately, and to experience passion from such an expert source can overwhelm the best of us if we aren't on guard. What we must realize is that for these men the fun is in capturing their prey, and once they tire of us they are on to the next big challenge.

The ability to conceal their motives and subtle manipulations is what makes a shark so dangerous. They can be devious, and many

86

are devious to the point they have fooled themselves into believing that every word and promise is an absolute truth. The shark often believes what he is telling you, but he hasn't recognized that his pattern is one of his own creation. He thinks that the women in his past have left him, betrayed him, and failed to satisfy his needs due to their own sexual shortcomings. He doesn't take the blame or responsibility for the pathway of destruction left in his wake. He merely wants to find the one who will be the reason to stop the cycle.

Girls, don't fool yourself. You are not it. No one woman can ever be enough for this man. He wants it all, and none of us, even the best of us, are everything he needs. This is a man who may profess to be a Christian and have a deep and abiding faith, but the truth is he is really looking for salvation in you. And as amazing as you may be, you are not, nor will you ever be, God enough to save someone.

How do you know if you are dealing with a shark or man who truly is in love you and is simply having a right response to your femininity? The first part of the answer is you don't. You will be so clouded by the intoxicating nature of it all you can have no idea of what you are really dealing with. This is where your network of friends comes in. Tell them everything about him, and if he objects to you sharing those details, lose him. You cannot navigate these waters without some help and support. Also, let your friends' husbands check him out. Men know men, and they aren't shy about calling out another man who threatens to hurt one of their friends.

The second part of this answer is to ask yourself these questions:

- How much pressure is he putting on you for sex?
- Can you spend an evening alone, watching a movie, going fishing, or walking the dog without feeling like that is all he is all he is trying to get?
- Does every conversation begin and end with sex?
- Is he pouty or angry when you say "no" one more time?
- Does he ever get physically aggressive with you, trying to overpower or manipulate you into relenting?
- Does he try to make you feel inferior or immature for not giving in?

- Does he push the boundaries just a little more each time you are together?
- Does he laugh off an inappropriate touch as a joke and expect you to laugh, too?

If you answer yes to these or even a couple of these questions, you may need to back off and reevaluate what type of relationship you are in, because one of two things are going to happen if you stay.

1. He will eventually become more aggressive, seeing your willingness to accept these behaviors as your tacit acceptance and even your endorsement of them. He will see your protests as a lie and eventually do as he pleases with your body. I don't think I have to tell you that at that point all the romance is dead. Despite what the romance novels tell you, a man who rapes a woman is not a man she can love, trust, or build a life with.

2. You will become desensitized to what you are doing. The little transgressions that were committed in innocence will cease to be exciting, and to keep that same level of adventure in the relationship, your experimentation will increase. Soon it is no longer his hand on the side of your breast as you pull away. Soon you will be turning your breast into his hand of your own accord. You cannot withstand this type of pressure, and you will mess up.

And honey, as much as I hate to tell you this, you are not smart enough or strong enough to win this. You can't change him anymore than you can change your instinctive response to him. There is only one way out and that is to leave it behind completely. The only way to get free is to truly make no provision for the flesh. You will feel like this is the most difficult thing you have ever done. I won't lie to you. The high you feel with this man is addictive, but in the end, he will be who he has always been and you will find that you have been used as just one more way he eases his wounds. So run, run far away. Don't believe the pretty pictures he paints of your future. Don't take your comfort and satisfaction from his appealing words. In the end, you will find out that they are all lies, and that is almost too painful to bear.

Rescue Me

The second type of man out there is the knight in shining armor type, or what George Strait so aptly described as the fireman. He seems so amazing, rushing in and saving the day, but gals, we need to be careful about falling for him. Men who want to rescue us are there for that reason alone. He's not doing it because is in love with us, but rather he is enjoying the ego trip. Over the years, as a single mom, I ran across a lot of these guys. They saw that I was struggling financially, emotionally, and mentally to keep it all together for my kids. They were moved by my story and suddenly realized that if they could just sweep me off my feet, put my world to rights, they could enjoy my undying gratitude. Fortunately, I was never the type of gal who wanted to be rescued. If any dragons needed slaying, I wanted to be the one holding the sword.

As I watched my friends who ended up with those men, I saw one of two things happen.

1. The men felt that the women owed them everything. After all he had saved her, hadn't he? He starts to believe that her every decision should be motivated by her undying gratitude. Her days should be spent anticipating his every whim, and keeping his ego properly inflated. I shouldn't have to tell you that the least interesting person in the world is a person who has no goals or dreams of their own, and she gave hers up in an attempt to repay him for her salvation. Eventually, he is as bored of her as he is of himself, and he will soon move on to the next damsel in distress, often leaving the woman in worse condition than he found her.

2. Or, once the woman is back on her feet, she begins to resent the control he has over her circumstances. The woman will fight back, lashing out, and emotionally attacking the man who has been nothing but loving. He is lost, unsure of why he is in a relationship where he is

no longer needed to play knight in shining armor. It won't take long before some other woman looking to be saved will catch his eye, and he will take his wounded sense of honor somewhere it can be better appreciated.

Girls, men love to take care of us, that's what they were designed to do, but it should never be at the expense of who we are, or even who they are. The care and compassion that flows between two people who are secure in their own identity is a grand and beautiful thing, but when it is laced with the poison of insecurity and self doubt or loathing, someone is going to get hurt.

Your Wish is His Command

The third type of guy is the grateful lover. He is the guy who is so thrilled that you deigned to notice him that he cannot do enough to please you. He arrives with flowers for every date. He asks you where you want to eat, every date. He wants to know what you think he should wear, every date. He wants you call to him twenty times *between* every date. He wants you to pick out his college degree, his job, and his lunch. He never ever wants to offend you. Gals, let me tell you something about this man – you don't want him. Not because he isn't sweet. He is, in the way that drinking straight waffle syrup is sweet. And this man respects you with every fiber of his being, almost to the point of reverence. In some ways, he is almost too good to be real. The truth is you don't want him because somewhere along the way, he lost his balls and may never reclaim them.

Sure, the presents and attention are nice, but for me, all the niceness wore off in about a week. That's about how long it took me to realize I did not want another child to raise. I wanted a man, and these poor guys qualify only on a physical level. The clinging nature of these men makes them obnoxious. Not to mention what they are really looking for is someone to take all the responsibility of this life from their shoulders. He will never be able to pull his own weight, nor does he want to. He wants you to do it all, and girls, that is not being evenly yoked. When you break up with him, and you will, unless you have domination issues you need to deal with, try not to crush him. And remember, no pity sex. No need to leave the little guy more emotionally devastated than he already is, and no, you can't fix him. This guy needs a man who will walk with him and teach him the things that men need to know, like how to pee standing up.

Just an FYI, many women in the Church are married to men like this. He was a sweet guy, and he said all the proper things so they were married quickly as teenagers. Now she is complaining that he has never done anything with his life, won't be the spiritual head of the household, and expects her to do all the disciplining with the kids. Often this woman is bitter and resentful of her husband, and as you can imagine, this doesn't make for a good marriage or a good sex life. Don't fall into the trap of marrying the sweet guy for security. It may seem wise at the time, but I can assure you that the years will prove what a mistake it really is.

The Call of the Wild

The most amazing boyfriend a girl will ever have is the bad boy. Adventure oozes from his pores. His devil may care attitude is exhilarating and can often seem like a breath of fresh air next to the stuffy Christian guys. His tattoos are sexy, his smoldering eyes can set you on fire, and that rough kiss is as intoxicating as well-aged moonshine. Deep down, I think almost every woman has wanted the bad boy at one time in her life. There is just something about him that speaks to us on a primal level. He is as raw and primitive as the modern man is allowed to be, and we are more than willing to let him drag us off to his cave by our hair. Who cares if he lacks the sophistication of shark, the urgency of the knight, or the tenderness of the sweet guy? All we know is that we want him, at a primal level that matches his own.

Okay, God made him sexy. We just have to agree on that. It's the truth pure and simple, but oh girls, beware. His lack of concern with himself bleeds over into every aspect of his life with perhaps the only exception being his Harley or his hunting dogs. We see him as the fixer upper, the man who could be perfect if he just had a woman's touch in his life, but the truth is he doesn't want it. And the even bigger truth, he wouldn't be nearly as exciting if he did. Girls, run.

Taming him just isn't an option. One day when he is older and wiser, he might settle down, but don't bet on it. He will love a girl for a moment, passionately and with a scorching intensity that will leave her burning long after he has relegated her to a pleasant if unfulfilling memory. His wildness draws us, but in the end it is his wildness that will leave us alone and hurting because he will never love us more than his freedom.

My Name's not Wendy

The lost boy is probably the most common one in today's society. He is the boy masquerading as a man. He loves his toys, games, and good times with friends. He doesn't know what he wants to be when he grows up, and really has no desire to find out. His resume reads like a list of summer jobs despite the fact he is pushing thirty. He loves you because you are fun, and he wants to keep having fun. Serious commitments are beyond him. He wants a girlfriend for the same reason he wants a new gaming system: his buddies all have one. He doesn't want a standing date on Saturday night. He doesn't want to plan a wedding or provide for a family. For him, keeping his schedule freed up so he jump on the next good time is all important. He is content living with his mama and watching TV. If he marries it will be because he wants to make sure someone will fold his underwear after mama's dead and gone. If he wants kids, it is because he wants someone new to play with.

Date him at your own risk. He is highly enjoyable to go to the lake with. Mud bogging on the four wheelers, the arcade, bowling, even karaoke, he's great at them all, but don't give into his boyish charm. He stops being charming after a year or so when you are trying to get him off the couch and into a job. He would probably be a good dad and husband if he ever grew up, but girls, don't hold your breath.

Draw Me like One of Your French Girls

The artist does more to our minds than to our bodies. We become entranced by their perceptions of the world and their amazing ability to communicate deep and profound truths. They are brooding and deep, and the sense of mystery is tantalizing. They speak of love as mystical event and sex as the poetry of the universe. They can set us a quiver with their dazzling visions. The realms of beauty they spread before us in paintings, words, and songs arouse our emotions with an intensity that compels a physical response. The artist shows us things in ourselves we never knew existed, and before them we can be the most amazing creatures ever created.

As an artist, I wish I could endorse these men wholeheartedly, but I really can't. They are brooding, given to bouts of depression, and terrifying in their angst. If you have the stamina to weather thrilling highs and bewildering lows, they can be a psychological adventure that surpasses even the bad boy, but if you aren't into drama, he isn't the man for you. Sexually, he is an amazing lover, creative and inventive. His approach is so completely and sincerely original, that even the best prepared woman can be taken off guard. Being a sensualist himself, he loves discovering the things that delight your senses and takes satisfaction in your pleasure. With him it is vitally important to monitor your response and reaction, because he won't break or pressure you to bend your rules. You will simply find yourself in a situation that you never wrote any rules for, because you never dreamed they could exist.

Howdy, Ma'am

Now I call this one the country boy. At one time he was the nice guy who grew up on the farm, wanted to live there the rest of his life with the girl of his dreams, daughters that looked like their mama, and sons that he would teach the same values he learned at his father's knee. Today, this man is few and far between and can be found just as easily in the cities as in the fields of the country. This is the man who knows what he wants in life. He has a vision that includes a woman but is not determined by her. He is prepared to love and honor her, protect her, indulge her to a point, but never forget that he is the head of the house. He's a good man, not overly concerned with appearances, but with a strong sense of honor.

This man has one goal in mind when he is dating. He wants to get married. He can run his love life like a business, farming or otherwise. He is looking for a specific set of qualities in a girl and if he doesn't see them he will move on. For him, men are men and women are women, and there is no confusion in his mind as to who shall do what in his marriage. He is looking for a wife who will wear a gingham apron and cook up a batch of fried chicken while he is off earning a living. She will be well provided for and in many ways will live a pampered life, if she never forgets her place – as he defines it. So girls, if you being a wife and mother are the sum of your aspirations you couldn't find a better man, but if you ever plan to do more than host a Church social, you may want to check him off your list. A woman with too much of a mind of her own is just too unpredictable for his world.

His sexual appeal is deeply rooted in his dependability, the strong shoulder to lean against, and the fact that he is never wavering in his beliefs. Someone that secure provokes an instinctual response from us gals, and honey, they don't build bank vaults this secure. Don't be surprised that while leaning on his comfortably broad shoulders you get hit with a rush of hormones that steal your breath and your reasoning skills. He's the one that won't instigate anything improper with a girl he plans on marrying, but won't turn it down from the girl who offers. Any sexual vibes he gives off are understated and charming, but just be forewarned that the girls who do give into his charm are out of the running to become the little missus.

Amazing Grace

Who among us good Christian girls hasn't hoped to get our hooks into the Church boy? He is the one we are supposed to want. He knows what he believes, why he believes it, and why you should believe it, too. He has dedicated his life to God and ministry, probably somewhere in the wilds of Zimbabwe, and he wants a woman strong enough in her faith to join him.

He is looking for a good little Church girl to fill out his team, erase any appearance of impropriety on his part, and squash all doubts in the minds of the outside world as to his sexual orientation or that he can be trusted with the women of a Church. He is zealous and passionate about building that Church, reaching the lost, and knowing more about God than any human has ever known. He knows what his faith looks like, how it should be lived, and shuns anything of even a questionable nature. His entire life seems dedicated to avoiding all appearances of evil.

Before he asked you out, he talked with his youth minister, pastor, prayed and fasted until God parted the heavens and told him you were the one for him. Now all you have to do is meet his expectations – which include, but are not limited to – never saying anything that might be objectionable, wearing anything that might be questionable, and rejecting all thoughts or ideas that might reveal that you ever wrestle with issues of faith. After all, he already knows all the right answers: why would you waste your time on something that he has already settled?

His life is a testament to self-control and self-discipline. Everyone in the Church adores him, and no one can imagine a stronger young man of faith. Life for him seems so simple, so defined in the black and white terms of right and wrong that there is no doubt as to what he should do next. He is a fountain of certainty, a rock of self assurance, an immovable pillar of piety. He seems to be the short cut answer to every question you may have ever entertained about God or what the Bible said. Why wouldn't you accept this God-ordained union as holy?

Simple. No matter how good he may be, he is still just a man, and that means that he can still make mistakes.

Dating the Church boy is never easy. There are way too many people pressuring you to do the right thing – get married, be his helpmeet, and support his ministry. Friends and family may see this as the ideal dating relationship, because they don't have to worry about you messing up with him. He is just too good, no matter which of the three distinctive flavors of Church boys you try. You just won't know what you got till you have a taste.

The first one is everything you see. He really is that devout, and he is looking for a woman who can match him. He truly believes that a mature, healthy relationship with God looks exactly like his and there is no room for deviation. And deviance is exactly what he considers it when your personal relationship with God plays out differently than his. And all those extensive talks about God, faith, and spirituality that you really wanted to have with someone who has such a deep relationship with the Lord? Well, don't be surprised when they don't happen, because this man is more interested in telling you what you need to know rather than exchanging ideas and insights. His mind is made up when it comes to God, and you aren't allowed to confuse him. Matter of fact, I doubt that God Himself would be allowed to meddle with what this man thinks. Be prepared for the sermon when you fall short, and when he dumps you because you didn't memorize you quota of Bible verses for the week.

Of course, these won't be your only shortcomings. The major flaw in you is the fact that you are female and human. An ever present temptation, reminding him of the one thing he doesn't want to think about – that he is human too.

Don't be surprised when everyone in the youth or singles group blames you when things just don't work out. Or worse, pities you for not being spiritually mature enough to keep up with this rising star of the Christian faith. When you tangle with him, you are leaving yourself vulnerable to crazy attacks on your faith and sense of self worth. He can never accept that he might have been the reasons things fell apart, so you must be the culprit, and he will be righteously indignant over the fact that you dared to tempt him away from God's intended purpose for his life. Did I mention it won't end well?

The second one is really trying to be in the first category, but he is struggling. Sure he keeps it together in front of everyone else, even you for a time, but all the denial he is carrying around about his sexuality is going to come undone. And it will, when you and he least expects it, typically sometime during an intense time of praying together. (You know that exercise you do in hopes of maintaining the purity of your relationship?) His inability to cope with his own sexuality means that he wants your help to remain pure. He needs you to fight this battle with him, to provide him with the support and care needed to kill this "sinful" part of who he is. Honey, do I need to tell you why this is never going to work? He was designed to be a sexual creature, with a sex drive, and a desire for a mate. This is a good thing, and you can't help him with this one.

He needs a man to teach him the truth about sex and who will hold him accountable for monitoring his behavior. All you can do is inflame the desire that he is trying to control. As for praying together, that is the worst thing you can do. All that spiritual intimacy can stir up desires for other types of intimacy – the types you should be waiting for.

The third type of Church boy is the one who believes that he has experienced some sort of divine communication from God completely sanctioning and sanctifying his sex drive. God has laid down the rules for sex, but He really meant them to apply to lesser people who fail to grasp the significance of this great gift. And since, no one else understands, except you, he cannot share these spiritual insights with anyone other than you. Being the great communicator that he is, he will bypass the words and try to show you exactly what he means. (The first insight is about how a "holy kiss" includes the "gift of tongues" – a gift that will be further utilized in the lesson about his "rod and staff" being a comfort.) Think these guys don't exist? Think again.

I have yet to be in any Church or Christian singles group that did not include one of them. In fact, I know several where the worst offender was the leader. So be on guard against him, because he will be well versed in Scripture and ready to use some very "Biblical" sounding arguments to twist your faith into a weapon against you.

Am I saying you shouldn't date a Church boy? I think maybe I am. Maybe what you should really be looking for is a man who truly loves the Lord, seeks Him with all his heart, and is willing to be submissive to the rules God set in place. This doesn't mean you won't find him in Church, it just means that going to Church, even knowing all the churchy ways of doing things, doesn't make any man an automatic keeper.

Decisions, Decisions

So if all of these guys have their flaws, which one should you date? Well, here's where we have to address some of our ideas about men. Honey, just accept there is no such thing as a perfect man. Each and every one of them has something very tempting in their sexual make up. And his sexuality is what draws us to them before we even know enough about them to make a proper or informed decision. Every red blooded male desires to have sex with a woman, and that's a good thing. Looking for a man without sexual desire is like looking for a gun with no bullets. It may be shiny, but it's pretty useless. I am telling you about the qualities that would make them dangerous to the unaware, not so you can shut these men out of your life, but so that you can adjust your defenses properly. And I am not talking about defenses against him. I am talking about the defenses we must build around our own bodies in order to stay focused when we are in their presence.

Secondly, each of these of men has a certain level of potential. There are good things in who they are and how they were designed that would make them amazing if only they would _(fill in the blank)_. Girls take it from me, don't date potential. Unfulfilled potential is the most infuriating and frustrating thing we will ever find in a man. Yes, he is so close to what we want. Yes, he is almost perfect. Yes, you can see what he could be, but if he hasn't figured it out and pursued it on his own, he won't do it for you. Okay, so he might do it for a day or two, even a few months, but in the end you will both wind up disappointed and angry at the situation – him because you won't accept him for who he is, and you because he doesn't love you enough to try. Don't make yourself miserable trying to do something we just can't do for another human being. Trying to change a person who doesn't want to be changed is a waste of time, energy, and of *your* potential.

In my opinion, the ideal man has a combination of all the qualities found in each type of man. He can be as suave as the shark when need be. He can keep his boyish charm, invite you on great adventures, shower you with sweetness, and is willing to rush to your rescue. He can be steady and yet be given to bursts of inspiration. He is wonderfully complex and profoundly simple. He loves fiercely, yet gives you room to be you. He is brave and wise, conservative and a risk taker, a mystery and a wonder in his revelation. He appreciates our beauty and yet knows that the most beautiful women are those who reserve their passion for their mates. He loves the Lord. He actively lives out his faith and desires a wife who will share his passion for God with him. He works to express his love and desire in the most basic of ways, but can find a bit of poetry for the woman who truly moves him.

Most importantly, he should love our God with a passion that is greater than passion he has for you. He should honor your faith, but the two of you should never rely on the faith of the other as substitute of what you may lack on your own. Secure in what he believes, a good man will give you room to work through and live out your faith as God leads you. He will be able to listen and share about this intimate matter as one whose truest desire is to learn, even if the lesson comes from the lips of a woman.

And so we date. We date so that we can learn to discriminate in our tastes. We date so we can find those elements that make a man appealing to us, and to discern between a hormonal rush and a true desire to share something significant with the man we love. We date to learn the things that make men amazing and the things that make men weak. We date so that we might discover how to respond to their desire in healthy ways, and when to deny it for the same reasons.

Lesbianism
or
The Missing Piece

Homosexuality is one the most hotly debate issues in society today. And like all sexual issues, I feel that much of the debate stems from a lack of Biblical teaching and open discussion about anything we deem to be too embarrassing. Yet, while we older gals are busy sticking our heads in the sand, our daughters and their friends are actively discussing this both as a lifestyle and as one of the normal experiments in a college girl's life. If you think that your daughter is immune, I want you to take a second and turn on the TV. It really doesn't matter which station, you can turn it off when you hear the first reference to homosexuality or see the first openly gay person on a commercial, sitcom, or talk show. Go on now, I'll wait, but I am betting I won't have to wait long.

If you tried that little experiment but gave up because you heard and saw nothing, we may need to tweak the parameters of our test just a little – like are you sure you weren't watching the preaching channel? And would you know an openly homosexual person if they shoved a rainbow flag up your . . . uh, nose? I didn't think so. If you have failed to note the prevalence of homosexual motifs within the media it might be time to let you daughter take the lead and teach you a thing or two, because I bet she can spot a gay celebrity in a matter of minutes.

Okay, I know once again some of you are horrified at what you learning in these pages, but gals, this is why I am here, because not only is the discussion about homosexuality going on in some distant city, it is happening everywhere. We all need to be informed about the truth of this issue from a Biblical perspective. Now before you start thinking that you know all that the Bible has to say on the subject and decide to close this book, I am asking you to listen in on some the conversations your daughter is probably having with her friends. No matter which side of the line you come down on, it can never hurt to be better informed about this controversial issue.

When speaking with young women, I have found that they are divided into three very distinct camps. The first camp is what we might expect among those who have been raised in the Church. They adamantly believe that homosexuality is wrong in any form. The second camp believes that the Bible is an archaic document, which while good for general moral teaching, somehow missed the boat when it comes to human sexuality. The third camp is the most interesting. This camp believes that since there is no specific command against lesbianism it must be okay and only male homosexuality is wrong. I would like to address each camp individually.

To the Church Girls

To the first camp, I must commend your faith and willingness to accept the Bible and its decrees at face value. I believe that you are right, and I make no apologies for being among your rank. However, I want to caution you against another a sin, the sin of arrogance. Too many of you think that since you got it right on this issue that your poop don't stink, but honey, if you ever start feeling superior because this is not something you wrestle with, you are guilty of an equally damning sin. Each of us deal with something, and I have yet to find any sin that God likes more than another. So resist the temptation to get on that high horse, and start living out some other tenants of our faith – like love, compassion, and humility.

Really girls, I hate to be the one to tell you this, but sometimes you can be harsh, and more than a little forbidding. And that makes it really difficult for anyone who might be struggling with this issue to turn to you for any of the love and support they might need as they go through what is often a very painful time in their life. We were never called to condone anything the Bible declares to be a sin, but we have been called to love. So we need to stop treating anyone who is honest and brave enough to share what is really going on in their life as if they were somehow inferior to us. And dear Lord, please, please, please stop preaching at them and claiming you are acting in love, because you're not. It's you on an ego trip, plain and simple.

If you have never faced something that threatened to rock your world, totally redefine who you thought you were, or had to make a choice between a love you could see and touch versus a God who can sometimes seem oh-so-distant, count yourself as very blessed and accept the fact that you have no idea of what that person is going through. In time, I am sure that you will. Maybe it won't be this issue that you face, but at least once in every life we will face a moment where our faith will be put to the test. I truly believe this, and I know that those who screamed damnation the loudest are often the first to fall when they face their own crisis of faith. So be careful what you say, because our words of judgment for another are often the very ones that come back to bite us in the rump when we fail.

So if you aren't supposed to pull away or throw rocks . . . uh, I mean preach at them, what are you supposed to do? Be their friend.

Really, that's it. Set healthy friend boundaries like you would in any other relationship, and stick to them. After all, I have friends who watch reruns of a certain sitcom about nothing, but I exercise the right to set a healthy friend boundary and refuse to participate in this evil deed with them. We all have a friend who over or under eats, but it does not mean that we have to follow their diet. We all have a friend who over spends, is a hoarder, or fills their house with cutesy porcelain figurines of bubble-eyed children dressed as Bible characters, but we don't shun or mimic their behavior – hopefully. (And honestly, there really should be a support group for the good Christian woman who addicted to those figurines.) Nor do we preach at them every time we cross paths.

The bottom line is, the Christian faith is about redemption, and we serve a God great enough and loving enough to redeem everything, including me and you. He desires to do the same work of grace in the lives of each and every one of His children, and each time we injure each other in word and deed, we injure the heart of our Father. We should stop being thankful that we are not a sinner like the other gal, and start being thankful for a God who loved us enough to save us from our own stupidity.

Alright, I know homosexuality is a way bigger deal than any of the "sins" I listed, and I am not trying to make light of the people who have wrestled with this issue. However, some of you need to put the eternal consequences in perspective. You are not any less guilty in God's eyes simply because your sin does not illicit the same societal consequences. And let's be honest, the consequences dealt out by us Church folk can be severe, and too often that is final straw that sends someone spiraling from temptation to action. I just never want to carry that around on my conscience.

Am I saying that we shouldn't take a stand on homosexuality? Absolutely not, and we should do so unapologetically. We are responsible for telling the truth, but it should be the truth told in love with no trace of smugness or disdain. This is one area where we need to be carefully weighing and judging our words, not to mention praying like mad because we need the Holy Spirit's guidance on this one.

In my experience, we really do not need to speak as much as we think we do, and I am not above shifting the blame for what others might call my offensive position right back to God. After all, He sent the message. I am just responsible to live it. So I typically say, when *asked* what I believe, and not a second before, "The Bible says that homosexuality is wrong, and that is what I have to live by. However, it also says that the lie I told my boss about being too sick to work is wrong, too, and that puts me in the boat right along with you." Believe it or not, this is a message that most people can accept. I've made my beliefs very clear, but I have not exempted myself as holier-than-thou. Meaning that I am still leaving the door open for anyone who might want to pursue a sincere conversation about why I believe what I do.

And guess what? More often than not, they do! They were just looking for someone to actually talk to them, not judge them or preach at them, but to actually share our beliefs in a calm and rational way. For so many, this was the first time that they heard anything other than the Church's wrath or the world's message about homosexuality.

I realize that for some of you the idea of sitting down with an openly gay person is about as appealing as sharing a steak with a lion, but ask yourself, where did you get that idea? Let's be honest, we know about homosexuals the same way they know about us – through all the outrageous stuff that makes it to the local news, and just how reliable of a source is that really? We know that only a few nut jobs posing as Christians blow up abortion clinics, picket funerals, or live in gun-hording communes, but they are out there and they do make the news. So guess what people outside the Church think about us? Ever stop and think that the same holds true for others?

I know that there are militant homosexuals out there. I saw them on the news, but I have some friends who are kind, sweet, funny, brilliant, and practicing a homosexual lifestyle. They know what I believe, and I know what they are doing. Sometimes we talk about it, most of the time we don't, but they know that I am willing to make a distinction between them and what they are doing. And anytime they desire to know more about my Lord, I am ready to share. In the meantime, I am praying that God will touch their hearts, because I do believe they would be great additions to the family.

To the Skeptics

To the second camp, well, why don't you just finish reading this book before you make you final decision on the Bible's view of sex? And while you are at it, you might want to peruse Song of Songs, Leviticus, and Ezekiel. I think you will find that God isn't as much a prude as you may have believed Him to be, neither has He ever shown any unrealistic tendencies about us as sexual beings.

Right about now, I could launch into a diatribe about the authenticity of Scripture, its authority, and why it is the most amazing thing ever written. I could make just about every scholarly argument out there, but we both know that it would fail to convince you. So I won't bore you. What I will do is pray that you have an experience with God that takes your breath away, because I know that He is far more compelling than any words I could write.

To the Confused

Now let's turn to the third camp. Girls, we really need to have a talk. I know that the word lesbian is nowhere to be found in the Bible, but there is no reason to think that God was silent on the subject. We need to remember that the Bible was written in a different language and a different time, so it doesn't always phrase things the way we are comfortable or familiar with.

The verses most clearly dealing with lesbianism are found in Romans chapter one. Now I wholeheartedly recommend that you take the time to read the entire chapter so that you can see the context, but verses 26 and 27 state,

> "For this reason God gave them up to dishonorable passions. For their women exchanged natural relations for those that are contrary to nature; and the men likewise gave up natural relations with women and were consumed with passion for one another, men committing shameless acts with men and receiving for themselves the due penalty for their error."

It really doesn't get much plainer than that.

I don't want to muddy the waters too much at this point, but I do feel like I need to address one of the lies that is going around out there about this passage. Many people are claiming that this has nothing to do with lesbianism per se, and that it is instead referring to idolatry. And while I must be truthful in acknowledging that idolatry is indeed an aspect of what is being addressed, Paul is being very specific about the fact these homosexual acts are "dishonorable" and "contrary to nature." There is almost a break within his address where he sets aside the initial topic of idolatry and chooses to focus very specifically on the issues of homosexuality before resuming his discourse. Furthermore, he continues to offer a list of sins that are both included in and a product of idolatry, and we all know that things like "unrighteousness, evil, covetousness, malice;" "envy, murder, strife, deceit, maliciousness;" being "gossips, haters of God, insolent, haughty, boastful, inventors of evil, disobedient to parents, foolish, heartless, (and) ruthless" are sins – no one in their right mind would dare to argue otherwise. So why do we quibble over the mention of homosexuality?

Another line of thought that says the Bible does not prohibit lesbianism is the idea that the Old Testament never speaks on the issue. While there is no specific law against it, the general concept that sex is reserved for the marriage relationship is stated over and over again. And since there was no confusion within the Jewish culture on the nature of marriage, there was no doubt that sex was to be between a man and his wife. We should also bear in mind that a woman's sexual purity was to be guarded by the men in her life, first her father and then her husband who would be responsible for insuring that she clothed, fed, and sheltered. A woman who chose a lesbian lifestyle would have no visible means of support, and be left at the mercy of a culture that would see her as neglecting the word of God by not fulfilling the command to be fruitful and multiply. It simply was not a reasonable option for a woman in that day and time.

Now, before anyone goes and gets their knickers in a knot, I am not advocating that the modern woman be wholly dependent on a man. I am simply explaining one reason why a command against lesbianism might be unnecessary at the time the Old Testament was written. Furthermore, we see that when lesbianism did become a concern for people of faith, God did see fit to have it addressed by Paul, so it is not simply a forgotten issue.

The final argument the Bible offers against lesbianism is by far the most compelling to me, even if it seems to be the most obscure to others. This argument is found in Exodus 20 in a passage that I am sure you are all familiar with. We call it the Ten Commandments. This is that list of verses where God says "Thou shalt not" a lot. Things like, "Thou shalt not kill," "Thou shalt not steal" or "Thou shalt not commit adultery." To understand why I consider this to be so important in our understanding about Biblical teachings on lesbianism we need to pause for a brief Hebrew lesson, but don't worry. I'll keep it simple.

Almost all Hebrew words end with a suffix that tells the reader whether it is referring to the male or female gender. You can't even count in Hebrew without it being gender specific. It's just how the language works, and any of you who speak Spanish or one of many other foreign languages are already familiar with the concept.

Now if we were to read the Ten Commandments in the original Hebrew, we would find, based on those gender specific suffixes, that they are all addressed to men. Women don't come up, we are neglected and so we must be allowed to do everything that the men have just been told not to do because we weren't specifically mentioned. Right? Of course not! None of us are stupid enough to even begin to entertain the idea that women are allowed to go off on random killing sprees simply because the Bible never specifically forbids us from doing it. If that were the case, no one would survive our monthly bouts with PMS!

As my grandmother used to say, "What's good for the goose is good for the gander." In other words, there are just some things that hold true for us all, no matter what sex we are, and when we add up all the evidence, we find that the argument for lesbianism as a God-okayed act falls apart.

Inescapable Genes?

Finally, there is the thought that homosexuality is predetermined by genetics and must therefore be alright since a person cannot do anything about the way they were born. I won't even bother to discuss the validity of that little bit of scientific research. although the studies that have "proven" this have come under fire not only by conservative Christians but also various members of the scientific community for the not being performed in a strictly scientific manner. What I will do is concede that for some people homosexuality is an easier sin to fall into than for others. What I will not concede is that this makes it all right.

Personally, I believe that we all have a "pet sin", sin which is either through nature or nurture more appealing to us than any other sin. It may very well be our genetics that cause certain sins to be more tempting and harder to resist. However, I have yet to see any one condone alcoholism as okay simply because someone is genetically predisposed to becoming an alcoholic. We all know that this is self destructive behavior, damaging the individual and those who love them. A predisposition towards being obese can also be genetically based, but once again, we all acknowledge that it is neither good nor healthy to let the genes rule the show.

One of the basic tenants of Christianity is that we die to ourselves and all of our unholy desires. As believers, this is a process that we should be engaged in daily. It's not always easy, and it's not always fun, but it is part of this life of faith. The good news is we don't have to wrestle with any sin alone, and we fight with our eyes on the prize – a deeper, life-changing knowledge of our God. For this reason, it is worth the fight to eradicate sin from our lives no matter what form sin takes.

Pornography
or
The Not So Beautiful Lie

Every time Christians fail to speak clearly on any issue we might as well send out engraved invitations for someone else to speak up, and we shouldn't be surprised when their message is louder and clearer than anything we may have ever said. Nor should we be shocked when their message is not the message that we would have spoken, and I know of no issue where this is truer than the issue of pornography. Women today are told by the secular media that only an insecure woman or a woman who is sexually repressed would have a problem with her man viewing pornography. We are told that pornography is harmless and normal, a celebration of women even, an aid to help spice up a boring sex life, and something we should all embrace as a sign that we have become liberated from the oppressive, puritanical ideas that made us believe sex was dirty in the first place.

Meanwhile there is a whisper, maybe more of a whimper, from the Church saying that pornography is wrong. Our lack of boldness and clarity has left our message diluted and muddled with no real impact upon our audience. I don't know why we haven't taken a stronger stand with our message, but our pseudo-silence has left many girls torn and conflicted about what they should think concerning what has become an accepted means of sexual expression in our society. As a result many women have accepted the idea that the Bible has little or nothing to say about the use of porn, and what it may say is dismissed as outdated and not applicable to this day. Girls, I hate to break it to you, but when the Church has spoken on these issues, she has been right, but unfortunately, too many of us were unable to hear her voice through the competing shouts of others and the proper Christian wording. I know because once I was caught in the middle of the confusion. So let's take off the gloves and get to the heart of a few troubling issues. Allow me to begin by sharing my experiences with pornography and its users.

I really didn't date that much growing up. The one man that I got serious enough to actually begin discussing marriage with admitted to me that he habitually used pornography. In my naiveté I blew it off as something that single men did. I had no concept as to why they looked at porn or why it held such a fascination for them. After all I had seen pictures of naked men, and I really hadn't seen anything to get all the excited about. I mean really, honestly, that has got to be the funniest looking piece of equipment God could have ever dreamed up. Don't get me wrong. I am glad God came up with the idea, but to just sit and look at a picture? I still have a hard time believing that any picture could be that all that thrilling, even knowing what I know now.

To my nineteen year old country-girl ears, what he shared didn't sound that bad. He lived alone, had been single for his whole life, and instead of sleeping around he looked at porn. Not that I phrased it that way, because I still had no clue as to what the hype was about. My then-boyfriend told me that he anticipated a great marriage and looked forward to the day that he would no longer need pornography because he would have a wife. Due to many and bizarre circumstances, that day never came.

I did, however, marry another man when I was just shy of twenty one. I could not write a book long enough to encompass the many dysfunctions of that relationship, but one of the primary problems was his addiction to pornography. Over the next three years, I would do a lot of research in this area trying to make sense of a marriage that was falling apart with porn being the number one reason. No one ever warned me that this simple act of looking at pictures could be so devastating, but in the end it almost cost me my life – literally.

First off girls, just in case any of you are as naïve as I was, men do not simply look at porn. Men masturbate to porn. The pictures used as way to aid and enhance their arousal. There are many different types of porn available, and with the internet it is all readily available to anyone who desires it. Recently, I ran across a reference to "Rule 34". Not sure what it meant I looked it up and found out that Rule 34 states, "If it exists, there is porn about it."

This rule is not far from the truth or, more accurately, is more true than I wish it were.

Typically men start viewing porn because they have a curiosity about what we gals look like. They just simply want to know what they have to look forward to, and honestly, that is a normal desire. However, for most men it doesn't take long to realize these pictures have a strange and pleasurable effect on them. They want to experience that feeling again and again. So they begin seeking out the images that arouse them.

None of this seems all that bad on the surface. After all as we have discussed, masturbation isn't *necessarily* a bad thing, but this is moving beyond the bounds of a simple physical release. People viewing porn have now included another person in their actions, and actively lusted in their hearts after the person in the image. The sin of lust is addressed in the Bible, and very directly by Jesus Himself as a sin equal to, if not synonymous, with adultery. Lust is a sin is so damning that Jesus says it is better to pluck out your eye than to allow it to lead you into further sin. (Matthew 5:25-30). Are we getting the picture this is a bad thing?

Okay, you say, but all sin can be forgiven and surely, once they are married it will all go away. That's what I thought. How wrong I was.

Sin, all sin, has consequences, especially when that sin is habitual. Just like there is no such thing as safe sex, there is nothing even remotely resembling a safe sin out there. And like all other sin the consequences never affect just the person who is engaging in the sin. Everyone around the sinner suffers, and this is worked out through a natural process of events.

What most of us fail to understand is that pornography is desensitizing. The initial phase of desensitization happens on a mental level. The pictures of naked women are beautifully tantalizing in the beginning, but eventually, most habitual porn users must move on to more stimulating images. This can include but is not limited to live action films. Since these do require some action, the woman needs to someone or something to interact with. Many of the videos a man may first choose will feature girl-on-girl action, but soon even this will not even be enough. From there, the user usually moves on to movies with man on girl or even multiple girls with a single man. I wish I could say it stops there, but it doesn't.

Some readers may find the next part of this horrifying, and it should be. The next step is multiple men with women, and while male homosexual encounters may not be featured the user is being groomed to accept multiple men in a sexual situation. The user may then progress to films that feature orgies that include multiple partners of both sexes and in scenarios where any type of sexual encounter is condoned and celebrated. For those who have never experienced a porno, they often think that these are all beautiful people enjoying uninhibited sex, but the truth is the people are not always beautiful nor are they the stereotypes we have come to believe fill these films. Age distortions are common, gender bending is easily and readily displayed, props including toys, other inanimate objects, and even animals are employed.

The list of atrocities goes on and on. There are films that cater to a wide variety of fetishes from amputees and feet to bondage and sadomasochism which can culminate in a mock death of one of the actors during the sex act. Lines between ages become so blurred child abuse can be portrayed, and bestiality is common place on the internet, as are all types of demeaning acts to women, children, and even other men. I wish I was exaggerating, but I am not, nor am I working from someone else's accounts of what they have seen. In the three years of my first marriage, I saw all forms of sexual violence and perversion played out in what many people consider to be a harmless, single-guy diversion. Pornography is not harmless, and it is not a simple diversion.

Granted not every man who ever views porn is headed all the way to the bottom of this rabbit hole, but how far is too far? Is it even possible to make a line of demarcation about what is innocent "boys-being-boys-fun" and what crosses into life altering realms?

Over the years I have spoken to several men about pornography, and I have been able to watch the progression play out time and time again. Men who were once too macho to even entertain the idea of watching gay porn, now have no major objections, and certainly there are none to girl-on-girl porn.

For many men, the desire for these images begins and ends with pornography. They have no desire to act out the sexual fantasies before them, but some men soon find that watching is not enough.

So they begin to seek out women who will act out these fantasies on their behalf or with them. Many Christian men know that their wives, or the type of woman they hope to marry, would never do some of the things they desire. So they seek out women who will, and several men have resorted to prostitutes in an effort to keep this part of their lives separate from all other aspects of who they are.

A number of men that I have spoken with have claimed that I am completely off the mark and deny that they masturbate while viewing porn. I make no apologies for not believing them, nor do I buy what they are selling when they tell me they watch it simply because it is entertaining and funny. If that is true, my basic premise that pornography is desensitizing still holds true. Sex may be, and occasionally should be, fun but to reduce it to merely being funny? Since when is it alright to turn what should be a sacred event into a form of casual entertainment? To view sex as merely entertaining, even between two anonymous strangers, cannot help but bleed over into how he views his own sexual experiences, making him a less than attractive partner to a woman who ever desires to share in a meaningful sex life with her mate.

Even if the porn obsession begins and ends with viewing pornography, there are still major complications. And this leads us to the second level of desensitization, mental.

If you haven't figured it out yet, sex happens mostly in our heads. The primary sexual organ for men and women is our brains. And just like women, men are wonderfully complex in their sexuality. When a man has an orgasm a whole series of events are happening in his body. His blood flow is being rerouted to his genitals and groin, his muscles are contracting, his heart rate is elevated, and his breathing is changed to accommodate the demands on his body, but the most amazing thing is happening in his head. (No, not that one. Well, okay, that one too.) At the point of climax, his brain is being bathed in almost every feel good chemical our bodies can produce. He is being overwhelmed with a sense of well being and will soon reach the point of complete relaxation that allows most men to promptly fall asleep in their lover's arms. But something else is also occurring, all of those chemicals are creating a chemical bond with whatever the man was looking at. Remember how visual guys are? This bond flags certain visual cues that essentially go off like a fire alarm when he sees this same image again. Immediately, the brain starts telling the body "That's the thing that gets you off, that makes you feel good. Go get it again! This is what you need!" Eventually that particular image becomes the most arousing thing a man can ever hope to find.

In an ideal world, this is the process that allows men to remain monogamous for decades. Men who marry and remain faithful to their wives, both in deed and thought, experience this sensation with only one woman and his brain becomes conditioned to respond only to her. Sure he might notice the scantily clad gal on the beach, but that's about it. When I have talked to men who have been married for twenty or more years, they tell me that they really have no desire for anyone but their wives. The biological system God put in place allows them to enjoy one woman at a depth and level multiple women cannot provide.

However, when the image a man is viewing at the point of climax is ever changing, he has no chance to become attached to a particular woman. Instead, his brain is screaming that he needs an ever changing variety of women kept captive on a page or screen. Given enough time a man will lose his ability to perform sexually with a real woman. And no, I am not making that up, nor am I sharing what someone else told me: that comes first hand straight out of my own true life story.

Girls, if you ask men about this they will tell you that this is not the case. They will say that porn is just something to help them cope until they can be with you. And honestly, they probably believe it. I have never yet met a man who was in the middle of his porn addiction who could honestly admit he needed porn to have an orgasm. I have met a number of men in the midst of recovering who are more than willing to admit that a normal sexual relationship is difficult after habitually using porn. Rule number one of any addiction is never admit you are addicted. And like all addicts unwilling to give up their addictions, porn addicts follow this rule to an extreme. Acknowledging that you have problem means you have to deal with it, and no addict, until they are ready to heal, wants to do that if they can avoid it.

Physical desensitization follows, and literally, some of the nerve receptors of the penis become deadened to regular stimulus, i.e. the vagina. Girls, the inside of us is a million times softer and gentler than a man's hand. Continual and habitual masturbation can damage the nerves leaving a man unable to physically feel enough in order to climax. And as most men are in denial about how much damage they have done to their bodies, guess who gets blamed for their sexual dysfunction?

Which leads us to the fourth level of desensitization, emotional. For us, this is the most damaging aspect of pornography. In porn women (and men) are presented for one reason, so that the viewer may use them for their own gratification. The men who use porn do not have to make allowances for the feelings of the people in the pictures. He doesn't have to respond to her needs or wants. His focus can remain self centered with no immediate repercussions or judgments. Sexual satisfaction ceases to be something that two people in love seek and discover together, but is reserved for him alone, and the woman should find her pleasure in pleasing him.

I shouldn't have to tell you that this does not make for a very pleasing sex life. In my first marriage, sex was strictly about his desires and wants. Now, I believe that we should try to please our husbands in the bedroom, but he should be equally committed to pleasing us. My wants and desires were discounted or rejected. He claimed that I expected far too much romance from real life and sex was not about that. Other women who have confided that they are married to men with a porn addiction have confirmed that I am not alone in my experience.

When men come to believe that sex is simply about them, and not about building and nurturing intimacy, they surrender all sensitivity to their partners' emotional and physical needs. Added to that is the tendency to justify their egocentric behavior by blaming their wives. Women have been accused of being undesirable because they were too fat, too skinny, had the wrong size breasts, the house not being clean enough, the meals not tasty enough, or some other lame excuse. My all time favorite, spouted by my ex, was my body temperature was wrong. I still have no idea how a person would fix that one.

But the truth is there is no fix, at least none that a woman can offer. The problem is not the woman's. It is his and his alone. His fixation on her flaws means that she will be assaulted verbally and emotionally in an attempt to change who she is and what she is willing to do all so that he can achieve his high. Women frequently and shamefully admit that they allowed themselves to participate in activities that are a direct violation of the Biblical mandates for sex. And I am not talking about wearing some sexy lingerie or playing out some erotic fantasy together (both perfectly legitimate within marriage). I am talking about women who have allowed another woman to join her and her husband in an act that should have been reserved for the two of them alone. I have known women who allowed their husbands to urinate and defecate on them because that is what happened in his favorite porno, and others who have had multiple sex partners so their husbands could watch the live action. Do I need to tell you that since that time they have experienced a decreased desire for their husbands and even resentment towards him, further complicating the situation?

Why do they do this? Because they have come to believe the lie that they are not good enough, sexual enough, or exciting enough to please their men. Everything they do is motivated by the desire to hang on to their husbands, and many believe that their submission, even to his degrading sexual desires, is in keeping with the Biblical admonishment to be submissive to their husbands. We will discuss more about this in the marriage section, but for now, you should know that a man who is sensitive to his wife's feelings will never place her in a situation that she is uncomfortable with or finds degrading.

Second, porn is wrong and dangerous because it cannot be made without the blatant exploitation of another human being. Yes, most pornography features men and women who have made the choice to cash in on their bodies and sexuality, or have decided to flaunt their bodies and their so called freedom before the world. Ladies, all of these people are someone's sons or daughters. They have an eternal soul, and when anyone purchases porn, they are contributing to an industry that deliberately takes advantage another person's poor judgment. I believe this is a sin as great as any other.

The average porn star can expect to have only few good years before a nasty STD, emotional breakdown, drug use, or suicide takes them out of the game. The ones who survive will have to live the rest of their lives knowing that they allowed themselves to be used in the most base and crude manner by anyone who had the $1.99 rental fee or internet access. Can you truly live with that on your conscience?

Men, real men, would never take advantage of another person's weakness or illness simply to fulfill their lust. They shouldn't do it with us in a dating relationship, nor should it be alright to do it to a stranger. If we see signs that a man is willing to behave in a manner that is completely dishonorable to our God and the people He created in His image, what makes us think that same man will treat the women in his life any better?

The third problem with porn is it allows men to avoid those messy conversations. They do not have to become intimate or vulnerable to meet their basic sexual needs. So they can completely bypass intimacy with the very one they should be intimate with. Sex is the glue of marriage, forcing us to make revelations about ourselves that are reserved for someone who can be trusted with our hearts, someone who promised to cherish us above all others. In the safety of this relationship we learn how to expose ourselves, physically and emotionally, to each other, but without the urgency of our sex drives, we have little if any incentive to bare our hearts in this manner.

Women who marry men battling with this problem find themselves alone in a painful situation where they have no one to talk to or confide in. They cover it up, keep it hidden, and slowly go insane trying to save a marriage where they are the only ones willing to take the emotional risks necessary to rebuild their marriages.

So why do you need to know this as single gal?

First of all, you need to know that pornography is not alright, even for a single man. A man engaged in this activity is laying the ground work for a possible life time of sexual dysfunction. Any sign of it in dating relationship is the sign to run.

I know that running may seem extreme, but we are talking about the rest of your life. We are talking about the man who may be the father of your children. We are talking about your emotional, mental, and possibly even your physical health. And if those reasons seem too selfish, you need to realize that your acceptance of it in a dating relationship is seen as a sign of approval. Men using porn need to know that it is not alright, and maybe by breaking his heart, you will be prompting him to get the help he needs to get out while he is still young. Don't stay and enable his addiction if you aren't already married to him. Save yourself, possibly him and your future kids the heartache, because above all, we are talking about a man who is systematically destroying his ability to know what is good and right in a sexual context and is opening the door for perversion to rule his life.

Secondly, you need to know how to look for the signs that this might be an issue. Here is a list of questions to ask about your man. A yes answer is not an automatic conviction, but it might mean you need to do some further checking.

- When you go to his home, are there girlie posters on the wall?
- Magazines lying around?
- Are there KY, lotion, or oils and crumpled tissues shoved "out of sight"?
- Can you drop over unannounced without him scurrying to hide "something" before you have a chance to see it?
- Are you kept out of the garage, gym, or other "guy" spaces?
- Is it okay to get tools from his tool box for yourself?
- Does he have a stack of unmarked DVD's lying about that he never plays in your presence?
- Is his computer off limits? If you are serious (I'm talking impending marriage serious), has he shared his email passwords?
- Does he erase the history of his computer each time he logs off?
- Does he have pornographic pictures on his phone?
- Does he keep his phone locked so you can't look through it?
- Does he have questionable photos on his social networking site?
- Does he make jokes about porn to you or with his friends?
- Do his friends watch porn?
- Does he approve or downplay his friends' use of porn?
- Do the other men in your life have concern for him in this area?
- Does he ever make degrading comments about women on TV, in the movies, or simply seen in public?
- Does he ask you to talk "dirty" to him over the phone?
- Is the trunk of his car off limits?

- Are there stacks of magazines in his home, and only the top three are Popular Science?
- Does he avoid any direct conversations you try to have with him about porn?
- Does he justify using it just while you are dating?
- In your network of friends, does the woman who has experienced this get a funny vibe off him?

Girls, I know that some of these things look like they are invading his privacy, but if we are talking a man you may one day marry, get over it. There is no such thing as privacy once you say I do, and you have a right to know if you can trust him or not. If you can't trust him now, don't expect things to change once you do get married. Another thing, trust is something that has to be earned, especially at this level, so looking for warning signs is something you should be doing. If he gets upset or offended that you want to check him out, you are getting a pretty good tip off he is hiding something, and it is not right that he expect you to be okay with secrets that can affect the rest of your lives.

If you have reason to believe that the man in your life is using pornography, and you decide to confront him, you need to be prepared. Men usually begin by offering what they believe to be a reassuring statement, "I prefer the real thing to a picture." If you don't feel overly reassured then they will say that they know that "porn is just a fantasy, and it has nothing to do with real life or you." "You have no reason to be jealous or feel insecure about what you mean to me." "You're prettier than any of the girls in the movies." If this isn't working for them, they may decide to go on the offensive. Honey, be prepared for some pretty harsh words at this point. You may be accused of being unreasonably jealous and having insecurity issues that you need to work on. Your faith may be used against you, and they may say that Christianity is a sexually repressed religion, or that the Bible is outdated, and my all time favorite, pornography isn't mentioned in the Bible so it must be alright. (My response to this is, Hmmm, then why does the word pornography come from the Greek word that is specifically used for sexual sin?)

Gals, it can get really ugly. Most of the things that are said in these situations are designed to shake us to the core, cause us to question our sexual identities and value. If you are a virgin, then you will be told that is why you do not know enough to appreciate men's needs. If you have had a bad experience in a previous relationship, then you are reacting to your scars. If you decide to get out, then you were intimidated by a piece of paper. Be prepared. Know what you believe and why you believe it. Know that you are not going to win the argument, you just aren't. Accept the fact that there will be a rebuttal, and it will sound logical to anyone who does not share our faith, experience, or ideals about sex. The good news is you are not required to fix him. All you are required to do is to make the right decision for you and to hold onto to the truth.

And don't expect to hear these excuses just from the men using porn. Today I sat in a waiting room reading a women's magazine and in it was a whole section over porn. One of the writers was a respected "expert" on sex and relationships. She advised that women should feel glad that their men are comfortable enough to engage their sexuality, and women were encouraged to be happy when he picks up a good tip for your love life by watching porn. The writer went on to say that a secure woman would never feel threatened by a photograph or movie. It is a harmless diversion, and we should join him in watching porn. We might even learn "a new trick for the bedroom."

Ladies, this is a lie. God designed us to experience a committed and respectful loving relationship, and I can find no way in which porn promotes either idea. Taking steps to defend that ideal even while you are dating is wise and courageous. And frankly, I resent the fact that the world is trying shame us into being silent about our beliefs and convictions. Never let the enemy's lies rob you of the peace and satisfaction of clinging to a God given vision for your sex life.

You also need to remember that since this is an addiction, a simple promise not to do it again is not sufficient. More often than not the problem just goes underground, but the addiction will always rise again if it is not dealt with. You may feel like you are playing the shrew (read that bossy, overbearing, opinionated woman), but the simple fact is you cannot trust an addict until they have proven they are willing to make the changes for themselves. So don't try to manipulate him by throwing a fit, making threats, or even by destroying his stash. It doesn't work. I know I've tried it all, as have multiple women who have been in this situation.

Girls, you need to know that men dealing with this often love and desire the unattainable. So if you are one the few women out there who are holding out for marriage to have that sexual encounter you are just as much of a fantasy in his mind as the porn. That makes you just as big of a turn on as that unreachable woman on the page of a magazine. For this reason, men addicted to porn will find you highly arousing. They will do just about anything to finally achieve this great fulfillment to their fantasy, and the result is they are ardent lovers to the extent that you allow them to be.

They will pursue with a single-minded obsession, and it is easy to get caught up in their fervor. The attention and devotion they show is on par with the greatest romantic fantasy we women ever had. They will do anything to get to you, including marry you, all in hopes that you really are their fantasy woman made real. Gifts, lavish praise, expensive nights on the town will all make it seem like they are willing to do and give anything to experience your love.

The sad thing is once they have had you, you are as disposable as last month's issue of his favorite girlie magazine, and they are on to the next visually stimulating experience. So guard your hearts. To be loved with all the passion and desire is something that every girl wants, but we need to be aware that for these men it isn't about us. It is about them, and their need to acquire what is just beyond their grasp.

One last warning, girls. You cannot be the one to help him with this. Help has to come through another man, and the help of Godly, trained counsel. Trying to fix him is not your job or your place, and during this time of healing he does not need to be distracted by your presence. Offer to help him make the connections, if you can, and then shove off. This is between him and God now.

And ladies, if you are in marriage where pornography is an issue or was an issue, please know that you are not alone and it is not your fault he has a problem. Your journey is much more difficult, but it can be made with the grace of God and support of good friends. Remember there is power in your story, and while it may not be the power to set your world to rights right now, maybe it is the story that will save someone else from this special kind of hell. Become a part of redeeming your story by speaking out and telling the young women in your life the importance of having a husband who is not wounded or scarred by this battled. Please, don't be silent and don't suffer alone. Find friends who will love and encourage you as you seek the right path. We are out here, I promise.

Surprisingly, despite the heartache porn has caused so many of us, the use of pornography among women is on the rise. Producers of porn have figured out that they can increase their sells if they managed to appeal to us girls and they are actively researching ways to do just that. They are marketing women's porn that have more plot and dialogue, but is still just as exploitive as the material they market to the men.

Ladies, we need to be on guard against any attraction that this has for us because we are not immune to the devastating effects that pornography can have on a person. All the things that it does to the male's perception of sex can happen to us, and the damage is hard to undo. And don't fool yourself into thinking that you are immune. Watching porn is like watching a train wreck. You don't want to see, but you can't help but look.

I know that when we think of porn our minds immediately flash to a magazine or DVD, but it doesn't always have to be. To be honest, women have always had their own type of porn. We just tried to pretty it up by calling it "day time TV" or a "romance novel." The truth is we have used these items the same way that men use a dirty magazine, as means of escape from the real life pressures and disappointment of a true relationship, not to mention giving us that sexual buzz without the risk of disappointment. The porn industry is just upping the ante on a game we have always played, and girls, we need to stop. It is rather hypocritical for us to throw stones at the fellows if we are engaged in the same type of behavior.

All of these books, movies, and shows have managed to pervert our perceptions of sex. And it is not uncommon to find things like rape, abuse, and casual sex romanticized in the materials marketed to women, and as we allow these images and ideas to influence our thinking about sex we are making it more and more difficult to engage in a sexual relationship where love and respect are valued. Our ideas of true manhood can become warped and twisted until the only men that excite us are the "bad boys" who shows no regard for our feelings or well being. We begin to think of men in terms of the "pirate," "desperado," or "mobster" and can't get past our own fiction inspired fantasies about men to appreciate a real one. Much like men who use porn think that we should all have double D breasts and fall moaning to our knees if they deliver a pizza to our house or if they stop on the roadside to help us change a flat.

Look, I think that every girl should have some healthy and hopeful ideas about sex. We should be anticipating (if we are single) or enjoying, if we are married, a sex life that is gratifying and enjoyable, but if our ideas are gathered from sleazy books or films, we are robbing ourselves of the opportunity to discover who we are as a sexual creature. And that is a travesty, because finding the joys of sex with a loving and devoted mate makes all the once, brilliant fantasies look like the trash they really are.

Abusive Relationships
or
Beating Him to the Punch

I recently read an article that said the good news is domestic violence in marriages is going down. The bad news is domestic violence in dating relationships is on the rise. Now, you might be tempted to skip this chapter. I know that if I was reading this when I was seventeen I would have. Never once would I have even considered that I might wind up in an abusive relationship, but girls, guess what? I did, and I don't think I was the only one surprised to find that I had gotten myself into this situation.

I never fit the stereotype of a battered woman. I was sure of who I was, confident to the point of cocky, and I knew what I wanted out of this life. Before I met my ex-husband, I said that if a man ever touched me, I would plant him in my backyard and water him daily. However, like so many other battered women out there, by the time he actually hit me, I thought I was in too deep to ever get out.

Abusive relationships do not start out abusive, and I think that is what most women fail to understand. We think that we are smart enough to know if a man is going to mistreat us or not simply by looking into his eyes, but girls, sometimes we can be terribly stupid when it comes to men. Especially if they are dressed well and treat us like the queens we know that we are. And that's how an abusive relationship starts – He thinks you are perfect, every little square inch and quirk about you is sublime. The praise is effusive, and he is so eager to please you that there is nothing he won't do for your smile. And what girl wouldn't eat that up with a spoon?

Every doubt, every fear that ever made us believe that we were not beautiful or smart enough to get a great man melts away in his arms. All the more intoxicating are his words proclaiming that you saved him, gave meaning to his life, and have shown him the beauty of this world that he never believed existed until he met you. The power you have over him is heady, feeding your confidence as nothing before. Being in his presence is a high like no other, and you cannot imagine life without him in it.

But girls, when a man sets you on a pedestal this high you just have further to fall, and you will.

The day will come when you mess up, when you fail to meet his expectations, and now you must pay for the pain you caused him. This time the price won't be blood. Instead you get cold silences, words of ridicule, or the threat that he is going to leave you. It doesn't matter if you did it on purpose or not, because in his eyes you had the power to do better, and you neglected to use it. The idea that you may lose him is terrifying. How could you survive if the one person who truly believed in your greatness was gone? You know you can do better. You know you should have been aware of how greatly you affected him. How could you have hurt someone who loves you this much?

So you plead with him, beg him not to go, promise to do better, and attempt to be that perfect vision of love once again. But honey, once you fall down there is no getting up. You ruined the illusion, and now you have to prove that you truly want to make him happy. You begin contorting to yourself to fit his expectations, no matter how unattainable they may be. If he says you have been mean and cruel, you become kinder. If he says you are a coward with no backbone, you try to assert yourself. If he says that you lack drive and motivation, you redouble your efforts to do the things he likes. If he says that you work so much that you never have time for him, you drop everything to be at his beck and call. But no matter what you do, he always wishes you would do something more. Something a little grander, a little more impressive or costly. And you never can get your footing, because each time you think you finally got the hang of this, he will change the rules.

Friends are warning you that you do not seem like yourself, and that they are worried about his constant criticisms of how you act or what you say, but you blow them off. They don't see how he treats you when you are alone, when they aren't around, because when it is just the two of you, he holds you close and tells you that you are amazing. You life is one of praise and adoration, full of presents and reminders of how incredible it is to have you in his life.

Eventually, you get tired of defending him to your friends, so you stop calling altogether, you never hang out anymore. You devote your time to the man who is feeding your ego instead of telling you things you don't want to hear.

Now, his is the only voice that fills your head. He is the one in control. And he did it without ever raising his hand, maybe never even raising his voice. His increasing control over you was all accomplished through grieved disappointment and genuine remorse over your failings in the face of his desire to help you reach your full potential. He was just loving you, believing in you, and helping you to be the woman he once believed you were.

But don't worry. Even if you aren't perfect, he still loves you. He still wants to be near you, and he will do whatever it takes to make this love work because you will be worth it, one day. One day when you stop forgetting to do the things he likes, when you learn how to be more considerate, more compassionate and giving. One day when you stop being selfish and immature, when you grow up enough to know that you need someone looking out for you the way he looks out for you. He is not giving up on you yet because he knows the greatness that lies within, and he will help you find it.

Little by little you begin to surrender more and more of who you are into his control, because after all, you are a menace to yourself. Conversations are now only a list of his "suggestions" for your improvement. You need a new hair cut or color. You should lose a few pounds, stop wearing those clothes, listening to that music, watching those shows, going to those places, and you shouldn't have had to have been told. What's more, you aren't really as good at something as you thought you were. And you can bet, whatever you are passionate about – writing, reading, painting, sports, Church, school, music, you name it, that is the very thing he will attack. Anything that diverts your focus away from him and makes you feel good about yourself is target for his discontent, and the better you are, the more you enjoy it, the more he hates it. Not that he will admit it. He is just trying to keep you from wasting your time, building up false hopes, or believing all those liars out there who would take advantage of you illusions.

Of course all of these suggestions are made with a concerned voice, and he doesn't get mad that you don't always listen to him, not yet anyway.

When you do make a mistake, he withholds his affection leaving you to feel completely alone. After all, you have no friends left. You cut ties with them a long time ago. His criticisms become more and more cutting, and you think it must be true. He begins to drive home the point that you are failure, worthless, and lucky that he loves you enough to put up with your selfish behavior. You betrayed his trust, you let him down, you lied to him, you misrepresented who you were, and you will never find anyone who loves you as much as he does. And, baby, he loves you.

His world revolves around you, he would die for you, everything he does is for you, and while you may not understand it, don't worry, he has a plan you are just too stupid to understand.

Before you know it, you feel as if you are on the path to full blown schizophrenia, but you have to keep trying because you were the one who screwed it up. You were the one who almost destroyed the perfect romance, and you can't live with the idea that you ruined a love that so many women long for – like you did before he came along.

Any objections you have to how he is treating you are overruled often loudly and vehemently. The intensity of it all leaves you reluctant to speak or act, because deep down inside you know you are one argument away from total disaster. You try to explain to him how he is hurting you or why you disagree with something he says, but he tells you that you lack the experience or wisdom to know anything. He may scream and roar, throw things, all just to make a point. He doesn't hear you when you say no, when you don't want to do something, be it going to the mall, watching a particular television show, or a sexual activity. He knows what is best, and he doesn't want you to forget it. His words are confusing mixture of how much he loves you and how unworthy of love you are. You are ugly, your family is trash, you are lazy, a liar, have a mental disorder, or are emotionally unstable. And by this time you have bought into so many of his lies, you don't even know who you are anymore.

One day, he goes too far. The words are just too painful to bear. Some primal part of you that still fights for survival can't roll over and play dead anymore, so you snap. You yell, you scream, and tell him you are done. You aren't going to take it anymore. How dare he say that to you? You know the truth now, and you are getting out. He is horrified, yelling one second, crying the next, threatening that you will regret it if you leave and pleading with you for one more chance. He is sorry. He loves you. He was tired, stressed, hungry, or the barometric pressure was wrong. No matter how lame the excuse is, you buy it because you want to believe it. You just want to make it beautiful again.

Maybe you know that this is the moment you should leave, but where would you go? Can you admit to your friends that you made a mistake, that this man who declared that you were a goddess is really a crazed maniac? Can you tell them that the man you love is destroying your sanity? Can you admit that the relationship was a failure, that you lost your heart and yourself to a failure? That you failed?

He can see you wavering. He knows he has to win you back, and he is willing to do whatever it takes. The sweet words begin to fall from his lips, gifts appear, soft touches, and whispered reminders of what you have meant to each other. He needs you, and he doesn't know what he would do without you. God created you for each other. The moment is almost as beautiful as the first day you met, in those sweet days and weeks before it all started to fall apart.

Proud of your ability to salvage the situation, to reach a mature conclusion to the matter, you relent. You accept him with open arms, and his return is a thrilling mixture of passion and contrition. This is the type of love you have always dreamed of, the absolute adoration of a man who believes you are so important and stunning. Your world is complete. All those things he said were nothing. He didn't really mean it. Surely, if you hadn't set him off he wouldn't have said it. Anyways, he is sorry now, and it won't happen again. He promised, and he always tells you the truth even when it hurts. He loves you that much.

What makes the abuser so effective is he knows what we want to hear, and he will tell us the exact words needed to make our hearts soar. I won't lie to you. This part of the relationship is greatness beyond all other greatness. Women who have never experienced it can't understand why we are willing to put up with all the other things that go on, but they have never seen this type of adoration in a man's eyes. In the moments when he is groveling at your feet, you feel like you have all the power in the world, you can do no wrong, and for a moment you can believe that you really are the most beautiful thing God ever created. And feels good to a heart that has been so bruised, like a cool cloth on a burn. His words make everything better, until the next time.

But we don't think about the next time. That thought is just too ugly to pollute this time. So we hang on to the beauty, the comfort, and the absolute security of this pristine moment. Really, weren't we taught that good Christian girls forgive and forget? He's just a man full of flaws, but with enough love you can fix him. You can change him, and you couldn't ever willingly leave someone who needs you so badly.

From here all the cycles become the same: you try to be perfect but fail, he explodes, you find your back bone, and he tries to make amends. The only thing is the highs are becoming higher, and the lows have become epic. As you begin to erode away under the constant pressure and stress of the situation, you need him to define you more and more. You cling to him even as he becomes more and more abusive. You feel like you owe him something, and you just can't figure out what it is. You stumble through the day trying to find the key, celebrating each little victory and dreading every failure to say or do the right thing.

As you diminish, he becomes greater, more sure of himself, and all along he has been doing everything he can to bind you to him. He may have even pushed you to bend your rules about sex, and plays off your guilt for giving that part of yourself to him. He probably has taken your faith and twisted it to mean that love and forgiveness means complete acceptance of anything he does. You have been convinced that you were too stupid, lazy, or ugly to hope for something or someone else.

Finally, he feels safe enough to shake you, push against a wall, and pin you down while he screams in your face, but you brush it off because he hasn't actually hit you. He didn't mean it. He told you he didn't. He had just been pushed too far, and you will vow not to push him again. Then one day it happens. He backhands you, slaps you. Maybe it is a stinging blow to the rump, and he reminds you that you deserved to be punished. Maybe today is the day that you realize that you vowed never to let this happen, but he is quick. Almost as fast as his hand flew out to teach you a lesson, he has a pretty apology, a gift, or tears of repentance. You have to forgive; that is what good Christian girls do.

Soon the blows are more frequent, but a busted lip equals a leather coat. Bruised ribs mean a necklace. A bloody nose is worth a new stereo, and passing out from being strangled gets you a car. A rape is a diamond cocktail ring. Surely he must love you if he is willing to make amends so tangibly? And after all it was your fault, wasn't it? He didn't mean it. He never means it.

Think it won't ever be you? Think again. I've heard numbers as high as six in ten women will be in an abusive relationship at some point in their lives. That's more than half of us who will become some man's emotional or physical punching bag, and gals, it could be you.

It never looks like abuse in the beginning. At first it looks amazing, and that is why we get sucked in. And like a frog in a pan of slowly heated water, we aren't always smart enough to jump out before we are boiled alive. So we need to be looking for the signs that we are heading down a path that we should stay far, far away from.

Ask yourself some things about your relationship, and ask your friends to help you answer them realistically. They aren't victims of the good times.

- Does he blame his parents for where he is in life?
- Does he blame you for everything that goes wrong?
- Does he claim that his bad attitude and moods are caused by others?
- Has he cut you off from your friends?
- Does he hate your friends or find reasons not to do group activities?
- Are you his only friend?
- Has he tried to get you to dress or behave differently?
- Does he discourage you from chasing after your dreams, especially if they don't involve him?
- Has he ever your used your faith and morals as leverage to forgive him?
- Does he call you names?
- Does he criticize you in front of your friends?
- Does he compare you to women who are "better" than you, including his mother and ex-girlfriends?

- Do arguments end with you or him begging for forgiveness?
- Does he try to buy your forgiveness?
- Is there a cycle of fighting and making up?
- Does he have a ready excuse for losing his temper?
- Has he said that you can save him, or that life is only worth living because of you?
- If you try to leave, does he threaten to commit suicide?
- Does he check up on you to see if you are where you said you were?
- Does he distort events from the past so that he looks better?
- Has he told you that the way you remember something is wrong?
- Is he constantly changing the rules of the relationship?
- Does he accuse you of being mentally or emotionally unstable?
- Do you feel off balance, like you can't get your footing with him?
- Are you tense and anxious to please him?
- Do you cringe if you miss one of his phone calls because you know it will mean a fight?
- Do you like yourself when you are with him, or are you worried about messing up again?
- Are the only good times after a fight?
- Has he accused you of misrepresenting who you were to him?
- Does he tell you must prove your love for him?
- Has he pressured you for sex and then told you that you were a tease for refusing?
- Do your friends think you have changed since you became involved with him?
- Are they worried about your well being?
- Do they complain that they never see you?
- Does he frequently ask you to ditch your friends so you can come and be with him?
- Has he ever invaded your personal space when you were in an argument?

- Can you address an issue without it turning into an argument?
- Are your imperfections turned into a reason for a personal attack?
- Does he tell you that you don't try hard enough or could be better with more effort?
- Does he promise he will be better when you get married, he has a better job, or some other future event happens?
- Has he thrown, broken, or destroyed things during an argument?
- Has he ever been abusive to animals?
- Do you cover up his bad behavior with your friends?
- Do you blame yourself for his outbursts?
- Is this the type of relationship you want for your daughter?

This is not meant to be a comprehensive list of things that definitely mean a person is or is not in an abusive relationship, but, girls, please use your heads. If you found yourself answering yes to more than few of these questions and can remember more than one incident that caused you to answer yes – you are probably in an abusive relationship. Once again, this is where you need a group of people who desire your best and love you enough to be honest. If they are concerned for your well being, physical, mental, or emotional, listen to them. An abuser often has us so confused that we can't see the havoc they are creating in our lives, and we may not be aware of the changes that are occurring in us. We need an outside perspective from people who are not caught up in the emotional chaos.

We need to remember the number one lie of an abuser is that this is as good as it gets unless we become a better person. And this is a lie straight from the pits of hell. Good relationships can happen, even for messed up people, and no one person is always the reason things go bad in a relationship. In a healthy relationship there is room for both people to make mistakes, and to move forward. Conflict doesn't fall into a cycle. Conflicts occur, but when they do both parties work for resolution and mutually extend forgiveness and compassion for the other.

Don't believe the lie or buy into the false hope that things will get better. Short of a miraculous intervention, they typically don't. Like a snowball going downhill, all of these behaviors just gain momentum the longer you hang on. You need to face up to the reality that you cannot save or change anyone. Rescuing someone is beyond your capabilities and there is no shame in recognizing your limitations. And no, you are not betraying your faith or being selfish by getting out. You are protecting not only yourself, but your future children. Never in a million years would a good mom willingly place her kids in this type of environment, so keep their mom out of it and you won't have to worry about the kids.

Getting out is a process, and the longer you have been in the longer it will take to disentangle your hopes, emotions, and identity from this relationship. You can't get free on your own, and you will need your friends. Isolating yourself is almost a guarantee for relapsing back into the comfort of what you have known. And even if it was bad, we still prefer what we have known to facing our fears and stepping out into the new and unfamiliar.

Remember, relationships like this are addictive, and you need to admit this to yourself. You were just as addicted to the cycles as he was, and now you are doing without your fix. No more adrenaline highs, no more comforting affirmations. You will crave the familiar, emotionally, mentally, and even physically. So make yourself some hard and fast rules. No contact, if at all possible. No last appeals to reconcile, and no lies about how dangerous things really were.

Tell your friends what has happened, everything you can bear to share, and then give them carte blanche permission to remind you of the truth if they ever see you wavering. Don't ignore them, and don't avoid the painful words. Yes, there were good times. You never would have gotten involved with him if there weren't. After all you aren't a complete imbecile, but right now you don't need to think about those times, and that's why your friends need to be speaking the unvarnished truth over you. Ask them to call you periodically at random times of the day, just to see how you are doing. Pay attention to when you feel the greatest draw to go back. For me it was always began somewhere around 10:00 pm, and by 11:00, I was trying not to cave. Thank God for my friend and her insomnia. We spent many nights on the phone or driving aimlessly while I worked through my angst.

Journal, journal, journal. Get all the crap out of your head on to the page. It doesn't matter if it is pretty or makes sense, just do it. Don't know where to start? Start telling your story, or write him a letter. Don't censor yourself, write it all down, the good the bad and the ugly. Write to God, tell Him how you feel, and be honest. Remember, this is for you to get it all out, so don't mail anything, just write. You don't need the contact, and he doesn't need the ammunition. So hang onto to what you are writing, and go back to them in a few weeks to see where your thoughts are. You might be surprised at the magnitude of your emotions.

And be okay with the fact you may need some professional help to get through this time. Who you were was devastated, and it may take awhile to rediscover that person. Honey, this is one of those types of crazy that needs professional management. Trust me, I know. And this is the type of wound that cannot be self-medicated through the proper application of books, no matter how brilliantly written. You don't amputate your arm alone. You leave that to the professionals, and how much more important are our hearts and minds than a limb?

Friends, if you have a loved one in one of these relationships. Don't ride them to get out. No one can rush this realization. They have to come to it on their own. Instead, document any abuse you see. If there is evidence of physical violence try to get pictures. Remind them that you love them, and you want them to have a happy life. Tell them they are beautiful and smart, and don't be hurt when they don't seem to hear you. Let them share as they see fit, with no judgment or suggestions on how to handle the situation unless they ask. Be the safe place for them to share their feelings, and they will keep coming back until they are ready to get out. And when the time is right, don't just say get out, offer them a place to go.

Recognize that this is an addiction and there will be a phase of withdrawal. Understand that it can take many failed attempts at separation before they can make a clean break. Don't cut them off before they can get there. Locate a good Christian counselor in their area and help them make the first appointment. Go with them if they need the support, but most of all just love them and be there for them.

Now, for you single girls out there who have never been in this situation, start making some steps to help you avoid ever having to go through this. Get that network of friends now. If you are a teenager who doesn't have a great relationship with your mom and dad, find an older Christian woman you can trust. She will help you see the signs, but you need to be familiar with the warnings. Make up your mind that you will not tolerate being abused, even verbally, and if a guy's behavior feels off – run. It is better to be alone than to go through the trauma of an abusive relationship. Know what you are worth, God Himself created you, shaped you, and gave His life so that you could have life more abundantly. An abundant life is difficult to find when the person who claims they love you is abusing you.

Inform dates up front that you will be introducing them to your friends, and that you expect any relationship you have to have room for the people important to you. Listen to how he speaks about his family, friends, and ex-girlfriends. Does he show them respect, even if he feels that they have mistreated him? Watch how he reacts to authority and boundaries. Be aware of how he responds when you disagree with him, see if he gets mad, immediately reverses his opinion, or carefully weighs what you have to say. Look for men who can kindly and firmly call you on your garbage without belittling or ridiculing you. This tells you that he is secure enough to realistically deal with the issues that arise in a relationship, and secure men are less likely to be abusers. They don't need your complete approval or devotion to use against you, nor do they feel the need to beat you into submission, emotionally or physically.

Ladies, if you have survived an abusive relationship wear your scars with the pride of a warrior returning from battle. Your presence in the war gives you validity to speak to this situation, your warnings carry more weight, and your encouragement is far more valuable than someone who has not been there. Don't hide what you went through. It might be your story that allows another to avoid suffering the same wounds, or be the source of empowerment to help someone else get out before she is destroyed.

If you are in the middle of a marriage marked by violence, keep reading. We will talk more about it in the marriage section.

Resetting Our Expectations

or

Real Men Don't Sparkle

For many of us our expectations of love, romance, and marriage have been highly affected by media images that bear little resemblance to the real thing. As a child I bought into the whole fairy tale idea, and I couldn't wait for Prince Charming to come and sweep me off my feet. As a divorcee, I believed that men were not to be trusted and any man over the age of twenty-five who wasn't married wasn't married for a reason. Unfortunately, that last observation often proves to be true, but I was using it as an excuse to grow cynical and bitter. Eventually, I resigned myself to the fact that I was doomed to be alone. After all, I am a package deal with two kids and a mountain of student loans. (So be sure to encourage all your friends to buy a copy of this book. Those student loans still need to be paid). It wasn't long before I made the harsh discovery that for most men, I am far more appealing at a distance.

In the end, I decided that even though I may never find someone it is better to be in the game than not. So I made up my mind to spend one evening a week devoted to me. Some weeks I went for a drive by myself, some weeks I went out and people watched, and other weeks I went to a friend's house and watched movies. I knew I did not want to end up alone, but I did not know how to find someone. On my thirty-fourth birthday, I took a leap and joined an online dating service, one of the most humiliating things I think I have ever done. I felt like I was admitting defeat. To make matters worse, the initial response to the grueling questionnaire was, "We have no available matches for you at this time."

If that wasn't bad enough, I was lamenting my unmatchable state to my brother, going on and on about how a stinking nationwide database did not contain one single man who could possibly be happy in a relationship with me. Nathan looked at me, then at the floor, cleared his throat, and said, "It's a global data base." At that point, I simply accepted defeat, but my friends propped me up. One of them told me, "Your man is somewhere in the hills of Afghanistan being groomed to deal with you." She wasn't too far off base, but that is a story for another book.

Little did I know that my future husband was right around the corner. In fact, I had already met him and dismissed him from my list of possible candidates for a future mate. (Of course, according to him he knew I was "the one" the very first time he laid eyes on me, but I think he is just trying to look like he's wiser than me). He wasn't what I expected, and he certainly wasn't what I was looking for. My casual dismissal almost cost me the life I now have and enjoy. The irony is that once upon a time, when I had made a list of attributes I wanted in a husband, I had described him right down to his toe nails, but I just didn't realize that this was him with a few goodies I wasn't smart enough to ask for.

We have been married over two years, and we have had a few bumps in the road, but what do you expect? He married a woman who had spent most of her adult life living and doing as she pleased, and some of his habits aren't so sweet either. Despite all the preparation I had made in hopes of one day being married, I was shocked at some of the things I have had to become accustom to – like just having a man under my feet again.

Girls, I almost missed him because my eyes weren't open. I thought that I knew what I wanted, and I did. I just didn't recognize the packaging.

Knowing what you want in a mate is a good thing, but honestly, some of you gals out there are really looking for the best roommate in the world and not a man. You want someone who will never leave the seat up on the toilet, who never smells, who likes the same movies you do, who has read Jane Austen novels, and loves kittens. I hate to break it to you, but if you find a man who meets all these requirements you should pray for him, not marry him.

You want love to be easy, simple, and beautiful. You want it to play out like a romantic movie, without all the drama. You want the adventure without all the risk, and most of all you want him to do all the work and all the adapting. However, you know you would also spurn a man who changes too much for being what you would deem as unreliable. In short, you want the romance without the heartache, and the adventure of love without the pain. You call it standing by your principles, holding out for the best, and refusing to settle, but let's call it what it really is, shall we? It's fear and laziness, and no, you won't get an apology from me on that. The truth is we both know what will happen even if you do stumble across this amazing figment of your imagination strolling around the real world – you would dismiss him for one of two reasons:

1. If there is no pain or heartache, you would say there just wasn't enough passion, and the sparks just didn't fly when you were with him.

2. If there is heartache and pain, you will say that it is not meant to be because it costs too much.

Hear me! You can't have it both ways, unless you reset your expectations of romance and love. I do believe that you can have passion and romance, and I do believe that it can be had without all the heartache, pain, and drama so many romantic stories rely upon. Sisters, wake up. We don't live life in a Disney sponsored bubble, and that is great news because it means we aren't locked in towers, worked as slaves, or running away from a wicked witch. But too many of us are so busy lamenting the loss of our Prince Charming that we forgot to be thankful we don't have to be the damsel in distress. So stop letting fairy tales, romance novels, and all those romantic movies dictate to you what romance should look like, because the real thing has little in common with the fantasies we have clung to.

So the question is – if our old understanding of love is warped, where do we find a new one? The answer is one that you already know, but we just never think of it in these terms. Remember that passage in Ephesians that all the feminists hate? You know the one that tells women we need to be submissive to our husbands? There is the key.

The problem is that too often we look at this passage upside down and backwards, with no thought as to the totality of what it is saying. If you grew up in Church you are thinking, "Yeah, I know it says that men are to love their wives as Christ loved the Church and He was willing to die for His bride." And you are almost there, but even that idea falls far short of the marvelous truth that is revealed in these verses.

We get all hung up on the death part, because ever since the first time we heard about Romeo and Juliette, we were convinced that true love is willing to die for us. And in part that is true, but when we focus only upon the death we fail to acknowledge the act of love that must come first.

You see, long before Jesus died for His bride, He lived for her, and it is His life that makes Him a fitting mediator for His Church before the Father and able to speak on our behalf. The fact that He took on flesh and blood allowed Him to spill that blood for our salvation. If there had been no life, there could have been no death. And if there had been no death, there could have been no resurrection.

So we must realign our ideas of romance in accordance to what the totality of His life as a man taught us. I believe in His life we find the greatest sacrifice that an omnipotent, eternal God could have ever made, and it here that we find the greatest expression of love ever to be lived. Death is a foregone conclusion for everything that has known what it is to have a heartbeat. Death was no surprise to Him, and yet He chose life, despite knowing how it would all end. In my view, His life is far greater sacrifice than His death.

I know that this is a radical departure from how most of us have been taught to view Jesus' life, death and resurrection, but let's think about it for a moment. Consider having spoken the world into existence, of shaping humanity with the same fingertips that hung the stars in the heavens, the wonder of being eternal, the splendor of your heavenly kingdom, and the glory of your majesty compelling all of creation to acknowledge you as Lord. Think of what it must be like to set aside that type of power, that splendor, and that glory.

What must it have been like for Him to willingly confine Himself to the womb of a woman? To experience an existence of a child wholly dependent on her care and love for His every need?

The implications are staggering, and yet He did it. He chose life for us because He loved us that deeply, that passionately. He was willing to go through puberty, in all its messy manifestations. He accepted the work of a man, sweating beneath the sun as He labored for his next meal. He endured the questions, doubts, and skepticism of those who should have loved Him best. He knew the pain of betrayal and the agony of rejection. He accepted our shoddy displays of affection and valued the love that His followers bestowed upon Him, even when it did not do justice to the God that He is.

His story does not read like a romance unless you have the eyes to see it, but He came to woo His bride, to demonstrate His worthiness of her in a language and form we could understand. He did all the things that a man needs to do to demonstrate his merit and value as a husband, and yet we miss it. We fail to see His brilliance as lover in His life. We discount the love that He demonstrated to His bride as He walked upon this earth, and we confine His passion to that final week of His life, the time when death is loomed large on the horizon. And yet what of the days before that week, the days He simply lived among us, learning about our lives, experiencing what it means to be human, and finding us worthy to be loved despite our many flaws?

I often wonder what those days were like. Did they compare blisters as they walked along the road? Was Peter the self-appointed fire starter for the camp, or did he have to fight James and John for the honors? When the boys told their fish stories, did Jesus have one of His own? What were their inside jokes? What things did they know about each other that no one else did? How many times did Mark get in trouble for being young and exuberant? How many times did Jesus indulge him? Could Jesus shake Matthew out of somber mood with a funny face or a witty retort? When Simon the Zealot was ready to slaughter everyone who opposed them, did Jesus toy with the idea for even a moment? Did He let them see Him as person? Could they see Him as someone who knew who they were but desired to experience this life, in this earth, with them because it wasn't sufficient to stand at a distance and hope that they would one day learn how to love Him?

Knowing and being known is the truest form of romance we will ever experience. Intimate knowledge is what Jesus extends to us in His life, and what we offer back to Him when we invite Him into ours. In Him, we experience a life exposed in flesh, not veiled in the shrouds of death, and it is here that we find the most powerful expression of love and romance this ever recorded.

We know that we are ready to receive this type of love when we are ready to be known by another, when we can find strength in the desire to reveal all of who are to a person who will have the power to wound us. And we have to give them that chance. We can't sit in our ivory towers and toss a handkerchief to the winner of some battle. You have to be willing to walk beside them when the sun is burning you to a crisp and your body is crying out for a reprieve, because real love means we keep going even when we hurt. When we see their weakness and their flaws, but don't condemn them or cast them away from our presence. Love knows the words that disarm us, and the secret look that communicates something known only to the two of you.

This type of love demands that you fight at his side, learn to cover each other's weakness, and allow him to see your wounds. True love compels you to walk the roads you would rather leave unexplored if it means that you can be with him when you do it. Love means blistered feet, long cold nights around a dying campfire, listening to his stories, and offering one of your own. Love and romance of this quality smoothes over the rough spots, allows the one you love to share his emotions with no judgment, and makes a place for you to experience your own emotions in the safety of his company.

Jesus has this type of love for us, for all of humanity, for you. He knows you, warts and all, but desires your presence anyways. He isn't worried about the messy house, but He desires that you learn the skills to cope with it. He doesn't care that you have bad days, but hopes that you will find the strength to transform them with His help. He wants to give you the tools to become everything He imagined you could be, and He will stand beside you as you learn to use them, no matter how many times you make a mistake. This is romance, pure and simple, and it is the best kind. The type that doesn't have to be sheltered in the realm of the mind, but can be walked out in the flesh. This is the example that He has given us, and standard of love for each other that He has placed before us.

It is time that we ask ourselves, are we brave enough to have this type of romance in our lives? Real romance? Not the animated types we watched as children, but the type that our Lord showed us as the ultimate expression of love? Can we respond to it as the gift that it is? Or are we content to settle for the beautiful lie that romance is only found in death and epic adventures? Can you love a man who may never kill any dragons on your behalf but is committed to walking with you down any road you may choose, no matter how rocky? Because I promise you, for a man that is the greatest sacrifice for love he can ever make.

There is something hardwired in a man that makes dying for love a far easier task than living for it. Most men could take a bullet for us far more easily than they can place limitations on their lives, or give up the things that make them popular and adored. Stepping in front of a bus for us is nothing compared to the sacrifice of waking up every morning and riding that bus to work. Swallowing the poison on our behalf is a trivial thing when compared to devoting your life to flawed woman and her ever-changing love. And their fear above all fears, is the idea of surrendering their heart, with no safety nets, to another who may betray or reject him.

Yet this is the man we fail to appreciate and honor. We think that he is far too tame, too docile and too subdued. He is too polite, too considerate, and too frightening. We know that he will require everything of us, compel us to be more of a woman than we had ever dreamed that we could be. We know that we will never be able to hide our flaws from him, and they will be revealed more clearly in the light of his love. A love that declares our worth, even as it exposes our weakness.

How often did Jesus' followers feel that their Lord was too tame? Too weak or too concerned with the mundane? Did they ever lament the fact that He did not simply destroy the enemies that filled their land? Were they upset that He fed only a few thousand when thousands more were hungry? Was it enough for them that he only healed one cripple at the pool or did they want something bigger, greater, and more worthy of their dreams of a Messiah? Did they crave a bigger adventure? Hope for grander display of His love for this world? Did they ever confuse His meekness with indifference? Or were they wise enough to know that love like this demands to known in the experience of the day to day lives of the men and women he came to save?

Many could not see the romance and passion in Him. They turned away because He failed to meet their expectations of the conquering hero. In their disappointment, they moved on and in doing so missed the greatest love of their lives. Other's stepped aside because they let their sense of unworthiness blind them to the fact He didn't care that they were flawed. He loved them as they were, and all He desired was to be a part of their lives, to know them, to experience them so that they could know and experience Him.

Even today, we step away from true love because we feel like we do not deserve him, or we conjure up reasons why the man before us is not good enough. Our images of romance never included anything as mundane as car pools and dirty laundry, but in the end this is what most good men offers us. He will not lock us in a tower or deny us the ability to grow and do for ourselves. Instead, he invites us to join in a life with him. A life that is full of heartache and tears, but heartaches and tears that are shared. He will dare us to grow and provide us with the support and encouragement to do so even when we would rather enjoy the comfort of the familiar. He pulls us out of the world that we have known, and shows us one that he is creating for us. This type of love is romance of the most sublime nature, but we have to be willing to embrace it.

Love like this does not sweep us off our feet or compel us against our will. It is inviting and sweet, wooing us gently but with confidence that we will find something greater with them than apart from them. And to do this, it must come from a man, a true man, with all of his flaws and blundering mistakes. A man who does not speak the same language we do, but tries to make himself understood the best way that he knows how. The man who can be so frighteningly strange and different, but so familiar and comfortable all within a single breath.

Girls, it is time that we stop looking for big scaly dragons for men to slay in order to prove their love. The dragon is the hardship of making a way for the two of you to be together in this world. We need to stop demanding they speak our language when they have barely mastered their own. And we need to quit expecting their clothes to be spotless, their hair to be perfect, and their demeanor fabulous every day from here on out. The good guys don't wear white hats any more, and I have yet to meet a man with his own set of armor except at the Renaissance Faire (and you might want to think twice before going out with him).

The first expectation that we need to crush is how we are going to meet him. Let me just say, it is never what you imagine. Never in a million years would I have dreamt that I would meet my man in a bar. Walking up and handing my future husband the beer he ordered wasn't the story I wanted to tell my grandkids, but yet there he was sitting at a table in the bar where I was working. And I certainly didn't expect my first words to him to be a demand that he give me a cigarette, but he did. He even listened as I griped about my day, even though I never thought I would be in a bear of a mood when he walked into my life. But guess what?

To make matters worse, remember that online dating thing? Well, it wasn't that one, but later I did find him through an online singles service for another famous social network. And that's how we wound up going on our first date. How's that for God's sense of humor? The two ways I least expected to find a good Christian man, and that's what panned out.

Be open to meeting people, anytime, anywhere. Who knows maybe that cutie that keeps smiling at you in the produce section is the great guy you have been waiting on? So what if you can't find a single romantic meeting over a cantaloupe in any of the fairy tales? This is your story. Write it the way you want it.

Remember our pattern for romance is in found in the life our Lord. No one expected to find Him in a stable, on fishing boat, walking on water or on a dusty road by the sea, but the ones with eyes to see Him knew that He had exceeded all their preconceived ideas about how it should be.

The second expectation we need to reset is how he looks. Girls, this is one time when biology works in our favor. We find men attractive on two levels. The immediate one is his appearance, but we follow up with one based on our knowledge of him. So if we see a so-so guy, but later find out that he is great with kids, guess how hot he just became? Or that downright homely fellow? His rating goes up immediately when we see how kind he is to his mother. And that kinda cute sweetie becomes an instant ten when we learn that he is a doctor.

We are all going to have our "type" and that will be what we are primarily drawn to, but we need to be willing to look beyond the superficial and see what a man is really about. We may find out that our type wasn't what we thought it was after all. I mean, I never thought I would date a sandy-haired, blue-eyed man, and yet here I am married to one when I swore I could only fall for a dark-eyed hunk. Now, I see I was completely mistaken, and my guy looks amazing.

And just in case you were wondering, Jesus probably didn't look the way so many people would have expected Him to look. He wasn't a king with a royal entourage. He was a carpenter who looked at people with such love they fell head over heels for Him.

The third expectation we need to reset is that there has to be chemistry every time you are around him. Look, contrary to what men want you to believe, they aren't always thinking of ways to impress you or seduce you. There are just some days when all they want is a shower and a good sleep. They love you and all, but hopefully, you aren't the only thing in their world demanding their attention.

When work is stressful, he is probably not going to remember to bring you flowers. And when his back aches, he isn't going to be keen on going shoe shopping. Sometimes when they have full and active lives, all they really want is to sit next to you on the couch and watch some TV, and we need to give them the space to do just that.

Keep in mind that this is not an excuse for them to ignore you all the time, but we just need to be aware that sometimes they need a little space, even from us. If we give them time to recharge their batteries, we might just get the flowers the next time we see them.

Being a man, Jesus did this, too. He was tired, and He took a nap while everyone else thought that He should be up and wowing them with His storm controlling ability. When they woke Him up, the atmosphere wasn't as sweet as you might have expected when Jesus was near, because like any man who is abruptly woken up from a nap, He was tad bit grumpy (Mark 4: 35-40).

The fourth expectation to reset is the idea that once you find love, you will never know sorrow again. Girls, no man is great enough to make this hope a reality. No matter how deeply you love someone, or how much you desire to make things perfect for them, there are just some things that cannot be avoided. Life will go on, even if you are insanely in love. And a life that is truly lived will be filled with emotions of all types: joy, sorrow, anger, and fear. Feeling them all lets us know that we are still very much a part of this world, and good man does not rob us of the opportunity to be alive. Instead, he offers us a place where we can experience it all, and he feels our emotions with us because love compels us to share in the life of the one we love.

Jesus did no less. He did not deny the ones who loved Him the chance to be alive or to know the emotions that define this human existence. He did not turn them into robots devoid of feeling or unable to be hurt. Instead, He felt as they did, joining into this thing we call humanity and all its messy manifestations. When His friends wept over the death of their friend, the Lord wept with them and in doing so validated the feelings of grief and loss as legitimate and no less appropriate because they were standing at His side. (John 11:28-35).

The fifth expectation is that everything in your life will fall into place now that you have found him. It won't. Usually this is when everything else falls apart, but if he is willing to walk through it with you and doesn't run because things are tough, he might be a keeper.

One word – Crucifixion.

The sixth expectation is that you will agree on everything. Haaahaaahaaaa! Not hardly. Sure, in the beginning there are a million and one things that you will discover that you have in common. You might even be thrilled to discover that you have the same number of eyes, but over time these things take on less significance, and you begin to show each other the things that really make you – you. Believe it or not, they won't be the same, and you will have to learn how to cope with the differences.

What's even more shocking is the fact that this is a good thing. Learning to navigate and appreciate each other's differences without losing yourself is a sign of a healthy relationship. So embrace it. Only a strong relationship between two strong individuals can endure the times when you will need to disagree with each other, maybe even point out when the other one is wrong. Calling someone on their garbage isn't a sign you don't love them, but rather it is a sign that you love them enough to risk upsetting them. And real love holds a mirror to our souls revealing both the beauty and ugly that we may not have known existed inside of us, but if our love is authentic we won't run from the revelation.

Jesus was constantly calling people on their bad ideas, attitudes, and behaviors. Not because He was trying to play the all knowing, all powerful, always right card (which He could have), but rather He wanted them to be the amazing people He knew they could be. And only those who loved Him the most and knew Him the best could handle His most direct speeches. (Matthew 19:12-15).

The seventh expectation is that people who are in love never fight. What a load of . . . manure. We fight. It's what we do. If you put two people in a confined space for very long, they will eventually get on each other's nerves. People have been this way since the dawn of time, and we will probably continue to be until Jesus returns.

Here's the good news about fighting. If it is done in a respectful manner, a good fight can help you express some things that really need to be worked out. Being willing to fight for a relationship shows that you both care about your future together, but only if you observe some boundaries and limits in your conflicts. Fighting should never be the norm, but it shouldn't be feared or seen as the death knell of your love either.

In fact, one piece of stock advice I give couples who are considering marriage is do not get married until you have had your first fight. You need to know if the other person is going to fight fair or completely lose his mind. You don't want to be stuck with someone who turns every conflict into a personal attack, but you also don't want someone who is constantly rolling over for you. We girls need a man who can call us on our crap without belittling or ridiculing us.

And it shouldn't be a big surprise that Jesus and the Apostles fought. They took sides on issues and told each other how they felt. Controversy and disputes were not avoided but embraced, and were eventually recorded as revelation moments that have helped guide the Church over the years (Luke 22:24-28).

Eighth expectation you need to crush: sex will automatically be amazing because we love each other so much. Sex, at least good sex, takes practice. You need some time to learn what makes each other tick, and to find your rhythm. For some couples this takes awhile, but hey, it's always fun to practice.

Now, I know that there are at least a few of you who are thinking about that mind blowing one night stand. Let me let you in on a secret, when sex is combined with adrenaline and the idea that it is "dirty", "rebellious", or "risky" it can be great, but you aren't really getting off on the sex. You are getting off on the danger of it all, and that's a risky proposition because if that is how you learn to have an orgasm, you are going to have to unlearn it to have one once you do settle down.

So girls, if you haven't had the hot and steamy bathroom sex with some random guy from the bar, just be thankful you don't have retrain your body on how to have a healthy response to your spouse.

Okay, I really don't have a good Jesus point for this one, nor am I going to fabricate one by stretching some obscure theological point to serve my wishes. Sorry.

Ninth expectation to be crushed, he will love everything I say and do if he loves me. Not by a long shot. If a man really loves you he won't let you be stupid, hurt yourself, or be less than who you are – for more than a day or two anyway. A man who loves you will tell you when you are out of line, and he will do it in a way that demonstrates the strength and character of his love. So don't be surprised when he speaks up when you do go all stupid, and let's face it, we all do from time to time.

Just look up some passages about Jesus and Peter. Just about any one will do because they all seem to go like this. Peter screws up either in word or deed, Jesus tells him to cut it out, Peter repents, and they walk in deeper relationship (Matthew 16:21-23).

The tenth expectation to throw out the window: if I love him I will find the strength and ability to be perfect for him. Do I really need to explain why this is so messed up? You are still you, even in love, and if he truly loves you he will be happy to be with you as you are. So do try to be better, to grow and gain the skills that you need to be the person you hope to be one day, but never forget that ultimately you as you is lovely thing.

See the Jesus point above, but add "Peter screws up while trying to be perfect or a know it all" (John 18:1-11, 21:15-19).

If we can reset our expectations more in line with the example Jesus has lived for us and in alignment with the real world, we are far more likely to find and keep an amazing man. But when our expectations are based on myths and fairy tales, we will find ourselves alone or living a life of disappointed bitterness. Love, true love, (please read that line in the voice of the *Princess Bride* priest), will never have a chance to grow and thrive in our world if are caught up in our illusions, and if we do meet someone amazing, we probably won't recognize him for the amazing man that he is. Be wise in this. Not everyone gets the second chance I did.

Marriage
or
More Than You Bargained For

After my divorce, I handed out a lot of advice to young men and women who were considering getting married. Allow me to start this section by saying, I am sorry. Not because I was wrong, I wasn't, but rather, I did not understand how difficult this advice would be to follow. Now that I am married, let me just say, I recognize the struggle it is to do what seemed so simple from my perspective as single woman.

Of all the chapters I have written so far this one is by far the most difficult, and the reason for that is the Bible has so much to say about marriage. There is just no way to cover all the beautiful and horrifying things that we can learn about this amazing union between a woman and a man. I was tempted to let this chapter become another glorified Bible study about marriage, but there are enough of those out there, and some really great ones at that. So I am going to stick to what I know, shocking and offending people, and maybe even saying something worthwhile.

I think that the first thing we need to accept about marriage is God created it. He ordained that men and women be uniquely united in this thing we call matrimony. He wanted us to have each other in a crazy intimate way, and He designed all the parts to make this happen on every level, spiritual, mental, emotional, and yes, (thank God, yes), even physical.

The key element that separates marriage from every other relationship is sex. Ideally, we do not have sex with people, even people we love and cherish, other than our spouse. As human beings we have recognized this for a very long time, even if we have failed to articulate it so bluntly. Church and ancient laws declared that a marriage was not legally binding until it had been consummated, and even today this reason can be grounds for an annulment, which says that in fact a marriage never took place – all because the bride and groom never got jiggy with it.

One key issue to address in any Biblical discussion of marriage, especially of its sexual component, is to dispel some of the myths we good Christian girls have about sex. First of all, it's a good thing. Contrary to what some quacks have been teaching, God was fully aware of what He designed our bodies to do, and He wanted us to do it. I have heard a few preachers declare that the fruit described in the book of Genesis was a metaphor for Eve's seduction of Adam. In case you didn't get that, let me break it down for you.

Adam was a good farmer, tending his garden, caring for his critters, and just generally minding his own business. He was happy and content with his life now that God gave him the little woman. She was pretty little thing, and she made a mean sandwich. Once beer and football were invented, his life would be complete. But Eve wasn't as happy as Adam. Making sandwiches didn't take up a lot of time and picking out an outfit wasn't an issue, so there weren't a lot of things to keep her from being bored out of her skull. Then one day she noticed the rabbits were playing some type of new game, and she thought that it would be fun to play with Adam. At first Adam wasn't too sure if they should, but it was Eve, and that sandwich she made tonight had been mighty tasty, so why not humor the gal? You can only imagine the poor boy's surprise when she started doing the things she did to him. He had no idea she could move that way or that he would feel the funny things he was feeling for her now! Oh God, this must have been the thing that God had warned him about. Now what was he going to do?

If you believe this version of the story, I must tell you that you have fallen for a load of hogwash. From the beginning Adam and Eve's purpose was to be fruitful and multiply. God says so in the first chapter, and if you can figure out any way they were suppose to fulfill that decree without getting it on – well, your imagination is a bit more twisted than mine. And that should disturb you.

God gave Adam and Eve to each other in a place of no inhibition and no shame. He did not clothe them or conceal anything about this new creation of Eve from Adam's sight and assuming that he was the man that God said he was – he had all of the male reaction that is right and appropriate for his wife. He was inspired by her presence, so much so that he utters the very first words of poetry ever spoken by a smitten man when he declares that she is "Bone of my bone and flesh of my flesh."(Genesis 2:23). (It is too bad that like all things we find in the perfection of Eden, poetic utterances by a smitten man also became corrupted thus creating the greeting card industry.) The remainder of Adam's response is lost to the sands of time, but I have a suspicion words weren't the only reaction Eve inspired.

The second myth we need to lay to rest is that since the fall our sexuality is somehow shameful. Now, I know that this is not how you heard it taught, but hear me out on this one, because I am pretty sure it is right. Adam and Eve did cover up once they realized they were naked, and for so long we have been left with the impression that being naked was evil. However, I think there is another and far more important reason they ran for cover. Since God was the one who neglected to give them even a fig leaf to begin with, I highly doubt that being naked with your spouse qualifies as a sin. Furthermore, they went on to be naked together at least a few more times after getting kicked out of paradise. Hmm, so what was it exactly that caused them to make a hasty cover up?

Obviously, the "I'm so dead when Dad finds out" factor plays a part, but I think that with the realization of evil also came the realization that they were vulnerable. Before they knew about evil there was nothing to fear, no need for protection, or shields of any kind, but suddenly, that rather fragile covering we call skin seemed a little insufficient.

Their sexuality was not hidden because it was evil. It was hidden because it was valuable. And you just don't flaunt things of value before someone who won't appreciate that value, or someone who might use the very thing you treasure against you.

Later God would give some rules about who we should and should not see naked, but our spouses are not included in that list. (Leviticus 18). Why? Because when someone loves us enough to commit to a lifetime together, they are saying that they value us, and it is to them we offer the greatest personal treasure we have to give to another human being. In the context of the covenant relationship of marriage we find a place where we can be free and uninhibited with another human being. A place where we can catch a glimpse of that paradise lost. Marriage is where we can remember that we are to be one flesh and shamelessly joined to the one who helps us fulfill the commission that God has given us.

The third myth is that sex was only designed for procreation, (read that as baby making). I have yet to find that anywhere in the Bible, nor is the idea supported in our biology. First of all, the Bible literally sings the praises of an erotic relationship in Song of Songs. This one book is chocked full of graphic imagery, and it is all about a couple who find delight in each other's bodies. The writing is so graphic that some people claim that its inclusion in the Bible was a freak accident, but since that can't possibly be true, there must be some reason why God has preserved it for our reading pleasure. And don't give me that "metaphor" line.

Sure, there are some great parallels between our intimacy with our spouse and with our God, but the book never says that is why it was written. In all other writings that use sex as metaphor the writer clearly indicates that he is using a poetic picture to share a greater truth, but such a caveat is not found in Song of Songs. Instead we have a shameless display of passion and desire between lovers.

If anything, Song of Songs is the "how to have amazing sex guide" of the Bible, answering many of the questions that Christians have about an appropriate sexual relationship with our spouses, once we push past some of the euphemisms and picturesque language. Unfortunately, there are few Biblical scholars who have been willing to go there, but before I step off that cliff, let's look at one other piece of evidence that shows that while sex may lead to procreation it was also intended for our pleasure. And by "our pleasure", I am specifically referring to us as women.

The answer is found in that little sensory powerhouse called the clitoris. What makes it so special is the fact that it has absolutely no biological function in the act of procreation. To put it plainly, the clitoris is completely useless when it comes to the baby making game. It is so useless that it can be removed without inhibiting or hindering our ability to have children. So why do we have it? The answer is simple, to make sex more enjoyable. For a large percentage of women, the clitoris is the key to an orgasm and only with proper stimulation can they achieve that mind altering state. If God had not expected or wanted us to enjoy sex, all He had to do was omit that tiny little piece of us, and yet He designed it in a way that gives us pleasure as no other part of us can.

As with everything God does, the reason we have this is far more significant than simply curling our toes. He is presenting us with an opportunity and a reason to grow in intimacy with our spouse. For many women, the need for clitoral stimulation is a source of great frustration because we have to have it for an orgasm, and intercourse, while good, simply doesn't provide enough direct contact to really rock our world. So now a woman has to choose: tell her husband what she needs or do without. Now a smart woman will talk to her man, and since the prize is so gosh darn spiffy, she has a really great incentive to let him in on this little secret part of herself. For many women, the idea of being this bold about receiving pleasure is scary thought. Speaking up about something so intimate puts us in a vulnerable place of teaching and guiding our husbands to those hidden parts of ourselves that no one else knows. But even in this simple act of vulnerability we learn how to open up in so many other ways that enhances our marriage.

And while we are learning to reveal more of ourselves to our men, they are learning how to respond to our needs and direction. He learns to read even our breath as a sign of our desire and pleasure in him. The light moans and sighs direct his touch, his pace, and his attention to our arousal and satisfaction, even as he finds his own. All aspects of who we are as individuals can now work together in fulfillment of the design God has put in place, a design that clearly demonstrates that we are to exist in unity with our mates, a unity of spirit that is replicated in the sexual act.

Furthermore, girls, something that no one tells us while we are still virgins is that we must learn how to have an orgasm. Guys don't seem to need any coaching on this (I think it all comes down to that easy-grip handle that they come equipped with), but for some of us an orgasm is about as mythical as a unicorn. Learning how to achieve a climax takes time and patience. Sex isn't always as mind blowing as we have been led to believe, especially when we are first learning. And that is precisely why we have honeymoons, so that we can learn how to respond to our partner's body free of any outside distractions, and so that he can learn ours. Don't be upset if it takes longer than the three days you set aside, and keep practicing – even that is fun. With a loving man, and a little patience, you can get there. Just give yourself the permission to enjoy this time of passion and unity. It's what your body was designed to do.

Now back to the Song of Songs, what does it have to teach us about sex? Sisters, hold on to your hat and grab your smelling salts. Like every great lover, God didn't hold anything back.

Song of Songs begins with something that flies in the face our traditional expectations of women's attitudes towards sex. The opening passage is the blatant and unashamed declaration of a woman's desire for her man. She delights in her man, not only because he is a person of power and influence, but rather because he chose her when she was not the stereotypical beauty of her day. She had mad skills in vineyards, and her work in the sun had left her skin darkened. (Believe it or not there was a time when a suntan was not considered a good thing.) She is not meek or docile, and she quarrels with her family, but he wants her despite her having the traits that would have been looked down upon in this culture. She wasn't the ideal woman, but she was the woman he desired.

I don't think that it is any accident that this particular book in Hebrew Scriptures follows the description of the Proverbs 31 woman. The Proverbs gal is the ideal, the wife that a smart man wants, but the woman in the Song of Songs is the one that really gets his motor running. She is the one who makes him feel alive, makes a king forget all the proper protocol and chase her about like a young buck who has nothing more than desire as a compass. And if you think Godly men are above being ruled by their penis, you have a lot to learn. She knows that the sex drive is a powerful force and instead of denying it, she embraces it. She sees his sex drive not simply a base desire to be fulfilled, but rather as the fuel for becoming the type of woman she knew she was always created to be. She celebrates the joy his desire brings to her in the act of giving herself completely to the man who loves all there is to love about her.

Gals, we need to take a page from her book. Our men love us, and they desire us even when we don't look like a swimsuit model, or all those girls on TV. They want us, and we should celebrate the beauty they see in us. We don't have to be the perfect woman in order for them to experience desire for us. And when a man, especially our husbands, sees beauty in us it can be one of the most arousing things we will ever experience, but we have to allow ourselves to accept their perceptions of who we are as legitimate.

This, however, is not an excuse not to improve on our God-given assets. The woman of the Song does not say, "Hey, he thinks I am great the way I am so I am just going to let myself go." Instead, she works to enhance that beauty and do things that please him. In return, she receives his uncensored praise. She takes great joy in her ability to arouse passion in him, and she brags about how he was pleased by her efforts.

I think we should note that she spares no expense in preparing herself to meet with her beloved. Too often as women we tend to think that we are being vain or selfish when we splurge on a bottle perfume, a tube of mascara, or those great skin care products. And if we are buying things just to please ourselves, we are being vain, but when we do it with the idea and hope of pleasing the men who love us, we are being good wives.

The Song of Songs woman tells us that she knows the secret to passionate love, because she has experienced it. She cautions the women about her to wait until the proper time to awaken and arouse your man, but she also makes no apologies for holding on to the man she desires, the one who reveals the beauty within her. Her friends celebrate her happiness, and she calls the day of their marriage his day of bliss. Why? Because she knows that she has something precious to offer her new man, she knows that he desires her, and she desires him. On this day they are united in all aspects, and the sexual expression of their love is proper and fitting. She is anticipating his delight in her body, and she is fully prepared to enjoy his.

For once, we are allowed to peek inside the torrid (read that smokin' hot) bedchamber and we are given a glimpse of what the two lovers experience with each other. This incredibly intimate moment isn't hidden away or given as a cautionary tale, but rather as an example of the how amazing the union between a woman and a man can be. And to be honest, she found a husband who was an incredible lover. He knew all the moves. He understands that as a verbal creature his wife needed to hear his praise, and he does not disappoint.

If we look at his first description of his new bride, we see that he begins with her eyes and her hair. He is recognizing her as a person, not simply as a sexual tool. He is enraptured in her beauty, even if it sounds a little corny to the modern reader, but we need to be honest – all declarations of this sort sound overly flowery to the person who is not in the middle of one of these grand love affairs. So cut the boy some slack. He makes a downward progression and spends a significant amount of time praising her breasts, and elucidating (read that being terribly specific and shockingly graphic about) what he desires to do with them. He acknowledges that she has made herself beautiful for him, and that even her garments are fragrant for him. His praise is such that any woman with half a heart would glow under its affect, and she receives his words with joy. He, in turn, is pleased with her response. (Song of Songs 4).

It would be easy to read this book as the fantasy love story. And I think many of us are tempted to think of it as the unattainable goal, but the truth is these words are far more realistic than we realize. The writer makes no bones about the fact that not everything is perfect. He (or possibly, she, because some scholars do believe that a woman may have written this hot little number) lets us know that at one time the woman was lazy and neglected her man. And like any self-respecting man, he walked away from her indifference. Girls, there are too many women in our churches who have been in the same situation. Good women who did all the right things for the Church, their children, and others in their lives, but when their husbands have made a simple request to be closer to them they have made the same plea as this woman – I am too tired. (Song of Songs 5).

Ladies, we have to be on guard against this. We need to keep some reserve of strength and energy that belongs to him alone. We have to get past the idea that we don't need to open the bedroom door for our fellows. If he requests a night of passion, and you feign a headache just to avoid having to expend the energy, you are asking for trouble.

Now our girl in the Bible realizes her mistake immediately, and she jumps up to go find him. Notice where she goes to look, the streets and town squares. She asks the watchmen if they have seen him. Do you have any idea of why she is doing this? Why would she search for him there?

I think the answer is simple, and to know it, all we have to do is ask ourselves one question. Who hung out on the street corners and in the town squares? The prostitutes, the women who made their living meeting the sexual needs of men, and these gals did not require that men humble themselves by asking for something they might not get. Remember, men do not handle rejection well, and every time a wife says no to his request for sex, she is setting the stage for him to go and find a woman he doesn't have to ask. As a woman, well aware of the power of sex, the woman of the Song wastes no time in grand delusions or deceptive hopes, she confronts the realities of what she has done.

Let me be a little plainer, she wasn't so stupid to think that a man who wasn't getting it at home wouldn't go elsewhere. Girls, this is not a commentary on whether a man who does this is right or wrong, it is simply an acknowledgement of how things work. Men do not go without sex as a rule. Good men will keep it at home, but if they are married to unresponsive women their temptations become more and more difficult to deal with. And ladies, if we love our men, we won't put them in this situation.

When she realizes her mistake, she wastes no time in enlisting help. Even she recognized the need for that network of friends. She appeals to them, and they join in her search for her lover. They ask her questions. The types of questions that remind her of her love for him, and they direct her heart back to the passion that was so bright on their wedding day. They encourage her to keep seeking him, even when she may be tempted to give up or harden her heart against him in her hurt. As she speaks his praises aloud, she is reminded of what she is fighting for, and in the end she is reunited with him. (Song of Songs 5).

Ladies, we all need these friends in our lives. Other women who will tell us when we are being unreasonable with our men, women who will remind us of why we love him, and who push us to keep seeking his love when we have alienated him with our actions. Many of the arguments that tear marriages apart can be averted with the help of these friends. Sometimes we need our friends to tells that we are being irrational and even ridiculous in our emotional reactivity. A good friend will let us blow off steam, regain some balance and perspective, and help us find the tools that can literally save our marriages.

With her lover and husband restored, we find some of the more interesting passages – these are the passages that answer some of those questions that many of you are afraid to ask. So let's look at chapter seven.

The passage opens with her husband watching her dance. Girls, think about this for a second. Her husband is watching her move before him. And guess what? Men are still the same. They like to watch our bodies move. There is something entrancing for them in the way we bend and sway, even our jiggly parts are fascinating to them. (Perhaps I should say that *especially* our jiggly parts are fascinating to them.) They love to see our beauty displayed before them. This is why they buy us lingerie. They are hoping that we will do a little fashion show, and not dive under the covers the second we put it on. Our men want to see us. The woman of the Song knew this, and she was fulfilling that desire.

Too many of us are way too hung up on the fact our bodies aren't perfect, but girls, we need to get over that. Men like to look, and so we should provide our husbands with some legitimate viewing material at home. If he doesn't buy you lingerie, he is doing it for one of two reasons: 1.) He thinks you won't let him look, so why bother? 2.) Or he would rather just see you naked. If you suspect it is more reason one than two, buy some yourself and surprise him. You might end up being the one who is really surprised, but back to our story.

The groom's second description is far more erotic than the first one. He praises her feet and legs, and her thighs are splendid things. Please note the upward progression here. Every bit of her is examined and praised in the order of appearance but then a careful reader will notice that something is out of place. He speaks of her navel and then her belly. Hmmm, that's funny, my belly button is slightly above the area I consider to be my belly. Shouldn't it read belly then navel to keep the flow consistent? Could it be that this woman is some type of freak? Even if she isn't, why make the distinction, aren't they in the same general area? Wouldn't it be enough to say one and not the other? And exactly how enticing is a navel? Makes one wonder if there was some type of mistake...

Well, girls, here's a fun bit of trivia that makes this passage great. The navel is a euphemism (read that a polite way to say something naughty). The Hebrew writers often employed this little device, because they knew that people would have a problem if they were a little too direct in their speech. So instead of vagina (gasp!), they say navel, suddenly the progression makes sense again – feet, legs, thighs, vagina, belly. Now, notice what he compares her "navel" to – a goblet.

What do you do with a goblet? If you answered drink out of it, you're a winner. And why do we drink out of goblets? Because they hold the best stuff, not your average day to day tumbler, or earthen mug, they hold wine. Wine is the drink of celebrations and something to be savored, not a drink to quench your thirst, but rather one to awaken you senses and desires. He even asks that the wine not be lacking! Talk about bold!

Some of you out there are still having a problem with the imagery, so let me break it down in our language. He is saying that her vagina is a great place to put his lips. He enjoys the flavor and hopes that she will always be wet for him. So, if you were concerned about whether or not oral sex is okay in a Christian marriage, consider this a resounding YES!

(And in case you missed it, she said something very similar in the second chapter. "Like an apple tree among the trees of the forest, so is my beloved among the youths. I delight to sit in his shade, and his fruit is sweet to my mouth." (2:3). Now that you are thinking a little more euphemistically, can you guess what "fruit" you can "taste" while "*sitting* in *his* shade"?)

And it doesn't end there, if we read some more in chapter seven she begins to talk about the things she wants to do to him, and I think it was safe to say they were well matched in the sexual arena. She tells him that she is turned on by his desire for her. She invites him to come and ravage her in the vineyards. She promises to give herself freely to him with a passion equal to what he has shown.

Their story ends with a caution. Yes, what they have is good, and they delight in each other, but it is only because they waited until the proper time for these expressions of love. They warn their readers not to indulge these passions until they have reached their proper time. Theirs is not a love for those who are too young, and as a family and community, we should be working to protect our girls from making unwise choices about sex. But when the time does come, the response should be swift and celebrated. (Song of Song 8:8-14)

So now that we know that God intended for us to enjoy and celebrate sex, we need to be able to apply these lessons. Some of them we have already alluded to, but let's take some time to be a little more specific.

One of the first things we notice in both Adam and Eve's story and Song of Songs are the beautiful settings. Now, I doubt that any of us are so lucky as to live in a picturesque garden or beautiful vineyards. In today's society, we cram humans into some rather cramped living quarters by comparison. Most of our sexual adventures take place in the bedroom, so we seem to have little in common with the Biblical lovers, but we can glean some good advice if we look past the obvious differences.

Any time we approach ideas in the Bible, we need to be able to sniff out the greater truths instead of always getting hung up on the literal facts. Obviously, we can't turn our bedrooms into gardens, but we can make our bedrooms places of beauty. Too many of us have fallen into the trap of using our bedrooms as that place where we shove everything we don't want our guests to see when they drop by. As a result, our bedrooms often cluttered and filled with a lot of things that have no business being in a bedroom. Our bedrooms are often the last place in the house we clean, thinking that those more public spaces need to be kept up more than this place of privacy.

Girls, this mindset is backwards. Of all the human relationships we have, our relationship with our spouse is the most important. One way we communicate this to our men is by taking the time to create a special and beautiful environment for them. Every man I have ever met has a problem with clutter. They find it distracting and emotionally taxing. As women, we have the opportunity to make a place where they can be completely at ease and we do this by investing some time and energy in making the bedroom the most inviting room in the house.

Some woman out there just got overwhelmed because all she could hear was a mandate to completely make over the bedroom, new paint, comforter, decorative pillows, and possibly even a new five piece matching oak bedroom suite. Honey, calm down and think smaller. Don't over complicate this.

Most men don't care what color the walls are, unless that color is pink, but they do care that the bed is comfortable, there are enough pillows (that can actually be used), and it smells good. They don't want to trip on laundry, and they don't want to feel like they are sleeping in a storage unit. So find some other place to put those things that you have been stacking in the corner, or get rid of it all together. He might not seem to notice, but I can assure you that somewhere inside he does. And I think that you will find that as you learn how to create this atmosphere in your bedroom, the effects will begin to spill out into other areas of your home, making your entire house a restful haven he will look forward to coming home to at the end of a hard day.

We should also keep the sensory clutter out of this space. In this room there should only be two people, you and your man. This means no televisions, computers, or other technology that would distract the two of you from the other. If you have ever had a television in your bedroom you will know what I mean. It is far too easy to spend an evening caught up in reruns of bad sitcoms instead of expending the energy to actually be with each other, and I am not just talking about sex here. Outside of those walls, there is a world demanding that you share your attention and energy. Bosses, friends, and even our children all want a piece of us and by the time we are ready to climb into bed we are physically and emotionally exhausted. The last thing we want to do is have another conversation, but if we want to keep our marriages healthy, that is exactly what we must do. For many couples, the bedroom is the only safe place to have those heart-to-hearts. So nip the temptation in the bud, and make it all about the two of you in this place.

And while we are on the subject, teach your kids that this is your and your husband's special place. They should be taught from an early age that a closed door means that you should be left alone except for emergencies, but even those merit a knock. And you should teach them what qualifies as an emergency. In our home, it is blood, fire, and vomiting. Everything else can wait.

Have a set bedtime for the kids. They need the structure, but the two of you need to get into the habit of spending some time alone each day, and for most of us that is only possible after the kids are safely tucked away. Do what you have to do to enforce it, and if you can, start it young. At our house the bedtime is at the ridiculous hour of 9:00 pm. Since my girls are older, they don't have to go to sleep, but they do have to go and stay in their rooms. Going to bed this early gives them a quiet time to wind down, read a book, do some journaling, and generally stay out of our hair. We also get the added bonus of not having to worry about who is in the living room, hearing what is going on behind our bedroom door.

The second thing we see in the Biblical accounts, particularly in Song of Songs, is that she kept herself beautiful. Ladies, some of us work with the public and some of us work at home, and most of us do both. Having done both, and currently getting to stay at home thanks to my new hubby, I feel like I am qualified to address this issue from both perspectives.

First off, most of us who work outside of the home take a lot of time making sure that we look presentable, if not attractive in the workplace. We do our hair and makeup, put on the hose and heels, and try to smell nice before we present ourselves to our co-workers and bosses. And then we get home change into our sweats, put in a hair clippie, and generally relax. Now, there is nothing wrong with this, but I want you to consider what you are doing when this is the only way you present yourself to your man. Believe it or not, you are sending a resounding message to him, and it says that everyone else in your life is more important to you than him.

After all, when we were dating we made sure that we were pretty for his arrival, and we always smelt good for his time with us. We were the ones who told him that he was important enough to dress up for, to be beautiful for, but so often, we fail to uphold the standards we put in place while dating. Soon he is feeling like all he is getting are the leftovers. Girls, this is not fair to him, and can end up causing some problems for you.

Should he be able to love and appreciate you even when you aren't at 100%? Of course, and do you need a place to let your hair down and stop worrying about how you look for five minutes? Absolutely, but we need to make some effort every so often to remind him that he is still the man we desire to impress the most. This may mean that you forego the sweat pants and opt for the yoga pants instead. (Still just as comfy, and the fellas love the way they hug our hips.) It may mean that you get rid of the comfortable, but hideous, stained and holey t-shirt and try out something a bit more flattering. Dressing to please our man's eye doesn't have to be all or nothing, but a smart woman works at finding a middle ground that works for her while still highlighting his favorite assets.

For us stay at home moms, we have to get up and get dressed. Too many of us have found out that we are more than capable of running a house without makeup, with frizzy hair, and in our pajamas. Ladies, you want to make a man resent you? Keep it up. When they come home and find that you haven't even bothered to put on those awful sweat pants, no matter how spotless the house is, they will still think you spent the day lounging around watching soaps. In his mind, working requires getting dressed. After all, every other woman he saw working today had some clothes on (we hope), and he can't imagine how or why you would be any different.

Don't forget, if he works outside of the home, chances are he works with other women. Women who did make an effort to be beautiful before presenting themselves to him, even if it was just in an effort to be professional. I know and you know that he shouldn't be making comparisons, but why should we make it so easy for him? We want him to know that we love and value him enough to desire to look good in front of him.

So kick it into gear, girls. Put on some real clothes, shave those legs, fix that hair, and put on some lipstick. It won't kill you, and you will feel more energized to take on the day. As women we like to be beautiful, and no matter who you are, you will feel better when you invest something into how you look. If you neglect your beauty, he will too. So remind him that he did marry a beautiful woman, and she really didn't get lost behind a mountain of laundry and dirty dishes.

Sure, it can be argued that this flies in the face of everything that feminism stands for, but I care a lot more for the reality and health of my marriage than I do about some idea that refuses to deal with the reality of human nature. How I look should be less important to him than who I am as a person, but part of who I am as a woman is the desire to look pleasing to the people who are important to me. Part of his design as a man is to see presentations of feminine beauty as our appreciation for his masculinity, and girls, we should be the first ones affirming that who they are as men is important to us. We are declaring that we love, value, and desire expressions of their masculinity in our lives, and such declarations are almost irresistible to any hot blooded male. When we celebrate that we are loved by him, and it is to him alone that we offer these expressions of love, in his eyes, we become the most beautiful creature to have ever walked the earth. We don't present our beauty to them because that is all we have, rather we do it as an expression that all we have is theirs.

Thirdly, we should be vocal in our praise of him and our desire for him (read that actively seducing our man). Men love to be loved. It is one of those things we have in common between the sexes. And if he knows that we can't wait to get him between those sheets, his appreciation of us often skyrockets (pun intended). So speak up, tell him what you love about him, and tell him how much you love what he does for you and to you. Be specific, and be graphic. Plant some new ideas in his brain, and confirm it when he has already had some good ones. Remember sex is all about being united, and nothing unites people like words of praise for each others' good points (yep, pun intended again).

Fourth, be aggressive sometimes. The words are good, but so many men have expressed their desire for their women to just grab them up and have their way with them. Girls, we have this right, and we should use it more often. Remember, when we get married our bodies belong each other, and they are no longer simply the property of the one inhabiting that allotment of skin. So take advantage of it.

Our girl in Song of Songs wasn't shy with her man. She let it all hang out, literally and physically, because she wanted him to know how much pleasure she found with him. She wasn't always content to wait until he made the first move, but that was okay because she wasn't above making a few moves of her own. His response proved that this was more than a little alright with him, and I am fairly certain that most men feel the same way. After all, we aren't the only ones who want to be swept off our feet.

Fifth, men like to look, so give him a show. Light some candles, or leave the lights on occasionally. If you are really adventurous buy a stripper pole for your bedroom, and learn how to use it. Go skinny dipping on a moonlit night, or just surprise him when he comes home from work with a wife who is wearing something revealing. Slip on a tank top and some Daisy Dukes, and then offer to pass him wrenches the next time he works on the car. Cooking him dinner? Do it wearing only an apron, but learn from my mistakes, make sure it's not a night you are serving fried chicken.

Bear in mind too, men not only like to look, they are most interested in what they can't see. So put that lingerie on like it was originally intended to be worn, like underwear, and manage to let him get a peek while you are out and about. (Hint: when you are climbing in and out of the car are great times to let him catch a glimpse of those garter belts). By the time he gets home, don't be surprised if that little glimpse of lace has turned into full fledged ideas about getting it off you.

Sixth, get away sometimes. The woman of the Song talks about running away with her man, and gals, sometimes we all need to do just that. I know most of us are dead broke and that can make it difficult, but most of us can afford a picnic lunch in a quiet park. Make time to get away and put aside all the responsibilities the two of you face. Getting away doesn't have to be an everyday event, or even every week, but set a date and do it. Having that time to look forward to is relief unto itself.

Seventh, don't neglect your man. Ladies, men will have sex. And if they are not getting it at home, they will find it somewhere else. Only the sainted and the asexual are immune, so don't go fooling yourself into thinking that your husband understands your lack of sex drive. He may get it on an intellectual level, but the part of him that speaks loudest on this matter (which certainly isn't his brain) is only feeling the rejection. Don't set him up for failure.

When you get married you are signing on for a life time of sex, unless there is a legitimate medical reason to abstain. And even those should be checked out and treated if at all possible. Paul says in the New Testament that we are not to deprive our spouses of sex (I Corinthian 7:3-5), and girls, we need to take that decree every bit as seriously as the one about not killing. Even if he doesn't seem to be all that concerned about not getting any, we have to remember that sex is a lot like air – one of our basic needs as human beings, and something that we really don't think about unless we aren't getting enough of it.

Eighth, enjoy having sex with your husband. Be fun, be adventurous, and be willing to do something besides the missionary position with the light off. Experimentation is okay, and it is okay to do some things that you might not consider proper. Sex is about the two of you and no one else, and if you discover that hanging by your ankles from the ceiling fan while covered in hot fudge and tickling his armpits with a feather duster turns you both on, more power to you – and let me know where you bought that fan. If you like to suck marshmallows and tobasco from between his toes while listening to Abba, I may not understand it, but hey, it's your party. I could go on, but I think you get the idea. If you both enjoy something, then go for it.

However, let me add a couple of caveats. I knew you were waiting for this, so here you go. The primary rule the Bible gives about sex with our spouses is that is to be with our spouse, no one else. This means no threesomes, even if he asks, and no porn, even if he insists. I know some of you are wondering why I would even have to make that clarification, but let me tell you I have known couples in the Church who believed that since they had both agreed, it was okay to do either or both. I have also known women who believed that they were fulfilling the role of a Biblical wife by being submissive to their men even in these areas. Girls, you have the right and obligation to refuse to participate in these behaviors. Our sexuality is a gift that you be guarded, and our husbands should be the first line of our defense, but if he fails to live up to this standard, do not hesitate to protect yourself.

I would also advise against anal sex. (Someone just dropped their book). Ladies, in case you haven't heard, this is all the rage right now. Our high-schoolers are using it as a form of birth control and as a way to remain technical virgins. The consequence is our boys are finding that they are really drawn to the taboo of the whole thing (no pun intended). The Bible never specifically addresses this particular sexual act between men and women, but it does condemn it between men.

That being said, I think the answer to whether this should be a part of a married sexual relationship is found in the design of our bodies. The simple truth is we were not designed to be rammed in the butt. The tissue is far more fragile, and you may be damaged internally. The sphincter muscle can be torn or damaged leading to anal leakage or worse (as if anal leakage wasn't disturbing enough). The bacteria in there were never meant to be released onto our other girlie parts and may lead to serious infections – it's why we wipe our bums front to back, to keep us healthy. The risks far outweigh the benefits, and I can't see how doing something that may lead to the perforated colon of another says I love you. Not to mention there are just some injuries you never want to see on a prayer list.

(For more information on anal sex, see the Scandalous Tidbits at the back of the book.)

Which leads me to the final caveat – if you feel uncomfortable or degraded by a sex act, you should be able to call a halt to whatever is going on. Sex is supposed to bring us closer to our spouses. A good sex life helps build unity, teaches how to trust each other, and how to communicate on an intimate level with another person. When it is not doing that, or is causing the opposite effect, you are damaging your marriage in more than just the sexual arena. A sensitive husband will respect your feelings and work through the issue with you. And don't be ashamed to seek out professional help if any sexual issue is bigger than you can address on your own.

Submission

or

The Fine Art of Getting Your Way, Sometimes

Of course, no Christian book touching on the topic of marriage would be complete without addressing that terrible issue of submission – as in "wives be submissive to your husbands." (Ephesians 5:22-33).

Now, there are a ton of really great Christian books dedicated to this topic. Books that offer great theological teaching and are firmly rooted in Scripture, along with some rather questionable books that offer examples of how to be a submissive wife, and books that defend a man's right to expect, even demand, that his wife fulfill this basic Biblical tenant of marriage. There are even books that explain why this passage is no longer relevant to today's woman. However, this is not any of those books, and I have no desire to rehash a topic that so many have already exhausted. The purpose of this book is to talk about those things that we don't talk about as Christian woman.

At first I was tempted to bypass this topic completely, but then I realized that there are things about submission that often go unsaid. Things that when said aloud sound rude, crass, and downright manipulative, and let's face it, if it is ever actually going to be said – well, it is going to take someone like me to get it done.

So let's begin with recognizing what we know about this passage depends on where and how we were raised. If you lived in rural Oklahoma your whole life, you hear about it a lot in sermons, Sunday School lessons, and even in admonishments from the women in your family. In the ranking of proper conversations for Christian women this one rates in the top three, falling right after the Proverbs 31 gal, tying for second with the Mary and Martha story, and just a tad bit ahead of banana pudding recipes. However, if you are from a more liberal environment then you may not hear about this verse at all, or you may hear it explained away as cultural mandate and no longer binding to us modern girls.

And this is the first issue we need to address, and it is simply this – girls, God told us to be submissive to our husbands. He did not offer any reasons. He did not justify His decree, nor did He leave any indication it was for a singular moment in history. This wording is not a mistranslation, a bad interpretation, or something snuck into the Bible by heretical women hating writers. So you are just going to have to get over it.

Sorry, girls, you don't get to bypass this one. As much as we may hate it, feel like it is degrading and archaic, it is still the word of God, preserved even for this day.

I freely acknowledge that there are some men who will try to abuse the fact that we are commanded to be submissive. I was married to one, once upon a time. And there is a time and place to set a boundary and even to "rebel", but we will return to that in another section. For now, let's just pretend that your marriage is merely facing the challenge of uniting a man and a woman in covenant relationship.

Having made that clear, let's move on to the fun stuff, shall we?

Okay, look, God is infinitely practical and fanciful all at the same time. Its part of what makes Him so great, and as a great God He has put in place some killer systems that boggle the human mind. On the surface they often fail to make a bit of sense, but if we take the time to pull back some of the layers and really see how it plays out in the real world, we discover that God isn't as off His rocker as we thought He was. Submission is one of these things in one of those systems.

Underneath all the hype and hoopla about marriage, it is ultimately about unity. In marriage we learn how to love another person so deeply that nothing in their life is unfelt by you, and nothing that touches you fails to touch them. Marriage teaches us how to be a part of something greater than yourself, even as you the individual become greater within it. Marriage is not about losing your identity. It is about deepening it and widening your identity until it requires another person to reveal the totality of who you are.

As human beings, we like to think that this can happen in the context of a fifty-fifty full and equal partnership, and by that we don't mean that both partners are equally valuable, we mean both partners have equal control. The idea makes sense in our minds. After all, mama taught us to share, take turns, and the importance of compromise, but guess what?

Fifty-fifty doesn't work in the real world where decisions are far more important than whose turn it is on the merry-go-round, who gets to be Mario this time, or which TV show to watch. I know, you thought all that time you were learning how to be an adult, nice to know you were being played, isn't it?

Okay, sure, there are times when compromises and negotiations work, but more often than not, forward progression is the result of one person seeing an opportunity and taking it, no matter what the people around them say. And girls, that person usually won't be us.

Something happens when we become wives and mothers, risks, chances, and daring moves just don't seem all that appealing anymore. So we stop putting ourselves in peril and learn how to play it safe. We become the defenders of the home, guardians of the nest, and basically the spoiler for every grand adventure that is waiting for our family. And honestly, most of us need someone to pull us out of that rut. We need a man who can drag us kicking and screaming over that unknown horizon because he knows that there is something amazing on the other side.

Somewhere in the back of my mind, I just heard a friend of mine, who shall remain nameless, who is hovering on the sixteen year old mark say, "Huh, not me." She may very well be right, and I hope she is one of us who never let that adventurous part of her die. But not all of us are going to manage to hold onto that sense of adventure, and since God knew individualized Bibles would be impractical, most of what He had to say had to be directed to the rule and not the exception.

And the rule is women tend to be more cautious, not because we don't desire adventure, but rather we believe the price is too high – especially if it involves our children. For this reason, God gave us men. Men who remind us that life is an adventure, one we don't have to face alone, and one that holds fabulous potential for beauty and growth together.

God knew that we would fight against the pull of the wild blue yonder, and that we would use all of our amazing logic and skills in rationalization to talk ourselves and our mates out of pursuing that adventure. And yet, adventure is what we crave. The desire for it is hardwired into our DNA and why we get caught up in that fairy tale full of knights and dragons or love that movie with the daring hero and his lady fair. When there is no adventure, we don't feel alive, our passion for life and love starves, and we cease to push the limits of who we can be. We need adventure to be completely alive as human beings and as women.

So our crazy, inventive God gave us exactly what we want and need, someone to lead us off into the wilds of life, and He calls that someone a man. God even made sure that we had a reason not to fight our men on this, simply by telling us to submit. Even more amazingly, He knew that the only way we ever truly become united with another human being is in the adventure, taking on a common enemy, and striving towards a shared goal.

What does this mean for us? It means when your husband comes home, hands you a leather halter top and chaps, and announces he is buying a Harley – go with it. Your man is recognizing his need for adventure, and he is asking you to join him. Not because he wants to endanger the love of his life, but rather that he knows that no adventure will be complete without the other part of him there in the middle of it too. It means when he suggests that you pack up and move across country, you start looking at real estate ads, and when he says he would love to see you in that red dress, you put it on. It means that when he says let's leave the kids with your mom and go to the drive in, you pack the diaper bag and put on your best push up bra. It means you stop making excuses to stay at home, guilting him into staying with you, or sending him out into the world alone.

Remember you didn't marry a house, your children, or your job. You married a man, hopefully with all his manly functions fully in place. If your man says you can put it all on hold to be with him, you can, and you should. The dishes will still be in the sink when you come home, the dirty clothes won't disappear, and the dust will only be slightly thicker when you get back. Your kids won't be permanently scarred because you loved their father, and if the job gets in the way you may need to consider getting a new one. Sharing the adventure with him, large or small, is what you committed to when you married him. So start doing what your God told you to do. As an added bonus, all that exhilaration you feel when you are sharing that adventure turns in "pure de ole hormones", making you ready for a different kind of adventure with your man.

God also knew that we are pretty good at getting our way. He had all the faith in the world in us and our ability to work the system. And any woman worth her salt will find a way to get what she wants, but it takes one with incredible strength, faith, and discipline to do it the right way.

A large number of us try to get our way by bullying and harassing our husbands into submission. I hope I don't have to tell you that this is a horrible idea. First of all, when we use the sheer strength of our will through fits, tantrums, or frozen silences to get our men to comply with us, we are one hundred percent completely and inexcusably violating God's Word. Girls, men do not always do what we want them to do immediately, and if you marry one, you are just going to have to accept this as a fact and stop your whining.

The second thing is we don't want a man who cowers before us. If he does shrink before you he is not acting like a man, and you will never be content with a husband like that – if you are content with that type of behavior there is something seriously wrong with you and should seek help, now. (No joke, ladies). When a man is nothing more than a glorified slave to our whims, he is not operating in his strengths, and will never be the type of husband that can be a spiritual leader in your home.

The sad truth is that too many of us have married some really great guys with all sorts of potential, and we have sacrificed that potential along with his masculinity on the altar of our wants and fears. These men fill today's Churches, and they are easy to spot. They are the ones who hold their wives purses, stand in abject silence after the service waiting for her to give the order that it is time to leave, the ones with furtive look in their eyes, and can't even make a single decision without their wives permission. Gals, if you are married to man like this, chances are a large part of the blame for who he is today belongs exclusively to you.

And no, I am not going to apologize for saying that. Yes, there are some men who are meeker and milder than most, but if you did not step back and you seized control of every situation before he could react, you were the one who helped in the creation of the person you are now married too. Yes, he should have put his foot down. Yes, he should have stood up to you, but what kind of tantrum would you had thrown if he did?

Does he have issues that need to be addressed? Absolutely, but this book was not written to him. And since I am addressing you, you are the only person who is responsible for making use of the information you receive. Right now, we need to address your problem – not his. Maybe the next book will be for the fellows, and I'll talk to him then. But sister, if I do watch out because your world might just get a little shake up.

Submission is one way God designed for us as women to protect and nurture our men's masculinity. We have an obligation to provide an environment where they can learn to flex their muscle in an appropriate way, where they know that their strengths are valued and desired. The world is full of people who are more than ready to tear a man down, make him feel inadequate, or wrong for simply being a man. We need to remember whose side we are on, and give him the freedom and support to step into that role of husband and leader of our families.

God knew that as real women we would want real men, and He put this system in place as a way to make sure we got what we wanted and needed. He did it for our good and our benefit. It wasn't to be cruel. It was and is a mercy to us and our needs as women. So stop fighting it.

So if I am telling you that you can get your way, and I am also telling you that bullying isn't an option, what do I expect you to do?

Well, here's the great part. Gals, we have already discussed that we have an amazing power over the men in our lives. As women we can inspire them to greatness, and we can provoke crazy fabulous responses from them, and all of this is a part of God's design for us as women. But we need to be careful, because with great power comes great responsibility.

Look, there are basically two things that every man reacts to on almost an instinctive and uncontrollable level. One is beauty and the other is respect. If you give a man these two things in his life you are giving him something that is more addictive than crack. He will do just about anything to keep the supply running and is capable of tremendous feats of daring and love to get more. Girls, guess who controls the supply lines?

Yep, that would be you, and every man with half a brain knows that. Ever wonder why he was so flattering and sweet while you were dating? He was trying to convince you to give him what he wants and needs, and if he is smart he won't quit just because you married him. A wise man will create every opportunity and give you every tool you need so that you can give him the desires of his heart. He will actively defend you from situations that would threaten your desire to be beautiful for him or rob him of your respect. To put it bluntly he will do everything in his power to remind you that you are loved and valued as the most beautiful woman in his world. And when he fulfills his role as a husband in these matters, we get what we desire. (All in hopes that you will give him what he wants without him ever having to ask for it, because after all, men hate to ask for anything.)

And what does every woman desire at the most basic level of who she is? To know that she beautiful and to know that she is loved. See how that works? You communicate love and respect for him in submission. He feels secure in that love, and responds by providing you with the love and support you crave – which in turn, feeds your desire to communicate love and respect to him through submission, et cetera, et cetera, et cetera. (Please read that in the voice of Yul Brynner as the King of Siam). See how God has instituted a plan that fulfills our distinct needs in a way that we would have never figured out on our own, but I guess that is why we trust Him.

In addition, if you are blessed enough to be married to a real man who truly loves you and the Lord, he will do everything in his power to avoid treating you like a doormat. He will consult you on the big decisions of life, and he will value your input and implement it. Not only that, don't be surprised if you overhear him singing your praises to his friends. Men love knowing that they were smart enough to marry a smart and loving woman. And let me tell you being appreciated like that feels great!

The benefits it has for us as women are enormous, and not just in the bedroom. (But girls, it takes a secure man to be a great lover, and what wife doesn't want that?) Submitting to our husbands brings out the best in us, making us even more beautiful and worthy of love in his eyes. Through submission we learn how approach him with kindness and in ways that don't attack his masculinity. We learn how make an appeal and still give him the freedom to do as he feels led. We honor his masculinity by reminding him through our submission that he is the head of the household. Submitting to him compels him to take responsibility and reminds him that he has an obligation and desire to care for our needs. A good man's response will be far above what we can do for ourselves.

Submitting gives us freedom from the emotional and mental stressors of being the only responsible adult in the house. And our faith is deepened in both our husbands and our God, as we live a life that becomes a bold declaration that God really does know what He is doing and we will honor our Lord as the master of our lives and this world. In this freedom, we find the strength and resources to be more of the wife, mother, and woman that God created us to be. As we grow in these roles, our deepening beauty will encourage our men to support us in our endeavors to develop our unique gifts and talents without the burden of trying to run the world.

Is my approach to submission manipulative? Yes, it is, and I will admit it freely. But manipulation isn't always a bad thing. We manipulate and are manipulated on a daily basis, usually with each party's full knowledge and consent, and that is what makes it alright. There is nothing dirty or underhanded in what I am saying. I am simply following the rules and being realistic about how they play out in my life, and Ty is completely aware of what I am doing. He knows that I am making a valiant attempt not be a domineering witch (read that as being a . . .oh, never mind), which for me is not the easiest thing I have ever done, and he loves me more for trying. At the same time, he knows that I am refusing to be his crutch, and that he has to rise to the occasion and be the head of our house, I won't allow anything less. As result, he moves confidently forward in his life knowing that I always have his back, and I am forever on his side. He does not fear that I will betray his trust or undermine his authority, and he honors me by making the choices that defend our marriage, even when I may not like those choices I never forget that I love my husband.

Even more, I am learning that my salvation and security do not rest on the shoulders of any man, even Ty's. I am forced to reconcile my life with my faith by reminding myself that even if I don't always trust Ty's judgment, I still trust the God who put the system in place, each time I determine to say, "Babe, you are big boy, and it's your call." (I almost always have to follow up with a prayer that goes, "God, you're a big God, and I sure hope you've got this one because my husband just went stupid on me.") And you know what? God has always been faithful, guarding and protecting my family in the midst of my obedience. Girls, honestly, when it is all said and done, the experience of God's grace and mercy is better than any argument we may win with our man.

(And in the interest of full disclosure, the times when I was tempted to resist Ty the most usually turned out to be the times when his decisions led to some of the most enjoyable blessings in my life. Don't tell Ty, but his crazy ideas have turned out to be fun and some of the smartest things we could have done. I just don't want to actually have to admit that he was right, at least not to him . . . not yet anyways.)

Also, knowing that submission is an act of faith given to my Lord helps me be a little more forgiving for those times that Ty does screw up. Because I don't expect him to make everything perfect, I am not disappointed when he can't, and I don't feel the need or desire to berate him for my unmet expectations. Instead, my husband and I can go together before the King and ask that He move on our behalf because my bitterness is not dividing us. The unity of our marriage is not threatened by resentment and has been defended by my conscious decision, allowing us to continue to grow in greater intimacy with each other. Not having unrealistic expectations of my man forces me have great expectations of my God.

I truly believe that submission isn't an awful word or an antiquated concept. Submission is freedom to women, even strong women, because it isn't about denying who you are as a person or rejecting your strengths and abilities. Submission is about making the choice to devote your strength to protecting the unity of your marriage. When we submit to our husbands we are using our power to build up the person who loves us enough to build us up in return, and growing together so that you can each become the men and women you could never be alone. And isn't that the reason God puts us together in the first place?

So to sum it all up, girls - we hold the nutcrackers if we want a gelding who is impotent, we can have one, but if we want a man who can meet our needs as women, we submit.

Divorce from a Biblical Perspective
or
When to Say When

Whatever you do, do not bypass this section. Even if you are in a stable, happy, and healthy marriage, someone you love has been or will be affected by this topic, and gals, we need to know some truth about it.

Divorce is one the big, ugly realities of our time. Statistics say that one in two marriages will end in divorce, and your odds aren't any better if you are a Christian. The numbers alone make it an unavoidable topic. And with numbers like that, all of you reading this book will probably be forced to deal with it one form or another, either by dating someone who has been divorced, being a child of divorced parents, having friends who get divorced, or more than likely experiencing a combination of all of the above.

Divorce was never the ideal, and is not highly looked upon in Scripture, but since it is a reality, God did not forget to address it. As someone who has gone through a divorce, it is a topic that I have spent much time on, and it is a reality that has affected my whole life and the lives of my children and current husband. No matter how much I might wish my experience could be different, it never will be, and that is a truth that my family and many others are facing.

Let me begin by saying, divorce is not always evil and can be an incredible blessing.

For some of you that is the most shocking and scandalous thing you have read from me to date, but before you put the book down allow me a chance to clarify that statement.

In case you haven't figured it out yet, no marriage is perfect. Marriage is a partnership between two flawed people living in a flawed world. Many of the things we love about our men are the very things will drive us crazy once we have to live with them. His quiet nature that made him so pleasant while you were dating becomes icy silences after the "I do's", and his exciting spontaneity can be seen as being unreliable. His great hygiene and impeccable grooming becomes vanity, and his relaxed attitude towards life can now be termed laziness. His ambition becomes greed, and his dependability becomes boring and predictable. No matter what traits you so adored in him while you lived in separate houses can become points of irritation once you have to live with it twenty-four hours a day, seven days a week. But no matter how annoying these things are, they are not reasons to seek out a divorce. Rather they are opportunities to grow as a person and as a couple.

The opportunity for growth is the main reason God designed us to be in a marriage relationship, and using that opportunity as an excuse to find an easy way out is both cowardly and lazy. However, there are times when the issues confronted in a marriage go far beyond annoyance or even inconvenience and these are the times when divorce is a legitimate option.

From a Scriptural perspective the first thing we need to know about divorce is God made provision for it (Deuteronomy 24:1-4). He did not like it. He did not want it. But He recognized that sometimes we as human beings get into situations where we need a life line and an open window (Mark 10:1-10). So often when divorce is discussed in the Church the only thing we are told is that God hates divorce, and this is specifically stated in the Bible. (Malachi 2:16). And why shouldn't He hate it?

Divorce runs counter to everything He ever intended for marriage and families. He knows the pain it brings to all parties involved, the scars it leaves on the hearts of His children and the lasting impact it has on families. The problem is no one ever seems to finish that verse, God hates divorce – "and I hate a man's covering himself with violence as one wears a garment." Anyone who has ever gone through a divorce knows that divorces are violent, leaving a bloody trail behind them. How could a God who loves us love something that causes so much pain?

I sometimes wonder if God doesn't hate the divorce so much as He hates the conditions and circumstances that lead to a divorce. After all, no one gets a divorce because things were just too good. We get divorces because someone betrayed our trust, abused us, or violated the covenant in some dreadful way. In short, we get divorces because someone hurt us, and God hates seeing His kids be the victim of another person's evil.

We should also know that despite what you may have been taught, getting a divorce is not a sin. God himself declared that He gave His bride, the nation of Israel, a certificate of divorce (Jeremiah 3:8), and if God is sinless . . . ? Well, you do the math. And if we go back and read through that passage, we find that He divorced Israel for the same reasons we humans get a divorce, and we can hear the pain this decision caused Him. He knows what it is like to sever an intimate relationship that was supposed to last forever, and as a good God, He desires to spare us from ever having to know what that feels like. But even He says there is a time to say when.

Adding to our confusion about divorce is the teaching of Jesus (Matthew 19:1-12). I believe that the root of this confusion lies in the fact the writers of the Bible assume that their readers would know a thing or two about what was really going on. However, since none of us have ever lived in first century Judea most of us have no idea that this whole scenario was just a plot to drag Jesus into the middle of one of the most heated debates of His day.

So let's just have a quick history lesson, and don't worry, I will just stick to the high points. In Jesus' time, there were two major religious parties, a lot like Republicans and Democrats. (Yes, there were others, but they rarely made the news, think Libertarians). And just like our political parties, they each had liberal and conservative members. So when the two parties weren't debating each other, the parties were squabbling among themselves. (See? Things haven't changed all that much.)

In Jesus' day, the debate was when could a man legitimately divorce his wife. Some of the liberal crowd said that it was okay to divorce a woman if she burned his toast. Others said that it was only okay to get divorced if she committed adultery. The question they were really asking Jesus was, are you a liberal or a conservative? And He was refusing to take sides. Instead, Jesus did what God always does and dealt with the heart of the matter.

First off, He acknowledged that women had few choices in His day – she could get married again or she could become a prostitute. There were almost no other options available to her and either one entailed having sex with another man. So He called it like it was and declared the awful truth that so many people had been avoiding – a man who divorced his wife was causing her to live a life contrary to that which God desires for us to have. He was placing the blame for a divorced woman's sin directly on the shoulders of a man who forced a woman into this predicament. He was forcing the men to acknowledge what they were doing to the women they had been entrusted with.

If you back up a little, you will find that one the things that Jesus has no tolerance for is a person who causes another to stumble or to sin (Matthew 18:5, 6). He is adamant that the guilt rests far more heavily on the person who creates an inescapable circumstance for another person than the person who must now live in that circumstance. And in His day and time divorce for a woman was just that – an inescapable circumstance. She could not fight for half of the belongings in court, nor could she demand child support for the kids she may have had to take with her, or visitation for those she left behind. If she was extremely lucky her parents might take her back in, but it was not likely. Having a divorced daughter was extremely humiliating to the family and often meant they avoided her like the plague. For the divorcee, her options were few, and Jesus was sympathetic to her plight.

Fortunately, this is not the last word we have on divorce. Paul goes on to explain that if one member of a marriage desired to leave the one left behind was innocent and free to marry again (I Corinthians 7:12-15). Girls, we need to remember that just because it wasn't Jesus who said these words they aren't any less important. God decided that Paul's words were valuable enough to keep in His book, and we need to honor them as significant to God.

God in all things is a realist. He never nurses an unfounded delusion about humanity or any of His creation, and one of the many ways He demonstrates that fact to us is the fact that He, Himself, made provision for divorce in the original law He presented to Israel. We need to stop and ponder that for a second because the law He gave to humanity was perfect. He didn't make any missteps or accidently hand Moses the rough draft. What He gave us was exactly what He intended to give us, and it included the reasons and proper procedures for dissolving a marriage in which something had gone horribly wrong.

Now as Gentiles who have been adopted into the Hebrew nation, we are not bound to those laws, but we know that they were given as an example for those of us who came later so that we might better know the desires of our Father's heart. What they teach us is still valid to this day, and in the matter of divorce we learn that God knew that not every marriage was destined to have a fairy tale ending because let's face it – girls, we aren't Cinderella, and we sure didn't marry Prince Charming. We are broken people trying to do the right thing, but in a marriage it takes two people consistently trying to do the right thing, and if one of them isn't giving it their all, marriage can be one the closest things to hell on earth we can know.

When we put all the pieces of what the Bible has to teach us about divorce together, we come up with something very different than what the world tells us and completely foreign to what we may have been taught in our Churches. God hates divorce, but He loves us enough to offer us an alternative to living a life bound up in a marriage that will cripple us spiritually, emotionally, mentally, and possibly even physically.

Hear me on this! Divorce should never be our first, second, or even our one-hundred-seventy-fifth option. It should only be considered when there is nothing else we can do, when we have sought out and utilized every type of help we can find, and when we know beyond a shadow of a doubt that legal proceedings are only telling the truth of what has already happened in our hearts.

And let's turn this whole issue on its head for awhile and consider some possibilities that I have found few Christian woman consider when thinking about divorce. We all know that there are some really great reasons for fighting it out and staying the course. No one in their right mind can dispute that, but have you ever thought that there are some really awful, even sinful, reasons to stay married?

When I have talked to Christian women about the possibility of divorce, they often cite the same two reasons for staying: pride and fear. The truth is few of us want to be the divorced woman in our Church, because let's face it, we Church women know how to gossip (we call it making prayer requests). We know what others have said, and what may have even come out of our own mouths about "that woman." Ever want to wound a good Christian woman's pride? Suggest that she may be a divorcee or headed that direction. Ever want to strike fear into the heart of Sister Goodie-Goodie? Let her think that she might be included on a prayer list for a troubled marriage. She would rather you pray that her herpes would clear up.

Girls, pride and fear have no place in our lives. And if that is all that is keeping you in a marriage, you might consider the fact that you are living a lie, not living out your faith.

The Three A's of Christian Divorce

For three years, I endured a marriage that was hallmarked with adultery, abuse, and abandonment – the three A's of Biblical reasons to consider getting a divorce, but I was not about to tell a soul that my life was in shambles, let alone "fail" at being married. I thought that I would rather die first, and I almost got my way. I know the power of pride and fear of being deemed a failure first hand, and when that is the only reason you refuse to get out of a bad marriage, you are living in sin just as surely as any wanton hussy out there. Learning to admit that is one the hardest things you will ever learn to do as a good Christian woman.

I mentioned the three A's as a Biblical reasons to consider divorce. I say consider, because there is no mandate requiring us to get a divorce if these things occur in our marriages. There is only the provision for a way of escape should we need one. Now, there is a common misperception out there that we know what these words mean, but ladies, I really think that we need to expand our definitions a little. So let's take some time to treat each one individually, but bear in mind that each one encompasses some aspect of the other two.

Adultery – More than Just Sex

Of all the reasons a Christian woman can seek a divorce, adultery is probably the most "proper" one in our Church circles. I mean who can dispute the wrong that was done to a woman when her man is out philandering with the town strumpet? (For those of you who haven't read any early English novels, read that doing the horizontal tango with the local slut.) We Christians like it because it is cut and dry, and easy to define. Either he is doing the deed or he isn't, but what if he is simply emailing a girl at the office every day? Talking to another woman about his hopes, dreams, heartaches, and disappointments? What if he is confiding in her what he should be telling you?

Gals, I hate to be the one who tells you this, but this is called an affair. And the same goes for you and any guy friend you have who gets the daily scoop on your heart – including the great gay friend who does your hair. Sure it may not have crossed over into the physical, yet, but this is why it is more specifically called an emotional affair. Don't think that is grounds enough to get out? That it has to be the physical act of adultery? Don't worry, it will get there soon enough, just give it time.

However, there is some good news. If you call it what it is soon enough, and ignore his protests, which he will make, you can nip this in the bud before it goes that far. Call the counselor, set up the appointment, and tell him that he had better be there or you are calling a lawyer. And don't you dare bluff on this one. Only do it if you mean business, because that gun only has one bullet – every threat you make after that is merely a stage blank, and he knows it.

A second form of adultery that is being overlooked in our Christian circles is pornography. After all he hasn't actually had sex with another woman, he has just had an orgasm to the image of another woman, and that isn't too bad is it? I don't know about you but knowing that my husband finds a piece of paper more arousing than my warm and willing body doesn't do anything to promote the intimacy or vulnerability needed in a healthy marriage.

Girls, you have to take a stand on this one, because if you don't you are in for the bum's rush to a living hell. Trust me, I know. The pure and simple truth is we will never be able to provide the variety that the porn industry cranks out on a daily basis. And your man isn't becoming addicted to sex. He is becoming addicted to the ever changing kaleidoscope of women before his eyes. There is no way on God's green earth you can compete, and over time you will cease to exist to him as a sexual and intimate partner, and as you diminish in his eyes, you will begin to diminish in your own.

Since the habitual use of pornography is an addiction, he will use the same excuse every addict since the dawn of time has used. "It's harmless." "I could be doing something worse." "I just wanted to have a little fun." "It doesn't concern you." and my all time favorite, "I am doing it for us." Honey, if your man needs to prime the pump with a little porn, he has a problem and chances are all of it isn't you.

When the excuses fail to convince you that this is acceptable behavior, be prepared for him to shift the blame, and guess who gets to catch it? It sounds something like this, "If you didn't stress me out/ were there for me more/ were more adventurous/ thinner/ had bigger boobs/ liked oral sex more/ weren't so tired/ take so much work to climax/ wore more lingerie/ had better breath/ were available at more convenient times/ cleaned the house more/ cooked better meals/ didn't have stretch marks/ shaved down there/ didn't make so much noise/ made more noise/ had two vaginas/ like threesomes/ smelled of lilacs/ had a higher body temperature/ looked more like my Uncle Mike, I would have no need to look at porn. It's all your fault."

Gals, when this is going on you are no longer in a marriage. You have officially just been demoted to uncompensated cook and maid. And who is getting the perks of being married? The expressions of love and desire? The joy of knowing that your man completely appreciates who they are and what they do for him? Who does he make time for, spend money on, and protect? Pictures and images on a screen of a hundred different women who will never scrub the skid marks from his underwear or pop that pimple on his butt, and yet we are reluctant to call it what it is – adultery.

If my words haven't convinced you, consider what Jesus had to say about it. Okay, so there weren't any copies of "Hot Harem Girls" being sold at the local oat station, but as long as there have been men, there have been men jerking off to images of naked women – even if they were forced to imagine what they looked like. Jesus called it like it is and said that if a man lusted (read that experienced and nursed arousal and desire) in his heart for a woman that he had yet to actually touch – he had committed adultery and was just as guilty as the man who had actually did the deed (Matthew 5:28).

So I don't care that your man isn't out there getting busy with any gal who will let him. According to the Bible, he might as well being do just that, and all of his excuses about how at least he isn't bring home a thrilling case of crabs to share with you doesn't make it any less hurtful to woman who truly loves her husband. And Biblically, we aren't required to take this type of abuse. Which leads us to the next topic –

Abuse - It Doesn't Always Leave a Mark

At one time spousal abuse was considered to be beating your wife with a stick that was bigger than your thumb. Then we became a little more progressive and abuse was anything that left a mark that a woman could not explain away by claiming to have run into a door knob. Over the past few decades we have become so enlightened that we know that hitting your wife is an inexcusable act, and with that abuse has become less of a problem – or so we want to believe.

The truth is there are several different forms of abuse, and not all of them leave a mark, at least not a mark that you can see. And since these types of abuse do not leave a tell tale black eye, bloody lip, or hand prints around your neck, many people do not consider them to be abuse at all. Girls, it's time to smarten up.

First off, let's establish that in any marriage relationship, no matter how good, one of you is going to do something stupid and hurtful to the other. We snipe at each other, say something mean, grumble and complain about something insignificant. We scream at the one we love most because they messed up our plans, scared us to death, or did something thoughtless. Whatever it is, there will be a time or two somewhere in the years you spend together when the two you will barely refrain from emotionally or physically eviscerating each other. (Read that as leaving him in bloody pulp in the laundry room floor.) But gals, most of us just need to learn how to forgive and forget these little tiffs and move on, because they are not abuse.

Abuse implies that there is some sort of pattern, some habitual behavior designed to hurt another person for the express purpose of bringing some type of enjoyment to ourselves. Abuse is not the occasional flying off the handle because one of you left the tools out in the rain, the rare rant for leaving the toilet seat up, nor is it the squabble over the cost of getting your nails done. Abuse isn't about an issue. The issue is really just an excuse. Abuse is about degrading and devaluing your partner to the point where they can be controlled and manipulated through an erratic pattern of indulgence and punishment, much the same way we train a dog but worse. In short, it is about inflicting pain on another in order to get your kicks.

I pray that most of you will never know what it is like to be in an abusive relationship, or to have to live the rest of your lives with the scars it will leave if you are blessed enough to get out, but the truth is many of you will know exactly what type of pain I am talking about. And what is even scarier, many of you will know that this is exactly what you are experiencing right now in your marriage.

Most abusers are smart and have a huge ego, one that they feed with daily doses of your soul that they rip bit by bloody bit from you until you have nothing of yourself left. They don't want you to leave, and they know that a physical blow might just set you over the edge and give you a reason to cut off the supply. They also don't want the attention that being labeled an abusive husband would bring. So they are far more subtle about it than simply giving you a right hook to the jaw. Instead they choose to do in words and deeds directed at you, not to you, anything that will make you flinch, and if you stop flinching they simply up the ante and find new and improved ways to torment you.

There is no way I can catalogue the varied ways that men victimize their wives. Each abuser has his own individual style that is uniquely adapted to their specific victim. They find out what hurts you the most and what violates you on the most intimate level. They are experts in determining which of our wants and needs they should stomp, all in hopes of finding that thing that will make you cry, rage, and finally give up all together.

So how do you know if you are being abused?

Unfortunately, many of "Biblically" based ideas of being a wife have made this a more confusing issue than it has to be. To begin with we have confused being a victim with being submissive. Girls, I make no apologies for declaring that we should be submissive. Submission is a completely legit Biblical concept, but husbands have an obligation in all of this, too. He is to love us as Christ loved the Church, and how many times did Jesus belittle, humiliate, or ridicule those around his Bride?

The correct answer is He didn't. He never attacked any of His followers for being who they were. He dealt with issues, honestly and sometimes harshly. He addressed what they said and did, but the entire time He was urging them to grow in wisdom and understanding.

If I were to isolate one common thread in abuse, it would be that you are being manipulated into being less than you could be. Sacrifices are a part of marriage, maybe it is foregoing that day at the spa, the nice new car, or a job that would separate you from your family for too long. It's what we do to show our love for our men and our children, but a sacrifice can only be given by one who chooses to give it. Sacrifices cannot be coerced or forced from us at the threat of violence, stony silences, or having our "allowance" cut off. Our husband's love and support should inspire us to give it our all, even in things we hate to do like cleaning and cooking, and we should never feel as if we would lose his love or incur his wrath if we did not comply with his demands.

Jesus never arm wrestled someone into doing it His way. The sheer force of His love would inspire those around Him to make the right decisions, and if they chose poorly, He let them bear the consequences of their decision. His goal was never to hurt or humiliate. Instead, He gave those He loved enough room to learn from their mistakes and was ready to restore relationship the instant they turned back to Him. As our example of the ultimate lover, He demonstrated what we should be experiencing from and providing to those we love. So ask yourself:

- Do you do what is expected of you because you desire to honor your husband?
- Do you do it out of fear of his rage, ice cold shoulder, or being denied something that you want or need?
- Do you try things you don't like in hopes of pleasing him or to avoid his punishment?
- Do you wait for him to come home with anticipation or dread?
- Do you actively fantasize about you or him dying so that you can be free?
- Do you tip toe around the house when he is home?
- Do you avoid asking him to help you?
- Dread the thought of when the kids are out of the house, and not just because you are going to miss them?
- Do you look forward to the time when you can just be his again?

How you answer those questions can tell you a lot about the state of your marriage, and if you are doing anything out of fear, you have a problem. If this problem is not addressed, don't expect it to get any better. In fact, you might want to brace yourself because it is going to get worse. And don't be surprised that after a few months or years of you being his emotional punching bag, he decides that it wouldn't hurt you to take a physical punch or two along the way.

Does this mean that your marriage is destined to be your own personal living hell or that divorce is your only option? It depends, and not entirely on you.

There is hope, but you need to learn how to set some boundaries, hard and fast. He won't like it, but why would he? Up until now you have let him get away with behaving like a spoilt child, and now you are going to have to undo many of the habits you nurtured in your naiveté. One word of caution though, if there is even the threat of physical violence, you should consider a temporary separation until he demonstrates that he is willing to work on the state of your marriage. Separation doesn't mean that you are getting a divorce. You are simply being wise and sending a clear message that you will not tolerate being bullied.

If you do stay, remember that you are probably going to be hyper-sensitive, after all you have just woke up from a deep coma of denial, and all that pain you have been stuffing is going to hurt in a fashion somewhat akin to ripping out your fingernails with pliers. Don't say you haven't been warned. You need to remember that this is not about exacting revenge. It is about learning the proper ways to love yourself and each other again.

And really, learning to love yourself will be one killer of a first step. You need to know that you are worth loving. After all, God said so – so quit arguing. You also need to bear in mind that you have been told an entire library of lies about who you are, what you are capable of, and why you deserve to suffer. Be prepared for him to reload every weapon he has ever fired at you and aim straight at your heart. He will be cajoling, sweet, shamelessly apologetic, and downright nasty all in an attempt to make you once more believe that he has done nothing but love you in the best possible manner. Don't be taken in.

The second step, almost equally as hard, is to learn how to set boundaries without being vengeful or spiteful. This is where most of us mess up. We have been taught that we are to forgive and forget. Well, I defy you to show me that anywhere in the Bible. Forgiveness, yes. Forgetting, no. Only God is required to forget, and even then we know that He doesn't really forget. He still knows that we hurt Him, and guess what? We remember when we have been hurt too. Remembrance is what helps us resist the urge to touch the hot stove, hug a cactus, lick a light socket, or give the cat a bath. Remembering is a good thing. It keeps us safe.

But since you will be tempted to make him pay, this is where that network of friends comes into the picture. They will help you determine what is reasonable and what is necessary. Ideally, you will have a friend who has a healthy functional marriage, one who has survived a situation similar to yours, and one who has done both. And I pray that you have a Mammie in the mix, because she will keep you straight. (If you need to refresh your memory on this one, refer back the network of friends in chapter 7.)

The third step is knowing when to let down your guard. After all, how many times did you take him back, forgive it all, only to wind up in the same boat again? You did, didn't you? Even when your friends told you not to, you thought you were doing the right thing, but now it is worse than ever, isn't it? Don't beat yourself up. I've done it too.

Girls, him being broken isn't enough. It's just not. Sure he is in pain. Sure he hurts and feels bad. He even cried and promised to do better, but guess what? Emotions change, and I am willing to put good money down that says he was just horny. So how do you tell when you should let him back into your heart fully? When he has worked at doing better for more than a few days, a week, or even a month or more, the recovery process takes time. Time for him to learn new habits, and time for you to heal enough to trust your decisions. If reconciliation is what you are working for, you need to accept the fact you are in for the long haul, because this mess wasn't made overnight, and there is no way you are going to clean it up tomorrow.

In extreme cases, an abuser will keep up the good boy act for as long as they deem it necessary, and it is only necessary until they believe you are back in their clutches. Months may pass with them treating you like a queen only to have it all change the moment you agree to move back home, share a moment of intimacy, or show any signs of dependence on them. My ex ran on three month cycles, and while at the beginning I was told I was nothing short of perfect by the end of the third month he was telling me that I was nothing more than a . . . well, it's a Christian book, so let's just say it was bad. Don't be in a hurry to believe that things are okay just because there have been no blow ups for the past several days. Taking your time is essential because running back too soon may undo any progress you have made.

With the help of your friends, and hopefully a trusted counselor, set some goals for your marriage, and envision how you hope it can be. Come up with some mile markers of success, and stick to the plan. Don't deviate, even when it seems like everything is wonderful the first three days into your plan. One of the primary things that will reveal his heart is how he responds to you not giving into him the first time he calls you baby. An abuser hates to be thwarted (read that stopped dead in his tracks with an emotional frying pan), and when he gets told no, don't be surprised when all those hurtful behaviors boil right back up to the surface. If he is really in it for the long haul, he will do the time to prove that he desires for the two of you to have a happy and healthy marriage.

If he doesn't, well, he was never in it for you to begin with, and you are better off without him. Okay, that sounds harsh, but when we have been beaten and battered, even if it was just emotionally and mentally, we need someone to speak the truth in love. God called us to be stewards of this earth and all that is within it, and guess what? That includes yourself, and if you are squandering your resources on a man who is using you up in order to feed his insatiable need for control, you are not being a good steward of yourself. Eventually you will have no energy to give to your children, your friends, yourself, or your God.

For many women this is a hard truth to swallow. They believe that as Christian women they are suppose to stand by their man, help him become a better person, find a way to bandage of his wounds, and help him heal from the scars that have left him emotionally crippled. And if your man is actively seeking out help and working towards becoming whole mentally, emotionally, and spiritually, then by all means stay, but remember ultimately you can't fix him. These things are for him and God to work out. All you can do is help, but sometimes when the scars run too deep, we need to step out of God's line of fire and give Him a clean shot.

And girls, this is not easy. We hate seeing those we love in pain, even self-inflicted pain, and especially when we think that we could have saved them from it if we had only tried a little harder. But we need to stop lying to ourselves. God sometimes uses pain to force us to change, to force us to turn to Him, and to get real about what we have been doing to ourselves. He will allow us to suffer here and now if He knows that it is for our eternal good. He loves us enough to make us face the truth. The question for us women becomes, do we love our men enough to do the same?

Sometimes that ultimate act of love is taking our hands off and turning our men over to God completely. Being able to do this is not running away or avoiding the problem. It is an exercise in faith. A faith that says, "God, I'm not big enough to do this, and the only thing I can hope for is Your divine intervention. So I'm stepping away, and I am entrusting You with the one I love the most because I truly believe that You will care for him better than me." It's a scary and powerful step, but oh girls, the freedom and peace it can bring if we are brave enough to take it.

Abandonment- Living Alone Even if He is Still There

The final "A" of this equation is abandonment, and if you haven't guessed by now, it is far more complex than simply having your husband walk out that front door and never coming back. Of course, if you are fortunate enough to have this happen then your Biblical answer is pretty simple. He leaves and according to Paul you are free to remarry or not, as you feel led.

Unfortunately, many women are still living in marriages where they were abandoned many, many years ago. Sure he is still sleeping in the recliner in front of the TV, but when was the last time you actually spoke to him? When was the last time he actually saw you? Cared about you? Or acknowledged that you shared a house other than to grumble about the fact you need to do a little more cleaning? When was the last time you made plans together? Dreamed together? Or simply enjoyed being in the same room with each other?

Look, every marriage is going through periods of time where you might feel like there is some major disconnect between you and your husband. Maybe you are worn out from a few toddlers running around the house, or maybe he is making a major shift in his job and he has no energy when he gets home. Perhaps there is medical crisis, an emergency with the extended family, but whatever it is, the two of you know that the other one is waiting for that time when you can come back together and enjoy each other again. Simply knowing this is a source of strength and encouragement for each other through the hard times.

But when this type of disconnect continues beyond a season, and no one, or only one person, is working at trying to reconnect, there is a problem. Ladies, if you are experiencing this, it is time to speak up. Let him know that you feeling alone and abandoned. A good man will express concern and start making some efforts to make things better. Fixing the problem might be as simple as going on a few dates, scheduling fifteen minutes each day where the two of you can look each other in the eyes, or maybe you just need to remember how much fun it is to kiss each other once again. However, if this has been going on for a prolonged period of time, it might be time to seek out some professional help.

I wish there was some fool proof formula in which all you had to do was say the magic word while performing the proper ritual with a chicken bone in the dark of the moon and all would be well, but God didn't create us to work this way. How well your efforts work greatly depends on how receptive your man is to the idea of working on your relationship and himself. Remember you cannot make him do anything he doesn't want to do, so do your part and then turn it loose.

So how do you know if it is time to consider divorce? You take inventory of your marriage by asking a few questions:

- Are you the only one working on your marriage?
- Does he refuse to participate in family events?
- Does he do his own thing with no thought or consideration the family plans?
- Have you been living like roommates instead of lovers?
- Do you frequently have no idea of where he is?
- Has he left you to handle all the family problems?

- Are you the only one bringing in an income?
- Does his money go only to his projects?
- Do you make decisions without consulting him because you know he doesn't want to be bothered?
- Can you go for days and weeks without speaking to each other?
- Have you ever faced an emergency alone?
- Does he know who you have become over the past few years?
- Do you go for long periods of time with no sexual contact?
- When is the last time he hugged you for no reason? Kissed you for longer than a peck?
- Is he actively avoiding you?
- Does he resent your presence or attempts to be with him?
- Has he ridiculed you for pursuing him?
- Does he have a room that is "his", where he frequently retreats?
- Is it easier to stay out of his way than engage?
- Does he use his temper to keep you at a distance?

Look, none of this has to be a reason to divorce, but it can be a good indicator that you are traveling in that direction. Some women have been able to create a life in the middle of what many of us would consider to be the barren wastelands of emotion, and they have chosen to stay because they feel that in staying they are honoring their God and the commitment they made before Him. I applaud their strength and tenacity. To stay in this type of marriage takes a special type of woman who is willing to be honest about herself, her husband, and the true state of their marriage. If she is dishonest about any of these three things she will become angry and embittered, but if she has the fortitude and courage to face her life as it is, she can live a life that is a testament to power and joy of entrusting God with our hearts.

However, there are times when this type of abandonment goes beyond just inconvenience or neglect and becomes an active form of abuse. When it crosses over that line, we are playing a whole new game, and it may be time to reconsider if staying in a blatantly unhealthy situation is really what God would have you do. Additionally, these types of marriages are the ideal set up for one partner or the other to get caught up in adultery. So if you see signs that your man is disconnecting speak up. Stop it in its tracks before it becomes a comfortable habit. You just might be able to save your marriage.

The Big "Church" Lie About Divorce

Finally, I believe it is time that we stopped telling our girls THE big "Church" lie that springs so easily from our Christian lips. I know that you have heard it. Shoot, I've even said myself, only to repent of it in the very recent past. It sounds like this –

"Divorce should never be an option." Or maybe a slight variation, "You should never even entertain the possibility of getting a divorce once you are married. Marriage is forever."

No, girls, it's not. Not always, and God knew what He was doing when He designed it this way. And I think He did this for three very specific reasons. The first one we have covered. It is the escape hatch for when things go terribly wrong, but the final two actually can help us have that safe and healthy marriage we all dream of.

One reason I believe we need to know that divorce is an option is to keep us motivated to protect our marriages. Nothing makes us lazier than thinking that nothing is required of us to maintain the status quo, and if we are arrogant enough to think that our men aren't going anywhere just because we have a ring, we need a reality check. He can pick up a phone and call a lawyer just as easily as you can, and given enough reason, he might. We need to remember that we can't take anything in this life for granted, including and especially our spouse. So treasure your man and hold on to him if he is a good one. Use your knowledge of divorce as a tool to motivate you into greater vigilance for your marriage.

The last reason I believe God gave us the option of divorce is just that, so that we have an option. And in case you haven't realized it yet, God is all about the choices. He created us to be beings who actively engaged in choosing our life paths, and being designed to make choices, we like to have them. When we feel like there isn't a choice, we start feel trapped and panicked. We can become angry and resentful, and I don't think I need to tell you these are not good for you or your marriage. When God, being that brilliant fellow that

He is, gave us an option, He gave us the tool to circumvented our all those icky feelings and left us with a sense of empowerment over our destiny.

Girls, we need to recognize that being married is not a onetime choice. Loving our mates is a choice we make every day. Each day when you wake up to that snoring, drooling, whiskery man with the morning breath and you give him that first kiss of the day, you have made a choice. When you cook a meal, watch what he wants on TV, do his laundry, and lay down at his side each night, you have made a choice. You may not have said the words out loud or even formed the thoughts, but you made a decision. And bravo to you for making it! But it is time that we owned it, ladies, as the honor and the blessing it is. You have been entrusted with this marriage, this man, and your children, and when we work to create a good life together with our fellow we are proving ourselves worthy of that honor.

The number one question Christian women have asked me about divorce is, "How will I know if it is the right time to decide to leave?" The answer would be so much easier if I could tell you to pee on a stick and wait for a blue line, but they haven't invented that test yet. All I can tell you is what I have experienced, and the day I left my ex-husband I knew beyond a shadow of a doubt that it was the only option that I had left. I packed boxes as I cried, but underneath all the pain there was a sense of peace and release. I knew in my heart that I had done everything I could possibly do to save our marriage, and I could go no further. Later, when friends asked me if there was any hope that we could get back together, I would remember that feeling and firmly say no. The people who loved me accepted that and supported me during this painful time.

With all my heart, I believe we should do everything in our power to preserve and improve our marriages. I don't think that divorce should be something that we take lightly or endorse as some type of quick fix, but when we have run out of options, when we are being degraded or abused, we need to remember that God has provided us with a way out. We are His treasure and sometimes taking care of what God has put under our protection means that we have take care of ourselves, even if it means doing something as hateful as choosing a divorce. Remember life isn't over even if your marriage is, but now it is time to heal.

Surviving a Divorce
or
A Time to Heal

There is no way I can address all the issues that face the women who have survived a divorce. The issues are far too many and way too varied. What I can do is encourage you to take some time to heal. As I have stated before, no one ever got a divorce because things were just too good. We only got out because we had to, and we need to tend to those wounds before we rush right back on the field.

For most women going through a divorce, the field they need to quit rushing right back onto is the marriage they just left. So often when I have talked with a woman who is trying to get out of dangerous marriage I have seen her run right back to the man who just hurt them, usually within weeks or days of leaving him in the first place. To the outsiders this is confusing and frustrating. After all, wasn't he the same guy who took a swing at her last week?

We need to understand that getting a divorce is one the scariest things a woman will ever do. Too many things are new and unknown. The world seems so much bigger than when you were single before, and that makes the world you knew – even a dangerous world, seem like a safe haven. I have heard it said that it takes a woman in an abusive relationship up to nine times before they can make a successful break. I think it took me a few more times than that, but who's counting?

Going back seems far easier than any other option out there. Not to mention that the spurned husband is making a dozen phone calls a day, showing up with roses, and promising to be superman from here on out. He is a whirlwind of passion and emotion doing everything from sobbing pitifully to threatening suicide. He seems so pathetic and broken, truly repentant, and ready to take your marriage and your feelings seriously for the first time in ages. And all the while there is the voice of Sister Goodie-goodie in the back of your head saying that a good Christian would forgive and return to the vows that she made. Meanwhile, you are feeling guilty for abandoning him, raising your kids in a broken home, and being an all around failure as a wife and a Christian. It's a deadly combination – and that's not a metaphor.

So let's call it as it is, shall we? The tears and gifts are just another attempt at manipulating you back into his control. At this point you need to remember why you left. Get some friends who are willing to keep repeating the cold hard facts of your life with him as often as you need to get the point. The threats are just his acknowledgement of defeat. He knows that he is losing his power over you, and he will try anything to scare you enough to yield. Don't do it. Get a lawyer instead and protective order if you need one.

As for Sister Goodie-goodie, tell her to take a hike. Chances are she is either jealous you have a backbone or she is trying to saddle you with the guilt she has felt when she thought of leaving her man. Either way, she isn't out to do you any favors. In fact, don't be surprised when she goes to your soon to be ex and offers him some words of encouragement. There is no doubt she is league with devil, and you should stay far, far away from her condemning voice.

What to do with the guilt you might feel about raising your kids in a broken home? Well, let's face it, home was already broken or you would still be there. Raising children in a violent or abusive environment is just as, or more, damaging than a stable single parent household. And besides that, if the ex is treating you badly you can bet it won't be long before he turns on the kids if he hasn't already. As a Godly woman can you live with that? I didn't think so.

But you don't want to be unforgiving or make the mistake of not giving it an honest try, do you? Okay, I get that, but the first thing you need to know is him being broken is not enough. We all feel badly when we are held accountable for what we have done wrong. We might even cry over having to face the consequences of our actions, but that is not the same as truly repenting. So how do you tell the difference?

You don't. Not right away. This is the time to call in a good counselor and set up a reconciliation plan. They will help you identify the mile markers that prove that the ex is making progress and truly committing himself to saving your relationship. This process should take place over months of therapy, individual and together, and you need to prepare yourself for the long haul. No moving back in, no booty calls, and no tolerance for the behaviors that got you to this point. It won't be easy, and he probably won't like it, but if he loves you he will submit himself to the process. If he refuses, run.

Which leads us to a universal fact about divorced women – we are screwed up nine ways to Sunday. And no, I am not apologizing for saying it. Look, we didn't marry the creep because we were perfectly sound and emotionally healthy. We married him because we were just as broken as he was. Emotionally healthy people do not choose emotionally crippled people to spend the rest of their lives with.

Knowing that you have a problem means that your job right now is to get better. So whether he is willing to go to counseling or not, you need to, because if you were messed up before you married him think of all the damage that has been done since then. Do you want that type of person to be the mother of your children? The example you live now will be the pattern they will live later, so make it a good one.

And guess what? This is a process that will take some time, and you need to set your mind to taking all the time you need. I know that there is something in you screaming right now, "But I don't want to be alone!" Tell it to shut up. Otherwise you are most likely in for a bad rerun of your first marriage, and if you think one divorce was bad, consider what two would be like.

If you don't identify the broken things in you that attracted your first husband to begin with those same broken parts are going to attract the same sort of man again, but in your current state you won't have the eyes to see it. Every bit of wisdom and common sense known to humanity is declaring that you need to put dating on hold for awhile. I know being alone is hard. I did it for eleven years, and no, I am not saying that you have to wait that long, but sit down with a good counselor and determine a timeline to healing. Your heart will thank you for it later on.

As a divorced woman, the number one thing you need right now are Godly friends, and I am not just talking about people who take up space in the pews on Sunday morning. I am taking about people who truly value and try to live out their faith. You need them to help talk you off the ledges and to encourage you in your new life. This network of friends will be your life line during this season in your life. They will speak truth over you and help you patch up that faith that may be a little tattered about now. They will also allow you to speak the things you feel, and let's face it, almost none of what you feel after a divorce is pretty. Emotions are wild and chaotic, and you will need a safe place to voice what is going on in your head and heart.

And as much as I hate to say it, don't rely on the women's group at Church to fulfill this role. Sure they want to be good Christian women, but honey, you just moved into a whole new category of woman – it's called a threat. For some Church women having a single woman in the mix who isn't a virgin is the scariest thing they have ever faced, and they will do whatever it takes to protect their men from you. I know you have enough going on without taking on someone else's problems of insecurity, but you need to show them some grace and stick to conversations about the weather when talking to them or their husbands. There is no need to give them any more ammunition to use against you when you are this vulnerable.

Given time, and if you conduct yourself properly, they will get over it, but in the meantime you need to be smart. Stay away from the men in the Church, particularly those who seem overly concerned with your situation, and continue to cultivate those friendships with women who can be trusted. Don't let a few rotten eggs sour you. Just remember that while you can't trust every woman carrying a Bible, there are some of us who truly do understand and want the best for you.

Once you have found us, get ready to feel some things you haven't felt in a really long time. It is amazing what can come out once you feel safe enough to actually let down your guard, and if we are good friends that is exactly what we are trying to do for you – creating a safe place for you to come alive again. Don't be taken by surprise when you find out that you are MAD, not just mad. And don't be surprised when you are MAD at the whole world, God included. There will be days when you will want to scream at the heavens demanding to know why God didn't show up and miraculously fix your husband. When they come along, just go with it. God won't be shocked, and I think He will appreciate your honesty. Being truthful with Him about your hurt will ultimately bring you closer to Him than you have ever been before, and it is really the beginning of that healing process.

During the healing process you will find you can't help but replay certain scenes of your marriage over and over again on that large screen in the front of your mind. Sometimes the images on that screen will be the places in your marriage where you were the one who screwed up. Resist the urge to think that you can rush back to the ex, plead for his forgiveness, and all will be well. It won't. As wrong as you may have been, it took two to tango, and maybe one day you will need to make a call or sit down face to face with him, but wait until the counselor gives you the green light.

In counseling you will discover new, healthier ways to deal with the conflicts of your life, coping skills, and relationship advice that no one ever told you before. While all of this is good to know, there can a tendency to feel guilty for not having gotten it right while you were married. Don't beat yourself up. You are only responsible for what you know in any given moment, and if you didn't know it when you were married, it is not your responsibility to time travel back to those times and fix it. Thank God for the new bit of knowledge and accept the responsibility for what you know in the now.

Another emotion that you should prepare for is grief. It will come, even if you were in the worst marriage imaginable. For a lot of women this is terribly confusing, and they even feel guilty for feeling this way, but you shouldn't. Yes, the marriage was awful and he treated you terribly, but at one time you loved him and you believed that he loved you or you wouldn't have married the jerk. You shared goals and dreams. You had hopes for your future, and I am sure that none of these included the divorce. So go on and grieve. Grieve the loss of that dream. Grieve the hopes that will never be fulfilled and grieve all the broken promises and lost expectations for your future. It's okay. In fact, it's normal. Feeling this way doesn't mean you want to go back. It means that you hurt because you couldn't go forward.

Use this time to discover your dream and vision for your life. Now is the time for you to move forward down a new path, a better one where you can be who your God created you to be. Rediscover who you are and what makes you tick. The majority of women who have been trapped in a bad marriage forget who they are, and even worse they have forgotten who God says that they are. Spend some time confronting and dismantling the lies that may have been spoken over you by the ex and replace them with the truth – you are the child of the King, you are loved, and you are precious to Him. If that is all you have to start with, run with it, you can get a lot of mileage out of those simple and profound words. You have a purpose in this world and it didn't disappear because you got a divorce. There is a very good possibility the divorce is what saved you so you can move into your destiny.

When it is time to move back into the dating realm, do so with caution and care. Go back and read those tips on dating in the first of this book. Come up with a plan and stick to it, because if you thought dating was rough before, it will be ten times worse now. And the main reason for that is you!

I won't lie to you. You are stepping into a mine field, and I am not trying to be discouraging. I just want you to be aware. Usually when we have been in a bad marriage one the first things that was destroyed is our sense of self-worth and attractiveness, and now you are going to be confronted with men who think that you are worth something – I mean they must, right? They take a shower, comb their hair, and put on cologne in an attempt to impress you, right? And to a woman who has not experienced any sort of affirmation of her womanliness for what may have been years, this is like gasoline on what you thought was nothing but cold ashes. You will be surprised at how quickly it can flame up.

To make matters worse, you know about sex now. You probably even had some decent sex somewhere in your marriage; you just thought you forgot what it was like. Guess what? Your body didn't, and it is aching for the chance to experience it again. I used to joke that all I had when I was married was bad sex, but sometimes I even missed that.

If that wasn't bad enough, there is this unwritten code in many Church circles that says it is okay (if not approved of) for a divorced woman to have sex outside of marriage. The justification is "well, it's not like she's a virgin." And while that statement might be true, I have yet to find anything in Scripture that says that sex outside of marriage is okay. Sorry to be the one to tell you, the same rules still apply for all the same reasons.

Set up an accountability group and give them permission to ask the hard questions. I know it may seem awkward being an adult and all, but you will need it now more than ever.

The hardest part in all of this is being alone, and I don't mean just sexually. I once offered a male friend of mine twenty bucks to just come my house and read the paper in my living room. I just wanted the presence of a man in my home again. I never found a fool proof way to get around the fact that I wanted a man's presence in my life, but I really don't think that we were intended to just get around that want. What I found instead was that all of God's great people had to go through a time of being intensely alone with God. Over and over again, I discovered stories of His chosen ones retreating or being chased into a desert or wilderness so that God could have their undivided attention, and out of these times came moments of great intimacy with their King. It didn't make the lonely go away but just knowing that I wasn't the only one to go through this made those long nights a little more bearable. In addition, knowing this gave me a new focus during those long and lonely times, and through them I came to know my Lord in a way I never would have if I had never had to face Him in the dark of the night.

Healing is a process, and processes take time. If that is the only thing you remember from all of this remember to give yourself time. I don't believe God ever has been in a hurry to do anything, but He always finishes what He started. A fact He clearly demonstrates each time it's His turn to dry the dishes.

A Passionate Love

or

The Gift of Sex

Long ago, I discovered that if you ever wanted to light off a powder keg in a Church discussion group all you had to do was to whisper the word sex. Immediately things would start to get interesting. No other topic polarizes a crowd like this one, and no one is without an opinion about what or how much should (or should not) be said. I have been politely, and not so politely, chastised for being too outspoken, and yet even during the censure there has always been a few brave souls that are willing to engage with me, to ask the questions and seek the answers that no one else has been willing to say out loud. Some would say that in writing a book such as this I am merely trying to exorcise my own demons and work through issues that solely belong to me, but I don't think so. I truly believe that there are women throughout the Church body that long to know the truth, to speak it, and to engage it. For that reason, I have written this book. Not so that you would agree with me (I couldn't care less), but rather to get the conversation started because no matter what you believe about these issues we cannot afford to be silent any longer.

For too long, we have viewed sex as synonymous with sin, shame, and disgust. We have confused being innocent with being naïve, and in our folly, we have left ourselves and our daughters defenseless in a world that is more than ready to use our sexuality as a weapon against us. Now is the time to reclaim the truth, not as I suppose it to be, but as our Father declared that it is. It is time that we stop thinking that simply teaching our daughters that saying no is enough, and we give them a vision of what God desires to teach us through this gift. For in doing so, we give them a reason to defend their hearts and bodies against those who see sex as something to be used simply for physical gratification.

Through the gift of sex God has chosen to reveal many and wondrous truths, but to see them, we have to stop shutting Him out of sex lives. We need to invite Him in, and ask Him to participate in this aspect of His creation. He is not shocked that we are sexual creatures. He is not scandalized that we deal with sexual issues, and He not is appalled that we find delight in expressing our sexuality. He knows who and what we are, always has known, and just as He desires to be our Lord in every other area of who we are, He desires to be Lord over our bodies. Our sexuality is no different and no less than the rest of us, but our little human minds recoil at the idea of a Holy God being involved in something so innately human, so raw, and so visceral as sex.

I believe that for women this matter is complicated by the brutal truths we know of our bodies. We know that our flesh is covered with scars, stretch marks, and fat rolls. Media images have confirmed that we will never be as beautiful or as perfect as we would hope to be. Thousands of products are sold each year, all with the marketing decree that we should be discreet, less aromatic, and require far more cleansing then our male counterparts. Every twenty eight days, we literally bleed with the truth that we are vessels of waste and gore, while our bodies seem determined to show they are the ultimate source of pain and betrayal as we double over with cramps. We know that in many ways we are slaves to our flesh which is constantly demanding to be served as we surrender to that craving for chocolate or salt.

The idea that God could create such a flawed being is difficult to swallow, so we chalk up our femininity to the fall because it is so much easier than believing that a good God would do this to us. Shouldering the blame of Eve, we refuse to let God close to this part of our lives, fearing that He would find it repugnant and disgusting.

And yet God paints a different picture, one we cannot escape, and He paints it in the form of a man who desires us so greatly the truth of womanhood does not dampen his ardor. For men see us as infinitely desirable, always longing to come closer, to touch and be touched by us. What we see as a source of blood, they see as the source of beauty and pleasure. For this reason, they set aside their natural aversion to blood to reach for us yet again. And for this reason, I must ask if a man whose love is flawed can find such passion for us, how can the God of love be or do any less?

In every aspect of sex, God is longing to teach us more of Himself, to offer one more revelation, one more part of who He is. Not simply to offer us mere information, but rather that we know He is a God who desires that we experience Him just as greatly as He desires to experience us. He knows such revelations require that we lay aside our self-created coverings to stand naked and vulnerable before His gaze, just as we do with an earthly lover. Sex is the picture of trust, where we declare that we know that His love and grace will see past the ugly to the beauty that lies within us.

And yet even as He longs for us, He waits. He waits with all the desire and expectancy of a groom awaiting his bride, knowing that even one day too soon would diminish the moment, leaving us scarred and hurt by His expression of love out of season. Nor should we miss that in the wait, God is there teaching us. Teaching us a love worth having is love that values our wholeness above any self-serving desire, and the wait is nothing more than a time of preparation so we can move into deeper intimacy with the one who loves us. Yet greater still, the wait itself is a blessed revelation of our Lord to us, for in waiting we are allowed just a taste of how greatly this time of self-denial must cost Him – a revelation of God's heart that will only be known by those who have experienced the beautiful anguish of knowing their lover is separated from their touch by only a few treasured and hateful days.

When we know this of our Lord, how can we trade away this gift for a few flowery compliments? A couple of cheap baubles? Or promises that will never be fulfilled? God has set the standard for love and the expression. He has lived it since the dawn of time and asks that we honor His love by doing the same for only few short years of our lives. He is, and should be, our standard by which all potential lovers live and die in our eyes, for ultimately it was His life and death that made ours worth living.

Am I reaching too far by making such bold comparisons? I think not. I have barely scratched the surface of what He has to say about our sexuality and His love for us. He loves us, and as women who love our God, we should love what He loves with a love that includes our bodies and all they represent. For we too present a picture of our Lord to the world. We are the ones who give life through our sacrifice, just as He gave life in His. Our hearts were designed to love and nurture those who have entrusted their hearts to us, just as He does for all who entrust their hearts to Him. We arouse men to be more than they dreamed they could be, just as God arouses the hearts of humanity to believe and hope for something greater than this reality alone. And as we offer ourselves in love to a heart worthy of ours, we demonstrate the sweetness of surrender and the joy being vulnerable before a God who desires to know His creation.

Even as I extol the virtues of our sex, my hope is that you know that this just a glimmer of the truth. A truth that surpasses our ability to understand here and now, flawed and falling so short of the love God desires to lavish on His people. For what He offers us is greater than sex, and the love He bestows is more powerful than what we will know here in this world. Sex is simply the picture, not the definition, and an old grainy snapshot at best, but in it is a lesson small enough for us to grasp.

Our sexuality gives us the ability to receive and communicate God's love as no other part of creation can, and it is a message whose truth and integrity we must guard. Yet, no message is ever complete until it is shared. For this reason we must be part of the conversation, telling our daughters and the world the truth of God's great love for humanity, no matter how undeserving we might be. We should not surrender our sexuality to our shame, or sacrifice it to the world to use as they see fit. As ones who know the truth our voices should be the loudest and the clearest – Yes, we are flawed. Yes, we are sinful, but a Holy God still desires to know and be known by me for His love is great enough to find beauty even in one such as me. That my dear sisters, is the most beautiful and scandalous message the world will ever know.

Miscellaneous

or

Scandalous Tidbits

Remember if you are hoping for a how to manual, you have the wrong book. Tons of them have been written, and written better than I could have done. The purpose of this book is to talk about the questions that single and married women of all ages have asked me. So if some of this seems a little random it is because it is. Remember, I am not claiming to have all the answers. I just want to help us have the conversations we need and the conversations our daughters need to hear.

Warning this gets extremely graphic. These are real questions that women have asked me and the answers I gave as best I remember them. You may not agree with what I have to say, but at the very least, it can give you an idea of what women, especially young girls preparing to enter a sexual relationship are concerned with. I applaud the girls who had the courage to ask, and I applaud the women who care enough to give an honest answer. So if you are single, but a sexual relationship is in your distant future, read with caution. If you are woman who is talking to other women about these issues, use this section to help prepare yourself for the questions you might encounter. And finally, don't just accept what I have to say. Pray about your responses and do as the Father prompts you.

How to Answer a Question About Sex

Women of all ages have questions about sex, especially our young women who have had little or no sexual experience. Often they don't quite know how to phrase the question they really want to ask, or they are just too shy. So when we are speaking to them about sex, we really need to do more listening that talking. Let me walk you through the number one question I get asked by high school and college girls, and share what I say, and what I know about the question they really have.

Question: What does sex feel like?

I really haven't come up with a great answer for this, because how do you tell someone what it feels like? Moms, aunts, and adopted moms and aunts, if you get asked a question like this it is a great time to work on your listening skills. Our girls aren't stupid. They know that you aren't going to be able to answer this question to their satisfaction, so they have to be asking something more. The clues in the rest of the conversation will tell you what that is.

Often what is going on here is a fishing expedition in hopes of finding some sort of loophole around the "no sex before marriage" rule. Girls come to me all the time hoping that I will show them one. They have a tendency to think that because I am so open I might not suffer from the same hang-ups that their parents, preachers, and youth leaders do. (I can be so very disappointing sometimes.) Knowing this is what they expect of me helps me answer the question in a way that reaffirms what they have been taught without preaching, and let's face it, no one wants to be preached at.

Answer: Sex is okay. Making love is mind blowing.

Did you catch how I set up the chance for them to ask another question? And guess what, they do! When a person asks a question, they are really signaling that they are ready for some more information, and this is great because giving anyone information before they are ready for it is a complete waste of time.

Question: So what's the difference?

Answer: Sex is a biological function in which two people exchange body fluids. So if you will allow me to spit in your mouth you will have a pretty good idea of what it's like. (Insert horrified scream here.)

Don't be afraid to ask them questions. By asking them to articulate what they are thinking or how they feel, you are helping them solidify what they believe and know to be true.

My Question: Why do you think that's gross? I have swallowed tons of Ty's spit, maybe more than he has, and it's fabulous. (Gagging to follow). Look, sex with just anyone is gross, because that is all it is, biology. Body fluids are disgusting when they belong to stranger or even a friend, because after all, I'm your friend, but you won't let me near you now. So there has to be some reason why we are willing to engage in this nasty event. If it is just hormones, we are no better than the animals following our basest instinct, and I can guarantee you that after they wear off all you are going to feel is gross. However, if you love them, if they really love you the body fluids are such a small part of what is happening. (At this point, my young audience is usually still hung up on the image of sharing body fluids.)

My Question: Have you ever held hands with a guy? Did you stop to think that even then you were sharing body fluids, your sweaty palm against his sweaty palm?

(Now they compulsively wipe their hands on their jeans, my furniture, or my carpet. Horrified they had ever done this with any guy ever.)

Think of this feeling only a million times worse. (Heads begin to nod with mystified horror and comprehension). But when it is someone you love, it is all about knowing them, experiencing them, even the gross parts and because when you love them it's not gross anymore. It's beautiful because they are experiencing you in the same way. But there is only one way to know if they are committed to loving you as much as you have to love them to give them this gift, a wedding ring, and the rest of their lives.

Question and Answer Time

Question: What should I expect on the wedding night?

Translation: What's will it be like to lose my virginity? Will be like all the romantic movies and books?

Answer: Not what you think. There is just way too much hype about how amazing it is going to be. Oh, don't get me wrong, it's a fabulous moment in your life, to finally get to be with the man who promises to love you forever, but nothing is like it is in the movies.

Look, the truth is neither one will know what you are doing. Even if you have been with someone else, everyone's different. So there will be a bumbling around, feeling embarrassed and awkward, but he will be feeling the same way. Only he will be dealing with a lot more pressure. The key is to focus on enjoying each other. Don't worry if it doesn't look like what you had hoped. And don't worry if everything doesn't go smoothly or as well as you planned. You get to try again, and again, to get it right. Practicing is part of the fun, so just relax and go with it.

Question: What if he doesn't think I am any good in bed?

Translation: My boyfriend is pressuring me to have sex and claiming that we need to know if we are compatible.

Answer: Then it is his fault. There is something wrong with him. Look, sex can always be better in some form or fashion. There are just too many variables to get all of it right all the time, but the truth is a good sex life is about discovering the things that make it good. If he thinks that you aren't any good, it's because he has some unrealistic expectations, and he needs to come to grips with the fact that his penis is not a magic wand. It takes practice on both your parts for it to be amazing.

If he is worried about it being bad, he is really worried about how well he is going to perform, or he is using a worn out line to get you in bed before the proper time. Tell him to think up some new material, and to get lost. A man who really loves you will be willing to invest the time and energy to make it good for both of you, including the time waiting until you are married.

And besides that, I have never met a man who said that any woman who allowed him to have sex with her was bad at it. A naked, willing woman is a great woman in bed, and usually, we don't have to worry about being anything more.

Question: What if I can't/ don't have an orgasm the first time?

Answer: Then we will throw a party when you get back and welcome you to the club. Most women don't have an orgasm the first time out. If you do, count yourself lucky. If you don't, don't sweat it. We have to learn how to have an orgasm. Believe it or not it is not something our bodies automatically know how to do. We have to learn how to respond to our men, and how to let go of our inhibitions long enough to be caught up in the sensations.

There are a lot of women out there who have never had one, because they never learned how. They don't know how their bodies work or what they need to set them over that edge, but part of the reason for a honeymoon is so the two of you have the time and freedom to learn how to please each other. So take that time to explore and discover what it is that feels good, and you do the same for him. If you can talk about it openly, the two of you will figure it out together.

And don't be surprised even you if have had an orgasm before that it doesn't happen right out of the gates the first time you make love to your husband. If you were waiting, like you are supposed to, he doesn't know all your "easy buttons" yet. But you will be learning how to please each other together, and that's what it is all about. This is truly something that gets better with time and experience. Ask any woman who has been married for more than 15 years – she will tell you that the first few years were nothing to what is going on in the bedroom now.

Question: Should I fake it if I don't have an orgasm?

Answer: Absolutely not! How is he going to get better if you are giving him false information?

Question: Is it really that bad that I've had sex even though I'm not married?

Answer: Yes. Sorry, I can't candy coat it for you. I couldn't candy coat my sexual history for myself. It affects us, and there is no way around it. I mean, I didn't catch any sort of disease or have any children outside of marriage, but I have those memories embedded in my mind, and they like to rear their ugly heads whenever I am least expecting it.

The part I didn't expect is how damaging the "good" memories are. You know the times when it felt really great. I expected the memories of the abuse to be worse, and cause me more problems, but that hasn't been the case. This is why it is so important not to give that part of yourself away even when it feels right in the moment.

Question: I was kissing my boyfriend and I got this funny feeling . . . uh, down there, was it an orgasm?

Answer: You will know an orgasm when you have one. You probably just got excited and maybe got close, but if you have to ask, you didn't.

Question: Is that bad?

Answer: Yes, and no. You had a normal response to a guy, but it is a sign you need to cool it before things go too far.

Question: Can I really be happy only having sex with one man for the rest of my life? Shouldn't I have some experience with at least one other man?

Answer: You can absolutely be happy with only having been with one man. I am not saying you will never see another man who might tempt you, but when you really love someone he will be the one you want. And as you learn to enjoy each other, he will be able to satisfy as no one else.

Believe me, it is far better to be someone who has few or no emotional scars, or attachments to a man or men in your past. Any sexual relationship not with your spouse is going to cause some problems for the two of you, some major, some minor. So if you will trust that God has a plan and purpose for a monogamous relationship in a covenant marriage, you will be much happier than any girl who goes out chasing some unrealistic dream we have been sold about sex.

Question: What if he isn't that big?

Answer: You just won the lottery! Guys with big penises think that they are fantastic lover just because they are big. So they have a tendency to rely on their size rather than on technique, and girl, you want him to learn his technique.

Your vajayjay is really only sensitive for the first one third of the way in. That's all he needs to reach. And since the average vagina is only five inches deep that means that he only needs one and seven eighths of inches of penis to get the job done. And since the average penis tops out at five and half, you really don't have that much to worry about.

Question: What if he's too big?

Answer: Highly unlikely. After all one day you will push a baby out of that same opening, so he will probably fit. Most men aren't over five and half inches, but even the enormous eight incher isn't too bad.

If it is uncomfortable, tell him. He doesn't want to hurt you, and he may need to shorten his strokes. He can do that and your body will learn to compensate for him. If it turns out to be a problem, then you both need to go to a doctor and get some help.

Question: What should I tell the doctor? How do you even begin to tell him what's going on?

Answer: The same way you would tell me. Just lay it out for him. He has been trained to deal with these issues and shouldn't be embarrassed by a patient describing symptoms.

Question: If I have a pelvic exam will I still be a virgin?

Answer: Yes, the doctor should ask you about your sexual history before he performs the exam and will use what you tell him to take the appropriate steps.

Question: I have only had one sexual encounter. Do I need to go to the doctor? He seemed like a clean guy.

Answer: Yes, because honey, clean doesn't prevent STD's and just because he didn't have any open sores doesn't mean he didn't have anything. You will need to have a vaginal exam and blood work. And don't think that just because you haven't had any symptoms means you are alright. Many STD's do not have any noticeable signs but can be quietly eating away on your insides. If they are caught and treated soon enough you might be able to avoid any long term damage. If not, you might be looking at fertility problems somewhere down the line. Go get the exam.

Question: What do I need to tell my boyfriend about my sexual history?

Answer: Everything. I don't mean details. He probably doesn't want or need a play by play, but you need to let him know the truth about what you have done. If you have fooled around, but not gone all the way, he needs to know that too. If there has been any abuse, you need to tell him that. And he needs to be honest with you too, because all this will affect your life together.

Question: Is sex messy?

Translation: How much "ick factor" is going to be happening? And will it totally gross me out?

Answer: Only if you are doing it right. Sure, there is some mess, but honey, you won't be thinking about it really. Put a hand towel, wash cloth, or box of Kleenex by the bed if you are worried, and go wash up afterwards. Better yet, wash each other up.

And be prepared for the post-sex positioning where neither one of you wants to lie in the wet spot. Use a towel, cover it if you need to, or if you want there are talc sprays available on the internet. Just spray it on and it is dry in five minutes, and they smell good too.

Question: Will it hurt?

Answer: Depends. It depends on how worked up you are, how sensitive he is being, and how you are made. Take it slow, and spend plenty of time on the foreplay.

Also, you should go to the doctor before you get married and have an exam. She/he can tell you if you should be concerned. If the hymen is too thick, they can tell you and may suggest that they do something in the office to make it easier. If you are okay with letting them do that, and aren't upset by the fact that your husband doesn't get to do the honors, it can alleviate some of you fears.

You should also know that you will probably be tender for a few days afterwards. You will be using some new muscles that haven't been exercised before. This is normal, and it shouldn't stop you from having more sex. I recommend a whirlpool tub to help you feel better. Also, don't be afraid to take a couple of pain relievers right before or immediately after - your body will thank you.

If your girlie parts are sore you can also use some Oragel to help. It doesn't take much and it is safe. Just remember if you wouldn't stick it in your mouth, don't put it down there.

Question: Can it really make you sick?

Answer: Yes, I have a tendency to get urinary tract infections, and they are awful. Start taking cranberry supplements the week before and right on through for at least the first month. Get your eight glasses of water a day, and always use the bathroom afterward sex.

Our urethra is really short and intercourse can act like a pump, sending all sorts of bacteria up to your bladder. It is important that it get flushed out.

Question: Every time I get excited, I feel like I have to pee. Will I pee on him?

Answer: Not really. Some urine may escape, but those muscles have been designed to clamp shut when we are excited, so don't worry. In fact, you may notice that it takes you awhile to go the bathroom after sex because those muscles are having to get the signal it okay to turn loose now.

Question: Will he think I smell bad?

Answer: Men are strange, and most men love the way we smell down there. So keep it clean, and that means actually washing out each crack and crevice intentionally, and you should be good.

Question: Should I douche so I won't smell bad?

Answer: No, the vagina is self cleaning. Douching messes with our natural pH and bacteria we need down there. So if the doctor doesn't order it, don't mess with what's not broken.

It's also a good idea to avoid all those feminine deodorant products out there. They aren't harmful, but our guys really do like the way we smell.

Question: Will he stink?

Answer: Everyone has some type of unique aroma from that area, but when we love someone we usually don't find it offensive. In fact, the way a person smells is part of what attracts us to them in the first place.

Don't be surprised when you realize that smell of your man coming in from a hot and sweaty day outside working turns you on.

Question: Will it smell when we have sex?

Answer: Yep, but you probably won't mind. If you think it is going to be big deal light some scented candles and use that sheet spray.

Question: What if he gets done before I do?

Answer: This is a very real possibility, but don't worry, if the two of you have been waiting, he will be ready to go again pretty quick. If not, he can use this as an opportunity to finish up with his hands. Don't take it as a bad omen for the rest of your marriage. It just means you get him that excited. The two of you can work together to extend the pleasure, just be sensitive and don't belittle him for being a little quick on the trigger. He probably needs some practice, too.

Question: What if I fart?

Answer: You will both laugh and keep going. And don't be surprised if you queef, otherwise known as a vagina fart. It's normal. With all that pumping action sometimes air gets forced into the vagina and has to come out. You will both laugh about that too, and some guys like it. They say it feels good.

Question: Will he expect me to go down on him?

Translation: I cannot imagine sticking that thing in my mouth.

Answer: Yes, every guy out there wants his woman to go down on him, but if he has any amount of consideration, he won't rush you. And when you are ready, wash it yourself. No one wants day-old dick in their mouth.

And remember, if you expect him to do it for you, you should be willing to return the favor. And trust me, you want him to be so generous.

Question: Do I swallow or spit, or do I have to deal with that?

Answer: It's up to you. You can just use in foreplay, so it doesn't have to be an issue. You decide what you are comfortable with.

Question: What if I gag?

Answer: Stop being so ambitious. Take smaller bites. He won't mind.

Question: Should we use toys?

Answer: Only if you are both comfortable with them. Just don't rush it. I would wait until you have had some time just the two of you. However, toys can be fun, and there is no Biblical mandate against them. Talk it over and decide what the two of you are comfortable with, and enjoy.

Question: Should we have anal sex?

Translation: Can I have anal sex before marriage and still be considered a virgin?

Answer: Why? Really? You have a vagina specifically designed for this purpose. Your anus wasn't. It can lead to some really bad tears, which can put you in the hospital, weakening of the sphincter which can lead to anal leakage, and can lead to some pretty nasty infections. It may feel good, but why take the risk?

And just remember, sex is sex. Whether it is oral, anal, or regular, it all leaves a mark, and the mark anal sex can leave is not one you want to have to explain to your husband, especially if he isn't the one who gave it to you.

Question: What about tying each other to the bed, food, and stuff?

Translation: Is it okay to be "kinky"?

Answer: These are all things that you two are going to have to work out and discuss. I don't think that there is anything wrong with any of it if you are both loving each other while you use the props. It can be fun to playfully torment each other with feathers or to tease the other person when they can't do anything about it, but just be sure you aren't degrading each other in the process.

And by the way, chocolate stains are a pain to get out of sheets, honey is miserable in your hair, and whipped cream needs to be cleaned up immediately or it can stink – or so I heard?

Question: Should I shave or wax before the honeymoon?

Answer: This is not the time to do anything majorly different down there. You will be doing enough new stuff without adding to your body's stress. Besides, stubble which you will have by the second day is a turn off. Not to mention, that hair was put there as a way to decrease friction and to add to the stimulus. Also, most men hate bare girlie bits. It is a sign of our womanhood, and they don't like feeling like they are with a little girl. Better yet, condition it so it is smoother. Later, you can see if it is something you both like.

Question: I think that it would be cleaner if he shaved before the honeymoon, should I ask him to do that?

Answer: I wouldn't. Women whose sexual partners shave report having less satisfaction with the event. Besides, the stubble feels like sandpaper and I don't think you need your crotch sanded, do you? But once again, if you decide to experiment later, that's up to you.

Question: Where is my clitoris?

Translation: I haven't found it, or I have, but I don't know if I can direct him to it.

Answer: Find the man in the canoe! He's the one with his head sticking up that makes you feel funny when it gets touched. If he can't find it, take his hand and guide him.

Question: What if I don't like it (sex)?

Answer: Then somebody's doing it wrong, and you may need some time as a couple to figure out what that may mean. Just don't close yourself off to having a great sex life. If time doesn't fix it or it is physically painful you need to see a doctor to check for a medical cause.

Use your network of friends to discover the tips that can help you learn and grow. Speak to your husband, share what you are feeling, and ask him to help you find ways to make it enjoyable. Just remember, that this is about your feelings and your experience. He may not realize that there is something wrong, and you need to approach him gently. You never want to make him fill deficient in this area. Remind him that you love him and you do like __(fill in the blank with specific things he does that you enjoy)__, and ask him to help you move into the next level. It can be a fun discovery, if you relax and go with the flow.

And don't let embarrassment stop you. God intends for this to be good for both of you. It is one of the ways we draw closer to our spouse and learn to be vulnerable with each other. It is how we learn to rely on another human being to meet our needs and how we learn to meet another's need. Work at it. Do what it takes to make this a fulfilling experience for both of you.

Question: I don't think I can be naked in front of him. What should I do?

Answer: There are three things to keep in mind. One: you aren't expected to walk in and do a striptease for him. You are going to progress to the state of nakedness, hopefully with some hugging and kissing and other things that send your head "areeling" along the way.

At this point, you need to do one thing and one thing only – shut off your brain. Your body will do the rest. Just respond to his touch and you will forget how awkward it is. Two: Buy a pretty negligee for the evening if one of your friends doesn't get you one, and light some candles. Bright lights can be overwhelming, so ease into it with some mood lighting. Three: We feel less naked in water, so take a bath. Use some bubbles to play hide and seek. It will take the edge off.

Question: I don't think I can even look at him naked. What should I do?

Answer: Showers! The stalls are typically small so you are right up against each other, and they don't really allow a lot of room for looking – until you get creative. Again you have the water, so you don't feel so naked. Wash each other's back. You can stand to check out his butt, especially since he can't see you. Let your hands do some meandering and soon you will find that he isn't too bad to look at.

Question: But don't "they" look funny?

Translation: I've never seen a penis, and I am totally scared of what it is going to look like!

Answer: I think God was high the day He made penises, but what do I know? Yes, it is one funny looking piece of equipment, but it is part of your man. And for most men a big part of their identity is wrapped up in it. So accept it for what it can do for you and the fact it belongs to the man you love. Before too long, it won't seem so strange.

Question: Should I touch his balls?

Answer: You need to ask him. Some men love it. Some men don't. So find out what he likes. He'll let you know.

Question: What should I call his . . . uh, stuff, you know his boy parts?

Answer: You can begin by calling them by the correct names, penis, scrotum, and testicles. As you guys begin to have conversations about your sex life, he will let you know how he typically refers to the "boys", so just follow his lead.

Question: Do we really need to talk about it?

Answer: Yep, you need to talk about your sex life. And you need to do it before you get married. In today's world, most men have had sex in their teen years, they have been exposed to all sorts of sexual influences, and they certain ideas about what sex should be like. You need to know what they are, and he needs to know what yours are.

And you need to be specific. I know this sounds improper, but you don't want to get married to a man and find out he is really into things you don't want to do. Talk about oral sex, positions, anal sex, and frequency. Does he expect you meet him at the door when he comes home from work? Or should you wait for him handcuffed to the bed? Morning sex? Night sex? How about some afternoon delight? Does he like costumes or does he just want you to curl up next him naked? Anything that concerns you or anything you especially want should be talked about.

If you are worried about the conversation becoming too heated or impassioned, ask a trusted friend or marriage counselor to mediate. If you just can't say the words, write letters, but don't go into this with your eyes closed.

Question: When should we have this conversation?

Answer: I think the answer really depends on you and the type of relationship you have with your guy. If you are both young, come from similar backgrounds (such as you attended the same youth group in high school), it is a conversation that can wait until you are engaged or at least, seriously moving towards getting married.

As a single woman in my thirties, I often had this conversation pretty quickly into the dating process. By the time men had reached that age, they were experienced enough to know what they were looking for in a sexual partner and spouse. Many had gone through marriages were their former wife was unwilling to even meet them half way in the sexual arena, and these guys had no intention of getting into that situation again. The conversation may not have been as detailed in the beginning of the relationship, but once things began moving towards something more serious, it quickly got there.

Question: What if he wants me to do something I think is wrong?

Answer: It depends on what it is and where you are getting your definition of wrong. If it doesn't violate a Biblical principle and you don't feel like he is trying to hurt or degrade you, give it a try. It might be your new favorite thing.

If it doesn't meet that criteria or you are not sure, ask him for some time. Truthfully, tell him you will consider it, but you need a chance to think and pray about it. If he loves you he will be okay with it, and you can do something else to fill the time. (Hint, hint, hint.) Then seek out some Godly counsel, and do some research.

As far as I am concerned there are very few things that are wrong in a sexual relationship within a marriage covenant. The number one thing is this is between you and him. No one else, so no inviting anyone else into your bedroom, and that includes films and pornography. Sex should never put you or him at risk for injury or infection, and you both should feel valued and loved in any sexual encounter. If he isn't asking you to do anything of this nature, you might want to ask yourself why you think it is wrong, and if that is a right conclusion.

If you don't believe that it violates a Scriptural principal, but still don't feel okay with it, talk to him. Let him know that you aren't ignoring him, and that you want your sex life to be good, but you just aren't ready to do that. Believe it or not, he will probably be okay with just knowing you are open to discussing new adventures with him.

Also men tend to be less adventurous than what they claim to be. Most men talk big before the wedding, but afterwards they are just so happy to be getting some that they forget about all their outrageous ideas and want to get down to business.

Question: What about birth control?

Frequent Translation: Can I use birth control and not get caught having sex before marriage?

Answer: I hate it, especially the pill, patch, shot and condoms. I think they are nasty inventions designed to make our lives miserable, but these are decisions that the two of you need to make together with the counsel of a good doctor. You need to take into account that there are side effects to hormonal birth control, including weight gain and mood swings. And you will need to start them up six months before you get married. With the pill, you will be locked into a daily dosage plan that cannot be messed with, or you have just messed up how effective it will be, and you have to be careful about antibiotics and even some foods. Personally, I never had a good reaction to having my body high-jacked by artificial hormones, but some women swear by them.

As for condoms, they are unreliable. Too many well educated and experienced people have had one break or leak, and I can tell you stories of women I know personally who now have children thanks to those happy accidents. And I never liked the way they felt, nor do most men. The goal of intercourse is to be united, and I think that takes away from the unity.

Whatever you chose needs to be a joint decision, and a part of at least one of those sex talks you have with your fiancée. This is something that will affect the rest of your lives, and you need to be in agreement over it. And no one else can make the decision for you. So do your research, look on-line, read customer reviews and what the doctors are saying. Be sure to take into account any medical conditions you may have, as well as, determining a time line for if and when you want to have kids, because all of this will play into your ultimate decision.

Question: Can I have sex on my period?

Answer: Sure can, and it can even help alleviate some menstrual cramps. Just be sure to warn him first. For some men it is no big deal, for others they just want to wait it out, and you need to respect his decision on this.

Some men deal with this by making this the time of the month for shower sex, or you can throw down a big bath towel first. Be advised that it can get pretty messy depending on your flow, and all those sex fluids can make it seem like there is far more blood than there actually is. Grab a wet washcloth or baby wipes before hand to handle the mess, and enjoy.

Also, you might consider using a menstrual cup. The disposable type can be used while having sex and they block the flow making it less messy.

Question: What is a menstrual cup?

Answer: My new best friend! A menstrual cup is a great alternative to tampons and pads. It is simply a cup that you insert vaginally to collect the fluid. And it can be left in for up to 12 hours. There are several varieties including reusable cups that can be purchased online, and while the initial cash outlay is pricey, they can save you a ton of money in the long run.

However, I would advise that you experiment with a disposable brand to see if you are comfortable with this method. Even though there is a significant difference between the reusable and the disposable, it is such a foreign concept to most of us that it helps acclimate us to the idea. And while I love them, many of my friends do not feel the same way. They can be tricky to use at first and can be messy to change since they collect the fluid instead of absorbing it. I recommend changing them in the shower until you get the hang of it. And even if you don't think they are for you, consider keeping them on hand if you have sex during your period.

Question: Is missionary the only Christian position for sex?

Answer: (Trying not to burst into hysterical laughter). Not if you are flexible – in more than one way. The Bible never prescribes a particular position or declares that another is wrong. So have fun, experiment, and find what works for you.

Question: Should Christians consult sex books for ideas?

Answer: You need to be careful about this one. Start with good Christian works about sex and see what they have to say. Now, I will be the first to say I don't always agree with them, but they will not lead you into any questionable behavior or recommend something blatantly wrong, like relying on porn to spice up your sex life.

If you do look at secular works, be sure you have a pretty solid grasp of the Biblical principles about sex. And a side note about the most famous sex book ever, the Kama Sutra. This book was written when the penis topped out about four inches, it was next to impossible for a man to hurt a woman by penetrating too deep. Over the years, thanks to better nutrition, that has changed, and some of the positions in this book can actually injure you, so be careful. Experimentation should stop if there is ever any pain or possibility of injury.

Question: I like to have my hair pulled, bite, scratch, etc., is this okay?

Answer: First know that as women our pain threshold increases dramatically when we are aroused. Things that we ordinarily could not stand, feel amazing during sex, but we need to be careful – after all, you don't want to have to explain some unintentional bruising to a boss or worried parents. And walking like a duck the next day isn't too much fun either.

Sometimes a little rough stuff is fun, if you know when and where to draw the line. Every girl wants to know that her man wants and needs her NOW with a primal need that leaves no room for niceties, but both of you need to remember that in your enthusiasm you might not realize exactly how rough you are being or being handled. If you do engage in some rough stuff, make sure you have constant verbal interaction, letting each other know how much is enough and how much is too much.

Remember it's all about being loved and valued, even in the rough stuff, because even then it's not about being forced to do anything – it is about raw desire and experiencing your love for each other in a very passionate, uninhibited way.

Question: Should I use sex toys if I am single?

Answer: I advise against it. As women we teach ourselves how to have an orgasm, and the stimulation provided by toys is not the same as the stimulation of real sex. Toys are often more intense, and if that is what we are used to it can make having an orgasm with the real thing more difficult. Not to mention, if you use a toy for penetration you run the risk of breaking the hymen, the technical sign of being a virgin.

Question: Is it true women can become addicted to vibrators?

Answer: I don't know if addicted is the right word, but vibrators provide a much more intense stimulation than a penis, hand, or tongue. Some have claimed that with repeated use over time the intensity can damage nerves to the point that only a vibrator will provide sufficient stimulation. So if you use them, use with caution, if at all.

Question: If I am married and we decide to purchase sex toys, where should I get them?

Answer: This one is tricky. While I don't believe we should be ashamed of pursuing a fun and exciting sex life, even one that includes various toys and aids, we still need to be careful about what we expose ourselves and our husbands to. So going to the local sex shop isn't always a good idea. Most of these stores have assorted pornography on open display, and I don't think it is fair to drag a man through that. And it probably isn't a good idea for a woman to go alone.

You can search the internet, but beware. You never know what you may find out there.

My best source has been lingerie parties in the homes of my trusted friends. Typically, the sales lady comes prepared with products for sale and of course, you can order out of a catalogue and have it shipped to your house in that plain brown package. An added bonus, she will explain how all that stuff is used.

Question: What can I do to make it better for him? Are there any exercises?

Answer: Yes, and they aren't just good for him. In fact, we should all be doing them on a regular basis. They are called Kegels, and they strengthen the vaginal muscles and the muscles that control the bladder. Simply flex you pelvic muscles as if you were trying to stop peeing, hold for a slow three count, and repeat until you are tired. If you want to step it up a notch, they make vaginal balls that you insert. Each ball has a weight inside that moves freely. As the weight hits the outer ball, it vibrates gently causing a reflexive tightening of the vaginal muscles. They can be used at any time, and no one will know except you. These can be bought at those lingerie parties.

Question: Is it true that vibrators can get "lost"?

Answer: Not if you use them only in the vagina. The vagina is closed off at the other end by the cervix blocking off anything that might want to travel out the other end. So you really don't have to worry about that. However, when used in the butt the answer is yes. Not only that they can actually travel up the colon and have been found buzzing away deep inside the abdomen. And that means surgery – wouldn't you like the pastor come visit you in the hospital for that one?

Anyway, bear in mind that should you experiment with any sort of anal stimulation, you should never use anything that might slip, because once the sphincter tightens down you are going to need medical intervention.

Question: What is "rimming"?

Answer: Rimming is the act of kissing or licking the butthole. I hope you know enough to know that this is a bad idea. I won't even try to list the different types of bacterial infections that you can contract from this practice – even if you are the one on the receiving. After all, I am assuming that if you are doing this with a fella, you are probably kissing him too. Now consider where his tongue has been and think about that image – how do you feel about swapping spit now?

Question: What is "fisting"?

Answer: Oh dear Lord, the fact that I even have to answer this question bugs me, but I hear it all the time. Fisting is the act of sticking one's fist – the entire thing up another person's butt (or vagina). I have been told that some people find considerable pleasure in this, but I keep thinking about the largest dump I have ever taken and the size of someone's fist. To me it just doesn't make sense, and no, the idea of doing this to someone else holds no appeal to me – that's where they keep the poop.

As far as vaginal fisting, well, the vagina is highly stretchy, and that's your call. Just bear in mind that it is not something you just do. It takes considerable time and preparation. From what I understand there is no worries about the vagina returning to its original state after being stretched like that, but it was never a risk I wanted to take.

Question: Is anal sex safe?

Answer: The research is conflicting, but no one can deny that people have been injured in the act. The butt was meant to be an exit not an entrance, so any time outside pressure is applied the sphincter contracts making entry nearly impossible without careful dilation (read that stretching out parts that weren't meant to stretch that way). Moving too fast or applying to much pressure can damage the muscles, not to mention that the parts on the inside of us are usually more fragile than the parts on the outside of us. Also, our bodies don't provide the same defenses against sexually transmitted diseases back there as it does in the vagina, so it is not a safe alternative to conventional sex – the only thing you might be avoiding is pregnancy, but even that isn't guaranteed because all it takes is a drip in the wrong place and one ambitious little swimmer.

Question: Then why do people do it?

Answer: Because no matter how we feel about all of this, there are a ton of nerves back there and they can provide a significant amount of sexual stimulation. What we need to bear in mind is there are risks and that God did provide a way for us to find sexual satisfaction in a way that doesn't require that we run the chance of a perforated colon (read that as a hole that lets the poop out to run amuck in your body).

Question: My fiancée says he really wants to try anal sex at least once after we are married. Should I let him?

Answer: I wouldn't, and I would tell him that before the wedding. Look, the anus is tighter than the vagina, after all it was designed to keep things in, and that means that it can be far more stimulating than the vagina for some men. However, if there are no medical complications, the vagina offers more than enough stimulation for a man to achieve a climax – in fact, most men's problem is that even the vagina is too stimulating and they have a hard time hanging in there long enough for us to get there.

If he isn't getting enough stimulation vaginally to get the job done, there is reason, and if you have ruled out all the medical ones, we could be dealing with a mindset that only finds the taboo or "dirty" aspects of sex to be arousing and can indicate a larger problem that needs to be addressed.

And I am assuming that since you asked the question you are not too comfortable with the idea, so tell him. If he hesitates to choose you over the hopes of anal sex – honey, show him the door.

Question: My boyfriend and I have already had sex. Does this mean I have to marry him?

Answer: No. Two wrongs don't make a right and marrying someone because you think you have to is never a good thing. If you don't want to marry him, get out now. If you do want to marry him, stop what you are doing and both of you find accountability partners of the same sex to help you relearn how to be a couple.

The truth is once unmarried couples start having sex, they tend to stop doing everything else, and that means you really have no idea of where you are in this relationship. You might discover that the two of you bypassed some really important developmental points in your relationship, and you will have to go back and work through them now. It won't be easy, because working through all the issues it takes to be a solid couple will be harder than just jumping each other's bones, but the quality of your future together depends on it.

Question: Am I still "pure" if I have been raped or molested?

Answer: YES. YES. YES. You did not sin, a sin was committed against you and there is no shame in that. The fault and blame lies strictly upon the person who would do such a horrible thing. In God's eyes you are as pure as the day you were born, and He does not see you as any less beautiful for what you have endured.

Question: I am a virgin, but my boyfriend is not. Should I break up with him?

Answer: I can't answer this one for you. You have to decide how you feel about this one and live with your decision. Ideally, I would hope that you have your mind made up before you get into a relationship so that your final decision can be the result of your convictions and not the product of your hormones or his charm.

I would encourage you to consider how he views his past, and go from there. Does he think it was no big deal? Does he believe that it was simply something that happened with that girl and may happen again, but he is willing to abstain for you because you are special? Does he consider memories of those times his standard for good sex or funny? If you answered yes to any of these, you probably need to get out. He doesn't put the same value on sex as you do and that is going to make for a messy and painful relationship.

However, if he sees it as a mistake, is truly repentant, and is willing to wait not just for you, but for his wife, he might be a keeper.

Question: How do I stop daydreaming about sex?

Answer: First off, stop telling yourself to stop thinking about it. That is the worst thing you can do. After all, if I tell you not to think about purple bananas, what's the first thing you think about? And I bet you never entertained a single thought about purple bananas before. What I did was come up with a list of things I liked to think about – things that had nothing to do with sex, so no weddings, no dream dates, no thoughts of future kids, nothing – and as soon as sex popped into my mind I switched to the assigned thoughts. No scolding myself for being a bad or weak person. No "why did I think that?" Just replace it with a new thought as quickly as possible. Pretty soon, I would skip the thought about sex and go straight to one of my other favorite thoughts. (These thoughts usually involved me playing an instrument, well, and singing to an audience so large I couldn't even see the last row for the stage lights – which at the time, was just about as likely, and ridiculous, as me getting to have sex. Now it's just ridiculous and still fun to think about.)

Question: Is it okay to date someone of a different race?

Answer: I can find no Biblical prohibition against it. So I would advise you to focus on the important things that make or break a long term relationship: Do you have things in common? Or are their major cultural differences that will pose a problem? Are your families supportive or is this going to be a point of conflict at every holiday from here on out? Are you dating because you truly care about each other or is it way to get back at your parents?

And these questions are good questions to ask in any relationship, not just one where racial differences are a concern because there is major cultural diversity even within a single race which can either strengthen or destroy a romantic relationship.

Question: Since I came to college, I have been experimenting with a lesbian relationship, and now I think I need to get out. Since we didn't have intercourse, would I still be considered a virgin?

Answer: What do you think? If you have to go looking for technicalities to feel good about yourself, you already know the answer. The truth is you had a sexual experience, and while you may still technically be a virgin, you chose to be intimate with another person and that leaves a mark.

The good news is God forgives anything that we are willing to lay at His feet, but we have to be honest with ourselves and Him about what we are bringing to Him. He won't let us lie so that we can feel better about what we have done. He wants full credit for your redemption, so don't try to short Him by skirting the issue.

You and Booze
or Dating Under the Influence

There are not a lot of dating scenarios out there that I cannot wholeheartedly endorse, nor can I say that I am guiltless, but I know that the reality is many of our girls will find themselves at least tempted to participate in what the world considers normal or typical dating behaviors. I am including this section not to encourage girls to engage in these activities, but rather I want our girls to be informed about how to be smart in the dating arena and other areas of their lives.

To begin with you should know that I was raised in a home where alcohol was strictly taboo. We did not drink, nor did we hang out with people who drank, and we rarely spoke about it. I personally do not believe that there is anything sinful about drinking in moderation, and I enjoy a good beer and appreciate a nice whiskey. However, if you are convicted about drinking, it is a pretty good indication that you should abstain, and those of us who do imbibe should refrain from throwing stones. As far as I am concerned this is a "meat unto idols" issue meaning that for those of us who are unoffended by it are allowed to partake, but those who feel a twinge of conscience should heed the warning.

I began drinking sometime after my divorce, and to be honest, it was an act of defiance. I knew nothing about alcohol, and I wasn't brave enough to actually go to the bars. So I chose my drinks off the liquor store shelves according to how pretty the bottle was – allow me to share this is an awful way to pick out booze. Over time, I simmered down, me and God made peace, and I carefully studied what the Bible has to say about drinking. Since then my selection method has become more sophisticated and my drinking has become more responsible.

Later, I became a bartender, and I learned even more about what it means to be a responsible drinker. I saw the whole gamut of drinkers from "a glass of wine with dinner" folks to the "puking on the floor drunk because they were too stupid to know when to say when" folks. I have watched men intentionally trying to get girls drunk and girls intentionally complying. I have seen good friends get together just for a chance to let their hair down and act a little goofy with no thought of getting into real trouble. I have seen idiots slam shot after shot in hopes of finding enough courage to start a fight. I have seen the casual drinker and the stone cold alcoholic, and I have learned that unless you have system and a code you can easily go from one to the other.

If you are going to drink, you need to do it responsibly. The problem is no one tells us what that is. So I want to share some of my guidelines about drinking.

1. Sleep where you drink. I am serious, if you do not have a friend that you would trust to take care of your most prized and valuable possessions, they are not to be trusted as designated drivers. So unless you trust them that implicitly, look around you and ask yourself is this sticky barroom floor really a good place to bed down. If the answer is no, then order a soda.

    Remember few people are really aware of how much they drink, or how deeply affected they can be by just few drinks. And you may think that you can have a few and go home, but the truth is too many times "one with the girls" becomes six. Not only that, you don't have to feel drunk or buzzed to be seriously impaired without you knowing it, and it only takes one time behind a wheel when you are not completely in control of your brain and reflexes to ruin the rest of your life.

    There's an old joke in the bars that goes, "I wasn't drunk until I stood up." And there is a lot of truth to it. For many people, the affects of alcohol won't be felt until they get up and stir around a bit, and many times it hits them sometime after they turned the key. So don't be stupid. If you drink don't drive, no matter how expensive a cab is. It is far cheaper than a DUI, a death, or even the false confidence that comes from making it home while intoxicated.

2. Only drink with people you trust, and by that I mean people who hold the same morals and values that you do. If they are not believers, or are only marginal in their faith, do not drink with them. Drinking lowers our inhibitions and a lot of the ugly we normally keep hidden can come out after downing a few. Being in bad company only makes it worse.

3. If you do go out with friends for a drink, set a limit before you get there. A bartender's or server's job is to sell you things. We have one goal – up the total of your ticket and hope that you know enough to tip the correct percentage of that number. So that's what we do. Its how we survive and the pay the bills. So we are really good at asking you if you want another, sometimes even trying to coax you into having just one more, and we know that we can get your friends to join in on the action. Before you know it, we have conspired to turn that one more into four more, but you won't realize it until I hand you the bill. And the more you drink, the more likely you are to drink more. Each drink I sell you makes selling the next one easier. The other added bonus? The more you drink the more likely you are to be generous in your tip because your fuzzy head will refuse to do the math.

   Some servers will even bring you another drink without you ordering it. If this happens do not feel bad about refusing it, or if you do want it, politely but firmly tell them this will be your last one. Other servers have even been known to add drinks that were not served to the bill if they feel the customer is wasted enough not to know the difference, so always check your bill.

4. Order your drink with the bread sticks. Don't drink on an empty stomach, and do drink while eating something high in carbohydrates. Alcohol on an empty stomach goes straight to the brain, and while eating won't keep you from getting drunk, it does slow down the body's absorption of alcohol allowing it to settle into your system a little more gracefully. Plus, it helps protect your stomach from becoming a flaming inferno.

   Also, if you are going to have a drink, do it early in the evening. Drink a drink when you first arrive, and then switch to something else. Be sure you have scheduled a few hours to stay in that location before leaving.

5. Alcohol is not a thirst quencher, soda, or fruit punch. It was not meant to be guzzled. So savor it, sip on it. Who cares how long it takes to finish it? It just means you are getting a little more of your money's worth (but not much, booze is horribly overpriced in restaurants and bars).

   And always order a glass of water with your drink if one is not served with it. Alternate between beverages. If you are really thirsty, skip the alcohol and stick to water. A dehydrated person gets drunk more quickly and more easily than one who is properly hydrated.

6. Never leave your drink unattended, and never accept a drink from anyone but the bartender. I don't care how nice he is or how cute the dimple in his chin seems to be, do not accept a drink from a stranger. Bar etiquette says that if a man desires to buy you a drink, he should order, or have the bartender ask your preference, and the bartender should serve it to you. You have the right to refuse any drinks from people who gives you the creeps, and you have the right to request an alternative drink such as soda or coffee.

   However, if he seems like a nice guy and you would like to talk to him after the drink has been brought to your table, simply raise the glass and motion him over. If you aren't interested, you can still accept the drink, and simply acknowledge his gift with a smile and a nod from across the room. Buying you a drink entitles a man to nothing, and accepting obligates you to the same.

   If you have any concerns about whether someone has tampered with your drink, talk to the bartender. Most of the time we are more than happy to mix you a fresh one, just to be on the safe side. We want you to come back and spend your money with us, so we will do a lot to keep you happy. Mixing a new drink is an easy solution and a great way to convince you to keep coming here.

7. Never try out a new drink in a public setting. Everyone reacts differently to different alcohols and combinations of alcohols. Give some people whiskey and they are ready to take on the world. Give that same person a glass of red wine

and they are the mellowest human being you ever met. However, tequila just makes everyone stupid.

So if you want to try out some new stuff, do it at home. Learn what you can drink that won't make you stupid and then stick to that when you do go out. If you absolutely see something terribly exciting on a menu or drink board that you want to try, split one with a few friends, or get the recipe (we typically like to share) and mix it up at home.

8. No drinking games. Do I really need to explain this? We can't keep up with the guys. We just weren't built to metabolize booze in the same way. Don't even try.

9. If you do get drunk, and sick, like so many of us gals are prone to do, don't fight the vomit. You body is saying that you poisoned yourself, and it needs to get rid of it fast. And puke in a bucket so you won't accidently drown yourself in the toilet.

10. If you do get drunk, but aren't puking, drink a ton of water and go to bed. One foot flat on the floor will make the world stop spinning and pray to God you didn't stop too late.

11. Do not drink alone, when you are depressed, or even to "help" you sleep. You will only feel worse. Alcohol is a depressant, so why throw more gasoline on that fire? And yes, it will put to you sleep if you drink enough, but this a sure road to alcoholism. Besides that, you will find yourself awake and staring at the ceiling in a matter of hours. There is a reason why doctors don't prescribe this as a sleep aid.

12. Do not drink several days consecutively, even in moderation. And if you ever feel like you "just need a drink" after going without for a day or two it is probably time to stop drinking all together for a while. You could be developing a dependence on it.

13. If you ever feel anxious or panicked at the idea of not being able to have drink, you should seek out help to deal with a

possible addiction. Do it immediately, before it gets out of hand. Some people, due to a genetic quirk, will never be able drink. If you happen to be one of these people, accept it and act responsibly. It's not worth ruining your life over.

14. No shots! People who do shots are out for one thing, and that is to get drunk. As a Christian, this should never be our intention for drinking. So just don't do it. I don't care if they are free, and everyone else is doing them.

   If you are given a shot, and are still under your limit, you can sip it, but don't slam it. The person who bought it for you probably has some evil designs in mind. Don't be stupid.

If you drink, be aware there will probably be a day when it slips up on you unless you are super disciplined, and you will make a fool of yourself. So don't think that this is something that you can play with – it's not.

A little warning about drinking: one of the most disturbing and disgusting things I have ever witnessed is the good little Christian girl who goes out drinking with her friends. She has a sip or two of wine and suddenly wants to challenge the town slut for her title. First off girls, if you get drunk off a tiny bit of wine or any other liquor, you are a medical freak or you have deluded yourself into believing that this stuff is way stronger than it really is. Secondly, we need to remember that alcohol does not have the power to change who we fundamentally are. It just brings out what was already inside of you. So if it turns you into a slut, guess what?

Using alcohol as an excuse to justify bad behavior is a cop out and a lie, and one that people who truly drink will not buy. The only person you might be fooling is yourself, but let's be honest – you probably weren't even doing that very well.

And really, it is probably just not a good idea to combine dating and drinking anyway. You need to have your senses and wits about you. After all, the reason we date is to observe and get to know the other person, and that is a difficult thing to do if our senses are operating under the influence. If you have already made up your mind that you really do like the guy, you don't want to sabotage it by showing how much you like him in an inappropriate way, especially if he has been drinking too. It is just far too easy to act on those biological impulses when the brain has been hobbled. So protect yourself and the man you love by holding off on sharing that drink. There will be plenty of time for that after you get married, and then you can shamelessly let him take advantage of your inebriated state.

If you haven't drank in the past, or haven't drank that much, you need to know the signs that you should put the glass down. When the room starts to feel hot, you've had enough. When your world starts to feel all warm and fuzzy, you've had enough. Any problems focusing, forming words, or getting your hands to do your bidding means you've had too much. Feeling amazingly happy, horribly down, or angry means you have more than enough. If you get the sudden urge to start posting random social status updates you believe are profound or hilarious, you know that you have gone overboard. And if you get the urge to call up ex-boyfriends and tell them how much they mean to you, dear God, find a bucket, because the next phase won't be pretty.

Listen to your friends, if they think you've had enough, you have. They are noticing the drooping eyes, the slurred speech, and the uncharacteristic behaviors. Remember, if you are following rule number 2, they are watching out for you. If they are really good friends they have already relieved you have your car keys and your cell phone. Remember to thank them tomorrow.

Phone Sex and Sexting

On several occasions I have been asked about phone sex and sexting. For those of you who don't know what this is allow me to explain. Phone sex is an erotic phone call where the two (or more) people on the phone describe sexually explicit actions, usually while masturbating. Sexting is more of the same, but this time the descriptions are sent in a text message, often accompanied by pictures.

While both of these behaviors are safe in the sense that STD's are not yet able to be transmitted via cell phone, and as of yet, we have had no reported pregnancies due these activities, they still pose some serious problems for Christians. Biblically, they violate the command not cause another to stumble, and these types of behaviors are designed to lead us into temptation while dragging along our partner. Also, Jesus Himself tells us that lusting after another person is the same as having actually engaged in the physical activity. From a Scriptural standpoint, I don't think we need any further instruction as to legitimacy of these acts for the Christian. However, we do need to add one caveat. If the person that you are having phone sex with or are sexting is a spouse, it is within the confines of a covenant relationship and violates no Biblical mandate. Of course, the wisdom of this depends on the integrity of your man, and how much you can trust him not share these personal revelations with his pals.

The more tangible problems with these pastimes are the fact that you cannot control what the person on the other end of the line is doing. In all reality, you can have no clue if he has ten of his best buds all sitting around listening to you pant on the other end of the line. And that picture you sent of you in your pretty pink thong – well, you can bet that it was passed around as quickly as his smart phone will allow. Even if it doesn't happen today, next week, or even next month, it will. Just wait until the first time he gets mad at you or he feels the need to defend his ego. And girls, let's face it if he doesn't have enough guts to pursue you face to face, his ego will need all the defending it could get.

What Every Girl Should Have in Her Honeymoon Kit:

1. The agreed upon contraception if you choose. If you are using internal devices like a diaphragm, the Sponge, film, etc, you should already be familiar with how to use them and be sure you have inserted it in the proper time frame. The last thing you want is to arrive at your honeymoon destination only to find out you should wait four hours to get busy. You should also do some trial runs to be sure you are familiar with how to properly use them. It is not a good thing to be standing in a bathroom knowing you have an anxious groom waiting for your appearance while you are trying to figure out if you got it in right.

2. Lubrication, both types. What I mean by this is, you should have some of the trusty standbys like Astroglide, one of the best, and some fun flavors. And don't be afraid to use it if you need it. Remember your body has to get used to this new activity, so it may not function as smoothly as you would hope. Nerves play fun tricks on us, don't take it lying down . . . well, do, but you know. . .

3. Bath products – bubble bath, body scrub, body paints, and lotions. Bath time can be good way to bond and get comfortable with each other's bodies. For some odd reason, we don't feel nearly as naked in water as do otherwise. And remember, don't put anything on your girlie bits that weren't designed for that purpose.

4. Candles – they provide a little light without being overwhelming and can help keep the place smelling nice. And don't forget a lighter or some matches.

5. Lingerie – all of us gals feel better about meeting a new situation when we are properly arrayed for it. I suggest something simple and easy to get out of for the first encounter, so you might hold off on that corset and those garter belts until you both get a little more comfortable. Also, don't forget new undies for when you do decide to actually get dressed.

6. A robe for quick cover ups.

7. Baby wipes, wash clothes, and a hand towel to clean up some of those little messes that are bound to occur. The towel is also great to throw over the puddles.
8. Breath mints for a quick fix to morning breath and maybe some fun experimentation with that minty sensation on other body parts.
9. Fun foods – chocolate syrup, whipped cream, honey, and other lickable items. This is supposed to be a fun time of learning each other's bodies, so feel free to experiment.
10. Quick energy snacks like fruit, granola, and candy bars. You will get hungry and chances are it will happen in the middle of the night after everything is closed.
11. Water, water, water – you need to stay properly hydrated, and you will want to urinate frequently to ward off possible urinary tract infections.
12. Cranberry juice or supplements – see above.
13. Make up, perfume, hair supplies, toothbrush, razors, etc.
14. Pain killers – you will get sore, but you probably won't want to take a break. So pack the anti-inflammatories so you don't have to slow down.
15. Oragel – it does the same thing for our girlie parts that it does for your mouth. So you can take the edge off if you get a little tender. Or if he is a little quick on the trigger, it can be used to help him have more staying power, but just use a little bit on the underside of the head of his penis. Too much and he can be numb for hours.
16. Throat spray – if you are planning on having oral sex and have a sensitive gag reflex. It numbs the back of your throat and lets you stop worrying, but remember not to be too aggressive.
17. Hemorrhoid cream– if you have them, they can be irritated during sex.
18. Pantyliners– to catch the drips if you go out after having sex.
19. Manicure set – because even though you remind him to do his nails before the wedding, he will somehow manage to have one nail that is way too sharp. Or you will discover that he has talons for toenails.
20. Music – help set the mood and cover up those awkward silences that will happen.

What not to bring on your honeymoon

1. Sex books or tapes – this is a time of discovery, so let it be about the two of you. Do your research before hand and now just go with the flow. There will be time to expand your repertoire later.
2. Cell phones if you can avoid it at all, or at least turn them off.
3. Kids. I don't care if this is your second marriage and the children are feeling left out. This is your time as a new couple, and it was designed as a time for the two of you to come together without any distractions or inhibitions. You can't do that if the kids are in the adjoining room.
4. Your mama – She probably doesn't want to think about what you are doing, and you don't need the image of her disapproving, shocked, or horrified face keeping you from enjoying the moment. So forget your mama for a few days and focus on this time of becoming one with your husband.
5. Pets – I know you love them, but having to stop and walk Fluffy just when things are beginning to heat up is not a good thing.
6. Anything to do with past relationships, so pack away those memories and stifle the urge to make comparisons – good or bad.
7. Tents – So you both love to camp, great. Go next summer. Trust me on this one, you will want access to your own private bath during this time. Don't make this more stressful than it already is. A great compromise is a cabin in the woods, but really, you won't see much of the great outdoors this trip.
8. Computers, video games, or anything else that is a solo activity. This is about the two of you, and if you don't think you can stand a few days with your man undistracted, why are you marrying him?
9. Uncomfortable undies or bras. The girls really need to be pampered right now, so unless it is something you think he will get you out of pretty quick, stick to comfy underclothes.
10. Untested bath products- your body is under enough stress. A new body wash can cause a yeast infection, and this is not a particularly good time to grapple with one. So stick to what you know for the time being.

241

How to Throw a Killer Bridal Shower
(and why you should throw two)

Years ago, bridal showers were given to help a young wife have the tools she needed to set up housekeeping. Gifts were blenders, toasters, and other assorted cooking utensils, but many of today's brides already have a home, and so does the groom. The problem isn't not having a blender, but what to do with the two you already have. And years ago, weddings were paid for by the bride's parents, but today many of us are footing the bill ourselves. So we are planning weddings that are far cry from the fairy tale vision that we had as children, and while that may not be a bad thing, some of the cuts we have to make for the sake of the budget hurt.

For these and more reasons, I think it is time to rethink the bridal shower. Traditionally, the bridal shower was planned by the maid of honor, someone about the same age and experience level as the bride herself. And I still believe this is appropriate for a traditional wedding shower, especially if the bride is young. Let her throw the one where all the aunts, mothers, and proper women of the Church gather to give the bride all the household items they desire, but there is no rule that says you can't have two.

If there is going to be a traditional shower, be sure to ask the bride what home items she and the groom already have. See if there are particular items that they lack, and tactfully inform the guests. Bridal registries are great for this, but remember that no one is obligated follow them – nor is the bride obligated to keep that tacky lamp great-aunt Gertrude knew she would love. Consider a themed shower, such as one that focuses on the fact the bride is decorating her kitchen in roosters, her living room in burgundy roses, and the bedroom in early Arabian harem . . . well, you might hold off on that last one.

Or you could consider a pantry stocking party, where all the guests bring some food staples for the new home like sugar, flour, baking soda, rice, dried pasta, or canned goods and condiments. Another twist on this idea is each of the women bring their favorite recipe with the distinctive ingredients needed like spices, flavored extracts, or something not typically found in a new kitchen. You can do the same thing with cleaning products and tools, but it is not nearly as pretty or charming. The point is that the shower not be redundant to what the bride may already have or provides something that will needed to be restocked.

Once you have had the safe shower, the one that won't give Grandma Myrtle a hard attack or horrify Sister Goodie-goodie, then have the real one and invite everyone else.

The Second Shower

My friend Joanna and I have thrown several of these showers, and we are biding our time until we can do our daughters. Honestly, I think we have more fun than the brides do.

To begin with we have a few rules, and they are non-negotiable. You must be over the age of twenty one, married, or have kids to attend. The content of this event is not kid friendly, and this should be a time when we gals can speak freely – hence, the no Aunt Henrietta's clause, unless she is just super cool and knows what she is getting into. And truth be told, the women who have been married for decades and are willing to share have the best advice, and are the most fun at these events. So if she is willing, invite her, too.

Now, we always serve one alcoholic drink at these events. And this constitutes the second rule, no out of control or wild drinking. We keep it light and fruity, and we serve it at the beginning of the evening. Alcohol is not required, but it does make the night feel like a little more of an event. If you chose to serve alcohol have a designated server, and that person's job is stand over the drinks and keep track of how many everyone has had. Be sure to have plenty of non-alcoholic options for those who don't drink and for those who have had their limit. We keep it to one drink apiece. No one wants to clean up after a drunk, and we definitely don't want anyone to drive home impaired.

The third rule is that the gifts are opened at the shower, and then left in the care of someone trustworthy. Ideally, the shower will happen only few days before the wedding, but we don't want to leave anything that might tempt the couple to do any experimenting before the proper time. Make sure that this person knows that their job is to get the gifts to the bride either when she is packing or placed in the car before the couple leaves the wedding.

Ordinarily, Joanna and I go in and buy one big basket of goodies that is a mix of practical and fun stuff. To begin with make sure that the basket, or gift bag, is sturdy enough to carry around. The idea here is that all their honeymoon goodies are easily transportable and in one place. Use tissue paper to keep it discreet if the basket is going to be delivered to the bride at the wedding. There are just some things her daddy never needs to see – this is one of them.

There is always a bottle of champagne for those couples who drink and two champagne flutes. Of all the things we put in, the champagne is the most expensive item. Almost everything else we get at a dollar or discount store. Shopping for these items is a hoot, and Joanna said that after making these trips with me she can't shop there with her kids anymore. The key to these baskets is to let you imagination go wild.

Be sure to include some traditional items like candles (and don't forget the matches), body wash, lotions, lip gloss, manicure sets, and bath poofs. Then move on to some more suggestive things like pain killers, band aids, energy drinks, candy bars, nuts, granola, and bottled water. Then go in for the kill with the powdered licking candies, candy necklaces, glow sticks, and an array of kid's toys like the sheriff badges, feather boas, and fairy wings. In the bath section, look for body paint and bath confetti. Plastic wrap and prize ribbons that say "I'm a big boy now" or "Princess" always get a laugh.

As the bride to be unwraps her presents tell her what they are all for. Some items are self explanatory, but others need a little instruction. Pain killers are for muscle aches the next day, band aids for carpet burns, energy drinks and candy for stamina, water to keep you hydrated. Everything that can be licked is for licking off each other, candy necklaces are for ring toss games, as are the glow sticks or they can be taped to the inner thighs to give him a lighted run way. Dress up toys are entire outfits, as is the plastic wrap (see Fried Green Tomatoes). The idea is to give them something fun to laugh about in their honeymoon hideaway and make those first moments a little less awkward. For more ideas on what to put in a honeymoon basket see the list of things a bride needs on her honeymoon.

Since we aren't the only one giving presents, we ask the rest of the bride's friends to bring their favorite sex items. Be sure to provide them with the bride's measurements and sizes in case they want to purchase lingerie for her. Also, let them know that they are expected to explain why they chose this particular gift and how it can benefit her on the honeymoon. Despite the overwhelming amount of sexual information in our culture, it still amazes me how little most women know about sex, and that's why we do this – to help teach her some of the things that will make this time amazing for her and her new husband.

Having recently remarried, Joanna and many of my other friends conspired to give me a great shower, but they put a little twist on it. They knew that Ty and I were paying for it all ourselves and he was laid off just weeks before the wedding. Many of the girlie things I had hoped to do for myself before the wedding just were too costly. With a multitude of phone calls behind my back, they coordinated their gifts to give me many of the things I thought I would have to do without.

I received gift certificates for a manicure and pedicure, a spray tan, the henna paints I wanted for my barefoot entrance, sunglasses to protect my eyes when my husband swept me away on his Harley after the ceremony, and full massage from one of my talented friends. They also gave me a multitude of lingerie, jewelry to finish my bridal attire, and many of the other things we would normally put in the basket. To top it all off, they invaded our honeymoon cabin and stocked it with enough food to insure we would not have to leave in search of sustenance while enjoyed our first few days of married life. In the end, it was their attention to what I needed and wanted, rather than being bound by convention, that demonstrated their love for me and commitment to supporting my marriage.

Really, this is the only rule we need to know when preparing a bridal shower, or to even be a friend. Know who you are trying to bless, and give them what they need – not what you think they should have. Do this and you are guaranteed to be a real blessing and throw the best bridal shower a girl can hope to have.

Handling a Compliment

Girls, girls, girls, we have a problem. Most of us do not know how to take a compliment. Now, I know that most of us think we can, but really, ask yourself a few questions.

1. When someone says they like your dress, do you feel like you need to explain that you bought it at the thrift store or it is just something old that you threw on?

2. When you do a good job or come up with a creative solution for a problem, do you try to act as if it were nothing when people praise you?

3. If a man compliments your eyes, smile, or even your walk, do you automatically think that he is a creep or pervert?

4. Is it hard to just say the words, "thank you," and smile?

5. Do you find some reason to discredit the compliment or, worse, the person who gave you the compliment?

6. Is a compliment an open invitation to explain exactly how, where, and how much something cost you or what you did to get it?

If you answered yes to any of these questions, you have a problem accepting a compliment, but don't worry you are not alone. Most of us have no idea of how to respond to another's favorable remarks about us, and there are few major reasons. Let's look at a few, the reasons match the question number, so see where you fall.

1. We often worry about seeming vain, especially as Christian women. We have been taught that our good looks are something that we should down play, when the truth is God created us to be beautiful and have great taste. So stop letting this false teaching steal your joy. If someone likes your dress, hair cut, or shoes, give them a dazzling smile and say thank you. It's that easy, and it's okay to enjoy the

confidence rush. Most of us can use the boost, and nothing does it for us gals like a sincere compliment.

If you're talking to a friend who would genuinely like to know where you found your outfit, then share, but otherwise don't bore someone with details they just don't care about.

2. This can be a little of answer one's attitude creeping in, or it may be the way you play the system. By constantly denying that what you have done or suggested was really beneficial to a situation, you are setting the stage for others to "convince" you that you did well. And let's face it, people who come up with brilliant ideas know that is what they do, and they do well.

So graciously accept your moment in the spotlight, and then step aside for the next person by giving that smile and saying "Thank you" once again. If need be, change the subject by acknowledging the people who helped or implemented your ideas.

3. Okay, contrary to what you might believe not every man is trying to get in your pants. Men love to look at beautiful women, and when we truly impress them, they often feel compelled to say so. If it begins and ends with some appreciative words, enjoy them, and appreciate the fact that he had the courage to speak up.

And keep in mind, men aren't as good with words as we are. So sometimes that compliment can come in the form of a wolf whistle or some poorly chosen words. As long as it is not blatantly sexual, give the poor fellow the benefit of the doubt. Remember that just as we haven't been taught how to receive a compliment, most of them haven't been taught the right way to give one. If you are feeling a little froggy, jump in and restate the compliment in better terms, and ask "Did you mean to say _____?" If you do it with a smile and light manner, most men will respond pleasantly and take the hint. If they don't, then you can write them off as a creep.

4. Look sometimes we just get stumped, taken off guard, or we simply haven't had that many people say nice things to us. So

see answer one, and be ready with sincere smile and a thank you. You aren't required to say anything else.

5. This response is false modesty on hyper-drive, not to mention a dash of superiority complex thrown in. If someone says they like something about you, they do. So accept it. Quit thinking that you know better than they what they like. You don't, and their manners are better than yours.

6. A compliment is a compliment, not an invitation to tell your life story. It should be a brief pleasant exchange that allows both participants to feel good about the moment. The good news is if you answered yes to this question, you aren't dealing with any sort of false modesty. You know that you want to be the center of attention and will do whatever it takes to get there.

    So knock it off, or you may soon find that compliments become few and far between because no one wants you to misunderstand or feed into your self-centered attitude. Again, big smile and "Thank you." That's all you need to say, and everyone will have a great day.

Every girl loves to know that someone appreciates the time and effort she has put into her appearance, and it feels good to hear positive things said about us. And as Christians we should be the best at dealing with positive, encouraging, and uplifting speech, so enjoy. Just remember to ditch the guilt or the pride, and by using the proper response you can make the giver's day better by making them glad they stop to acknowledge your beauty in looks, presentation, word, or deed. And who knows, maybe the good feeling will encourage them to keep encouraging others through these thoughtful words? Think about how great it would be to live in a world where we all appreciated the good in each other, and said so. So don't stop the flow.

How to Handle Unwanted Advances

It is almost guaranteed that at some point in your life you are going to receive some unwanted attention. The problem for most of us is we just don't know how to handle ourselves when the fellows start saying things that make us uncomfortable. In order to determine the proper response, first you need to assess the situation. Ask yourself these questions:

1. Is he trying to be offensive, or is he sincerely trying to compliment you?
2. Are his remarks sexual in nature, or simply an observation about your hair, eyes, or dress?
3. Is he invading your personal space while he is talking?
4. Do you have suspicion he just really doesn't know how to talk to a woman?
5. Is he really being inappropriate, or are you just uncomfortable with a compliment? (See above).

Look, most guys are really inept (read that blithering idiots) when it comes to saying the right thing to women. Most of them really, really want to say something that will impress us, but usually, they just don't know how. If you think he is *trying* to pay a sincere compliment but is just really bad at it, smile and say thank you. More than anything, he is probably just trying to find some way to draw you into a conversation. If you are single, you might want to take this opportunity to get to know someone new.

However, if you are certain that he is not someone you want to encourage – smile, say thank you, and walk away. No need to be rude or unkind. Simply do not entertain further conversation. If he pursues, unwilling to take a gentle let down, kindly but firmly tell him something along the lines of, "Honey, I appreciate that you think so highly of me, but you are making me uncomfortable. So save your flattery for someone who would enjoy it." Usually, this is direct enough to put a stop to their advances, and when said with a smile, nice enough not to crush them.

Unfortunately, not all unwanted attention comes from guys we can avoid. We can have bosses, teachers, and co-workers who find it amusing to say things that can make us extremely uncomfortable. Usually, it starts out as a joke – something not really offensive, but maybe just a bit suggestive. Girls, this is your time to take your stand. When they start doing this, they are on a fishing expedition, trying to see how you will react. If you are too polite to say anything at this point, the remarks will continue to escalate both in frequency and in impropriety.

How you make your stand will can greatly influence whether things get nasty between the two of you or not. Hear me, no woman is to blame for a man's inability to control his thoughts, mouth, or actions. The only one who has any control over what he does is him. All I am doing is offering a few tricks that I have used over the years – tricks that allowed various men to back out of the situation with their egos intact while still maintaining my boundaries.

1. Do not belittle him or berate him for making the offensive remark.
2. Do keep your sense of humor about you. Play it off as a joke he is telling you.
3. Don't stop smiling.
4. Maintain direct eye contact.
5. Stand to the side; preferably their right side.
6. Have an arsenal of prepared witty retorts. Some of my favorites:

> "Darn my morals and ethics – they always get in my way."

> "Sounds like fun. Will you be bringing your wife?"

> "Not without a note from my doctor."

> "I don't know what I find cuter in a guy – blindness or the lack of good taste."

> "I don't think I can get that drunk."

> "Mind if I bring my twelve kids/cats?"

"You're right, we would be great together, but I don't think the world is ready for that."

"Gees, with your big ears and my crooked teeth, think of the children."

"I see you are wearing a wedding ring, and that cuts off circulation in more than one way."

"I'm sorry, but I never out grew that three-year-old phase. I am not very good at sharing, especially when it comes to men."

"You know, I just don't think that is exciting enough to make me want to shave my legs and I already have three weeks worth of growth."

"Ahh, did you forget your meds this morning?"

"Let me see if you are still interesting after I get out of rehab."

Or my all time favorite, just launch into a vivid description of what type of wedding you want and how the colors you picked will really bring out his eyes. Tell him you can't wait to have a son who has his eyelashes. That usually sends them running.

7. Above all say it with a laugh. It allows them the chance to play along, and typically, they are grateful you offered them such an easy way out of the hole they just dug.

However, be prepared this is will not work with all men, just the ones who have a modicum of commonsense and social graces. Some men force us to take a very blunt, to the point of rude, stand. We have to let them know in no uncertain terms, we are not interested. And you do that by saying just that.

"Joe, I'm not interested. No more."

Billy-Bob, I've played nice until now, but you need to back off. I don't want to hear it any longer."

"Look, George, I can't be any plainer. I will not tolerate any more of those types of remarks."

Use their names. Stand squarely in front of them. Look them right in the eye, and don't stutter. Once you have said your peace, leave the area. Give them time to digest what you have just said, and when you do return, maintain a professional distance.

If you have further problems, tell them that you have given them a chance and if they say anything more that is inappropriate you will be reporting them to the proper people. In a job situation this is the Human Resources Department. In a Church this the pastor, elders, or leader of your particular group. On social networks, simply block them. If it is a neighbor, don't hesitate to call the police. No woman should have to live in fear or dread of being harassed. I know that this feels like you are committing the dreadful act of being impolite, but gals, we are not required to polite in every situation – sometimes all we need to be is appropriate, and in these cases, it is the men who dictate what that is.

My personal rule is every man has a right to be told no once. After that, I take no prisoners. Feel free to use it as your own.

What to do if you are Raped

This is never an easy topic to think about. Deep down, I think most women live with a dread that they can never quite shake, and if you have had a history of sexual violence, it makes it that much worse. But we need to know what to do if this ever does become a reality, and we need to know before it happens, because what we do in the moments immediately following a sexual assault will effect everything that follows.

First off, we need to know that women never deserve to have this happen to them. I don't care how sleazy a girl might dress, though unwise; men are still responsible for their actions. And gals, and by gals, I mean you goodie-two-shoes out there who think you are immune because you keep it all hidden, you need to know that you are just as likely to be a victim as anyone else. So don't you dare sit in judgment of anyone who has ever had this happen to them. Our response should always be one of compassion, because if you have never gone through this you have no idea of the depth of pain that it causes.

Second, we need to realize that most rapes are not committed by strangers. Typically it is someone we know, someone we have invited into our lives. Knowing this is important for two reasons.

1. When it is someone that we have known and even trusted, there can be a false sense of guilt and a tendency to blame ourselves. Many attackers have mastered the art of convincing their victims that she somehow "asked for it." It is their defense and excuse. Don't buy it.

    If any man disregards your no, he is the guilty party. And I don't care if he is the nicest, most respected man in town, or even if he is a preacher. You did not do this to yourself, and you are not capable of forcing a man to do this to you.

2. We need to pay attention to our "spidey senses", and if any man gives you the heebie-jeebies, be on guard for unwanted advances. Make your concern known to your trusted friends, and avoid situations where you feel vulnerable.

Yes, you might offend somebody who is really an alright fellow, but girls, it's not worth the risk. If it makes them mad or uncomfortable, they should take it as a sign they need to work on their people skills, but chances are, you are picking up on a warning you should listen to. Too many times, rape victims have told me that they knew something was off with the person who attacked them, but everyone else seemed to think that they were a great person. So be wise, and don't cave.

The third thing we need to know: rape is not about sex. It is about violence, control, and the degradation of another person. Men who rape are typically trying to prove that they can take whatever they want, when they want. It has nothing to do with your sexuality. It has everything to do with their warped and twisted need to dominate so that they can feel powerful. The truth is sex is available on every street corner and bar. If all a man needed was a way to get off, he could have gotten it legally and less dangerously, but that is not what he wants. He wants to hurt another human being, and you just happened to be in the wrong place at the wrong time. You did not cause this. You were the victim.

If you are raped, these are the basic steps you need to follow.

1. Get to a safe place.
2. Do not take a bath or shower. Do not even wash your hands.
3. Do not change your clothes.
4. Do not eat or drink anything.
5. Do not brush your teeth or use any mouth wash.
6. Call the police – Immediately.
7. Call one of your trusted friends to come and be with you.

I know that this all sounds so very simple, but if you have been attacked your first instinct will be to wash away the awful evidence that it has happened. Women have scalded the skin from their bodies and scrubbed themselves raw in an attempt to make this feeling go away. Girls, it doesn't work, and what's more you would be destroying the evidence needed to possibly catch and stop this man.

Once the police arrive, you will be taken to the emergency room where a doctor will use a rape kit. A rape kit allows them to collect semen and hair samples so that the attackers DNA can be used to catch him. You will also be treated for any injuries, and all injuries will be documented. They will want to take pictures to use later in prosecution. You need to let them do this. Don't fight the system. It has been designed to be as gentle but as thorough as necessary.

The medical team will assess and advise you on what steps to take concerning STD's and possible pregnancy. Having a friend who can help you navigate through all the information they will be presenting to you is a tremendous help and blessing. Don't be ashamed if you are having trouble comprehending everything that is happening around you. Let the professionals and the friends you trust guide you.

The truth is at this point you will probably be in shock, and that's okay. It is God's protective system at work. You will feel numb and maybe even disoriented. So trust the officials, doctors, and nurses to do their job. They want help you and stop this from happening to anyone else. If you have any concerns or doubts about what is going on, ask for an explanation. If you have a friend, tell them that you are mentally checking out for awhile, and ask them to watch over you. They will do it, and you can lay aside a little bit of your stress for awhile.

The police will interview you about what happened. Tell them everything you can remember. You will be asked to tell your story several times. It is not that they do not believe you, the rape kit will have confirmed that you were raped, so don't be defensive. They are simply hoping that you will remember something new and important with each retelling, and let them decide what is important. Don't filter what you remember. Just give it all over to them.

You will be referred to a trauma specialist upon release. Take advantage of this service. Rape is too big to handle alone. Get into counseling, preferably someone who specializes in this field. The next few months are going to be difficult, but they are easier if you get the right tools to help you cope.

Journaling, telling your story, and art therapy are all tools that will help you come to terms with your emotions. Whatever you do, don't just rush back to life as normal. Accept that your life has changed. As you begin to heal, you will find that it didn't destroy you and that you are far stronger than you thought you were.

Give yourself the freedom and permission to feel all the anger, hurt, and betrayal that will be flowing through your veins. Work through this time of healing with people who love you. Cry, scream, break a few things, whatever it takes, but know that there will be a day when you will laugh again. And there will be day when you won't feel the way you do today. There is healing, I promise, but it is a process. Give it time, and when you don't have the strength to believe it for yourself, let those who love you believe it for you.

From here there will be a time of limbo, where the police are looking for the man who did this, and the process of law is sometimes slow. Don't be discouraged or tempted to give up. This is one time when anger will serve you well, and no, it is not a sin. Let it be the fuel for making sure this heinous excuse of a man never gets the chance to do this to another woman again. You take back control, you decided your future, and you fight on behalf of the women who will never know what you saved them from. It is not vengeance. It is justice, and the fulfillment of our God given obligation to protect others.

One final note: Many women believe that being raped affects the status of their sexual purity. Girls, that is a lie straight from hell. You did not commit a sin, a sin was committed against you, and God sees you as innocent. No one has the right to contradict Him in this manner. So do not become a victim a second time by succumbing to the guilt and shame the enemy would like to throw at you.

Women who have survived sexual violence have gone on to be a loud and effective voice in the healing of others. In time, your story could be the story that helps another. And you will be able to point to that event, not as a time of shame, but as a time when you were strong enough and brave enough to survive.

Emily Dixon is an artist, writer, and teacher whose unique style is the direct result of her ability to combine the abstracts of faith with the demands of a real world. Born into a heritage of faith, Emily's childhood revolved around the church where she learned disciplines of a Christian life. However, when faced with a devastating marriage and divorce at the age of twenty-three, she recognized the need to move deeper into her understanding of God's love and purpose for her life.

Returning to school, she added a degree in Psychology from Southern Nazarene University to her previous degree in Fine Arts from Bacone College. Later, she continued her education and received a Master's degree in Biblical Literature from Oral Roberts University. She supported her daughters through this time by working in sales, teaching art, bartending, and as an adjunct instructor at Bacone College's Christian Ministries Department. Each of these experiences deepened her conviction that there is a desperate need for the truth of God's love, mercy, and redeeming power to be shared with the world in bold new way.

In June of 2010, Emily married Ty Dixon who encouraged her to quit her day job and pursue her passion for sharing her love of the Lord and His word. Thanks to his support, Emily's dream of becoming a full time writer and speaker have become a reality. Together with her daughters, Lauren and Lydia King, they live on the same family farm where Emily was raised.

Along with her brother, Nathan Underwood, she is co-founder of Pagus, a ministry dedicated to exploring the role of the arts and education in the experience of the Christian faith. To learn more about Pagus, its members, or to book an event, visit our website:

www.lifeonthepagus.com

Made in the USA
Columbia, SC
19 January 2021